God's Sabbatical Years

The Story of Alan Weiler

By Peter Harris

Published by JewishGen

**An Affiliate of the Museum of Jewish Heritage - A Living Memorial to the Holocaust
New York**

God's Sabbatical Years - The Story of Alan Weiler
By Peter Harris

Layout: Joel Alpert
Cover Design: Nina Schwartz

Published by JewishGen, Inc.
An Affiliate of the Museum of Jewish Heritage
A Living Memorial to the Holocaust
36 Battery Place, New York, NY 10280

"JewishGen, Inc. is not responsible for inaccuracies or omissions in the original work and makes no representations regarding the accuracy of this translation. Digital images of the original book's contents can be seen online at the New York Public Library Web site."

The mission of the JewishGen organization is to produce a translation of the original work and we cannot verify the accuracy of statements or alter facts cited.

Printed in the United States of America by Lightning Source, Inc.

Library of Congress Control Number (LCCN):   2017950323
ISBN: 978-1-939561-56-5 (hard cover: 234 pages, alk. paper)

Front Cover Painting by Samuel Bak

JewishGen and the Yizkor-Books-in-Print Project

This book has been published by the **Yizkor-Books-in-Print Project,** as part of the **Yizkor Book Project** of **JewishGen, Inc.**

JewishGen, Inc. is a non-profit organization founded in 1987 as a resource for Jewish genealogy. Its website [www.jewishgen.org] serves as an international clearinghouse and resource center to assist individuals who are researching the history of their Jewish families and the places where they lived. JewishGen provides databases, facilitates discussion groups, and coordinates projects relating to Jewish genealogy and the history of the Jewish people. In 2003, JewishGen became an affiliate of the **Museum of Jewish Heritage - A Living Memorial to the Holocaust** in New York.

The **JewishGen Yizkor Book Project** was organized to make more widely known the existence of Yizkor (Memorial) Books written by survivors and former residents of various Jewish communities throughout the world. Later, volunteers connected to the different destroyed communities began cooperating to have these books translated from the original language— usually Hebrew or Yiddish—into English, thus enabling a wider audience to have access to the valuable information contained within them. As each chapter of these books was translated, it was posted on the JewishGen website and made available to the general public.

The **Yizkor-Books-in-Print Project** began in 2011 as an initiative to print and publish Yizkor Books that had been fully translated, so that hard copies would be available for purchase by the descendants of these communities and also by scholars, universities, synagogues, libraries, and museums.

These Yizkor books have been produced almost entirely through the volunteer effort of researchers from around the world, assisted by donations from private individuals. The books are printed and sold at near cost, so as to make them as affordable as possible. Our goal is to make this important genre of Jewish literature and history available in English in book form, so that people can have the personal histories of their ancestral towns on their bookshelves for themselves and for their children and grandchildren.

A list of all published translated Yizkor Books in the project with prices and ordering information can be found at:
               http://www.jewishgen.org/Yizkor/ybip.html

Lance Ackerfeld, Yizkor Book Project Manager

Joel Alpert, Yizkor-Book-in-Print Project Coordinator

JewishGen
Yizkor Book Project

This book is presented by the
Yizkor Books in Print Project
Project Coordinator: Joel Alpert

Part of the
Yizkor Books Project of JewishGen, Inc.
Project Manager: Lance Ackerfeld

These books have been produced solely through volunteer effort
of individuals from around the world. The books are printed and
sold at near cost, so as to make them as affordable as possible.

Our goal is to make this history and important genre of Jewish
literature available in English in book form so that people can have
the near-personal histories of their ancestral towns on their bookshelves for themselves and for their children and grandchildren.

Any donations to the Yizkor Books Project are appreciated.

Please send donations to:
Yizkor Book Project
JewishGen
36 Battery Place
New York, NY 10280

JewishGen, Inc. is an affiliate of the
Museum of Jewish Heritage
A Living Memorial to the Holocaust

I wish to express my profound gratitude to Peter Harris of the Manchester Evening News, without whose encouragement, advice and invaluable help this book would not have been written.

Alan Weiler

About the Author

Peter Harris is a writer and journalist who for more than 25 years was Health and Medical Correspondent of the Manchester Evening News, former sister newspaper of the revered Manchester Guardian, now the national daily, The Guardian. He was born in the seaside resort of Cleethorpes, near Grimsby, coincidentally, in the same county of Lincolnshire where Alan Weiler settled when he first came to England. Now semi-retired, Peter and his wife, Wendy, live in the historic small market town of Sandbach in Cheshire. His leisure interests include oil painting, gardening and country walking.

Peter Harris

FOREWORD

Two of my most indelible memories of Alan Weiler are that he never felt cold even on the harshest winter's day and that he always enjoyed eating heartily and shopping for food - understandable legacies from the unimaginable hardships he suffered in Nazi captivity.

After gathering information for this book, I would often leave his Manchester home in the early hours of a bitter winter's night and he would stand chatting by my car in an open-necked short-sleeved shirt. "Alan, you get back inside. You must be freezing," I would say. "If you have been forced to work outside in sub-zero temperatures digging ditches for hour after hour without food, you would know that this feels like a summer's evening," he would reply.

He also often used to tell me that when he first tasted freedom he vowed that he would never go hungry again. He was never without his favorite pickled herring, dill cucumbers and bread from his local Jewish delicatessen and would enjoy making canapes of anchovies and egg and smoked salmon for guests.

His late wife, Betty, was one of the first young women he met when he first arrived in England, settling for a time in Grimsby in Lincolnshire, coincidentally my own home county. When we first met, they lived in a neat semi-detached house with their two children, a son Steven, and a daughter, Lesley, and were well integrated in the Jewish community of North Manchester. Betty I will always remember for her wicked sense of humor so it was especially sad when she became mentally ill and had to be admitted to hospital where she remained until her death in 1988, aged only 58. Alan moved into a nearby ground floor flat where he surrounded himself with photographic memories and which he always kept in spick and span order.

Alan Weiler was an intelligent man who could speak many languages – German, Russian, Polish, Hebrew as well as perfect English and his native Yiddish. Had his early year been different he would almost certainly have been a successful professional man but for all the years I knew him he had to be content with working as a manager in discount mirror and wallpaper stores owned by Jewish friends in Manchester.

Time plays tricks with one's memory but I believe that we first met over a lunchtime drink in a city center restaurant bar – sadly long-since closed - that was a favorite watering hole for Manchester's newspaper and television media. At the time I was a journalist at the Manchester Evening News, the former sister newspaper of the revered Manchester Guardian, now The Guardian.

I was both instantly inspired and motivated by his story and, in the light of my own family history, found that I could empathize with everything he told about his and his own family's life. I did not know the finer detail at the time, but had always been aware that my own Jewish grandparents had fled persecution in Eastern Europe and had settled at the end of the 19th century in the mining valleys of South Wales where they ran a clothing shop selling requisites to the local pitmen and were responsible for establishing the region's former thriving Jewish community.

Over a period of more than year, now more than 40 years ago, I would visit Alan in his home and chapter-by-chapter would record his memoirs on tape which I now wish I had retained for posterity. Eventually, after several bottles of his favorite brandy and gallons of black coffee, the manuscript was completed and we discussed numerous possible titles. But Alan was always adamant that it should be called "God's Sabbatical Years," explaining that if there is a God in Heaven "he must have been on holiday" during those long years of suffering. In 1997 he suffered a heart attack at home from which he did not recover. He was 68.

There were originally three hard-bound manuscripts: one was sent by Alan to the Russian Embassy in London where he hoped it would be used "for anti-Nazi propaganda," a second was destroyed in a fire at a magazine office in Germany and I retained the third on a bookshelf in my study. Earlier this year, conscious of the fact that it contained accounts of the Holocaust years previously untold, I donated the manuscript to the Wiener Library in London where it has now been added to their archives and, to ensure that it reached the widest possible audience, I was advised by the archivist, Sarah Putz who urged that it be published and to contact Yizkor Books Project of JewishGen who instantly agreed to publish it.

Peter Harris
June 2017

....

Acknowledgements

As Peter Harris mentioned above, he contacted me to offer the book for publication on the Yizkor-Books-In-Print Project of JewishGen, of which I am the coordinator. A significant problem presented itself in that the only version of the material was a copy of a 40-year-old typed manuscript that was not presentable enough for publication. There was no electronic version of the manuscript, only a scanned version, which did not lend itself to the Optical Character Recognition (OCR) process (which converts such typed material to text that can then be manipulated into a presentable form for publication). Several valiant OCR attempts failed. Frustrated, I resorted to requesting volunteer typists on the JewishGen listserve to retype ten pages each. I was overwhelmed by the responses and we had the 300-page plus manuscript completely typed in less than two weeks. It was only with the assistance of these volunteers who believe that this material is valuable to publish and preserve were we able to proceed. I want to thank those volunteers, who rose to the call and enabled this publication.

Joel Alpert
Coordinator of the Yizkor-Books-In-Print Project

Jennifer Alford

Juliana Berland

Hannah Bloch

Carole Burtch

Ellen Caplan

Malka Chosnek

Michael Diamant

Susan J. Eansor

Joyce Eastman

Naomi Finkelstein

Judy Floam

Ina Getzoff

Irene Goldstein

Sharon Grosfeld

Logan Kleinwaks

Malka Kontogheorgis

Paul Levit

Sue Levy

Sandra Lilienthal

Susan MacLaughlin

Susan Mann

Maurine McLellan

Susan Miles

Ruth Morrow

Rebecca Page

Marilen Pitler

Ingrid Rockberger

Irit Rosin

Stacey Saiontz

Patty Shore

Judith Singer

Barbara Sontz

Tammy Weingarten

Notes to the Reader:

A list of this book and all books available in the Yizkor-Book-In-Print Project along with prices is available at:

http://www.jewishgen.org/Yizkor/ybip.html

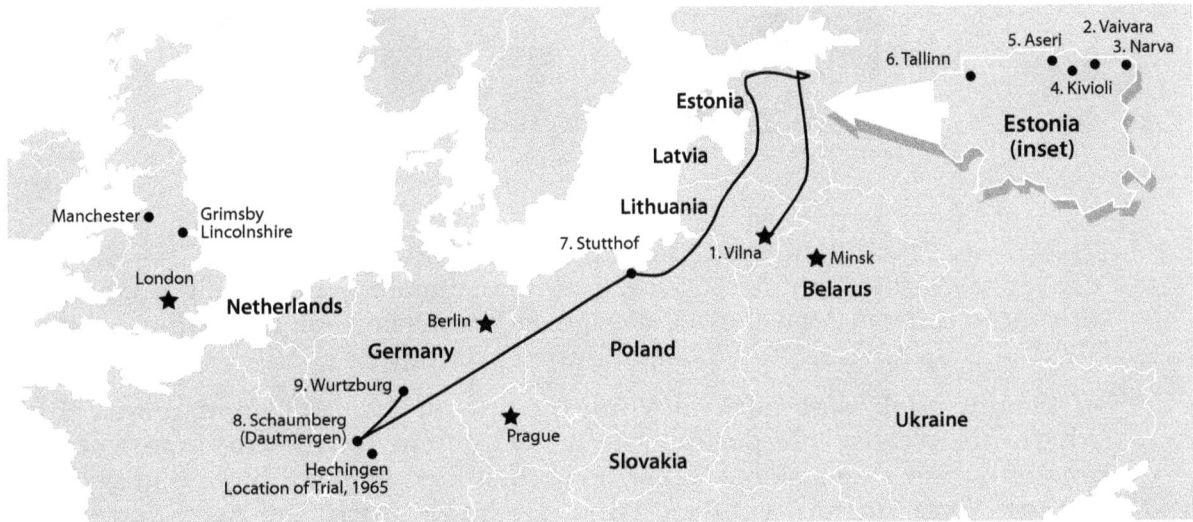

Alan Weiler's Journey, 1941–1945

About the Artist Samuel Bak

We are greatly honored and privileged that internationally-renowned conceptual artist Samuel Bak, who was a schoolboy in the Vilna Ghetto at the same time as Alan Weiler, has given permission for his iconic painting, "With a Blue Thread", to be used on the cover of this book.

Samuel Bak, was born in Vilna on August 12, 1933 and it was there where his creative life began with an exhibition of his drawings when he was only nine years of age. Since 1959 has had solo exhibitions in galleries in New York, Boston, London, Paris, Berlin, Munich, Tel Aviv, Jerusalem, Zurich, Rome and many other major cities. Samuel Bak never painted direct scenes of mass death but much of his work was influenced and informed by his personal experiences during the Holocaust.

In 1948, he and his mother emigrated to Israel where Samuel studied at the Bezalel Art School in Jerusalem and he completed his mandatory service in the Israeli army. Later he studied in Paris, lived in Italy and Switzerland and eventually settled in Boston, Massachusetts. Whilst he and his mother survived the Holocaust, his father and four grandparents all perished at the hands of the Nazis. In 2001, he returned to his hometown of Vilna for the first time and in November this year *(2017)* he and his wife are planning to return to the city of his birth for the opening of the Samuel Bak Museum, a branch of the Vilna Gaon Jewish State Museum. Several drawings from his childhood in the Ghetto will be included in the collection.

GOD'S SABBATICAL YEARS

Table of Contents

PROLOGUE

The Trial At Hechingen

There are those who argue convincingly that it was fate that took me back to the little village of Schomberg in Baden-Wurttemberg in August 1965. I was returning from a motoring holiday in Italy with my wife and our two children and, in spite of some very real misgivings because of my wartime experiences at the hands of the Nazis, I decided to return home to England through Germany.

Some 20 years had elapsed since I had previously stood on German soil, and in heading towards Schomberg I was deliberately breaking a promise to myself never to set foot in the country again.

The main reason for my change of heart was that two years earlier I had discovered that just a short distance from the Dautmergen concentration camp on the outskirts of Schomberg, the French, in liberating the area, had come across the communal grave of hundreds of civilian prisoners who had perished under the barbarous regime of the Third Reich. The French Commander had ordered the local German population to carry out a mass exhumation of the corpses and establish a properly kept cemetery with separate graves and headstones for each of the 1,755 victims.

The names of all the victims were known, and among them was that of my own dear father, Szolem Weiler, who was beaten with the butt of an SS guard's rifle at Dautmergen on November 23rd, 1944. As a result of that beating he died the following day. He was only 38 years of age. For this reason, above all others I decided reluctantly to tread once again on this bloodstained patch of German soil, and visit the cemetery in which my father was buried, and which in effect is a memorial to my kith and kin.

Night had fallen by the time we reached the village and there was no alternative but to postpone the visit to the cemetery until the following morning. There are two small inns in Schomberg, and we managed to obtain rooms for the night in one of them.

My bed was soft and comfortable, and I was feeling tired after a long day's drive, but nonetheless I found it quite impossible to sleep. As I lay awake, all the unhappy memories of my previous visit to Schomberg came gushing back into my mind. I saw demented, emaciated men knocked viciously to the ground as they stopped marching to pick up rotten apples lying in the gutter. I heard the cries of Hungarian Gypsies so insane with hunger that they were driven to eat the flesh of fellow prisoners minutes after they had died. I suffered once again the physical agonies of typhoid, of dysentery and the unrelenting ravages of lice and vermin.

I marched again with blistered, aching feet for four nights on roads that led us back to the same spot time and time again. I relived the misery of sleeping on damp earth in unfriendly forests. I trembled with fear of coming face to face with a party of armed German as, with six fellow prisoners, I made my final escape and felt the intense relief when they told us they were deserters and intended us no harm. I saw all the faces that to me personified the most evil regimes ever experienced by mankind. In that wakeful nightmare in that little German hostelry, all the people and the places, the agonies and the anguishes, the loves and the hates of those wicked days struggled for a place on an animated, confused canvas that seemed to be hanging in the darkness above my bed.

I recalled clearly how after the four nights of marching, following our evacuation from Dautmergen, the six fellow prisoners and myself decided that we would attempt to escape from the column – the remaining 750 inmates of the Dautmergen hellhole. Our opportunity came on April 21st, 1945, when, during the general confusion of an Allied air raid, we slipped unnoticed into the undergrowth of a forest along the roadside. The following day we reached the haven of Bad Saulgau and were greeted by the comforting sight of French troops. For us – the "Lucky Seven" as we called ourselves – the war was over.

Since then, however, I have often wondered about the fate of the other prisoners on that march, as I had good reason to believe that they may not have been as fortunate as I was. For before we made our successful dash for freedom, we had seen the bodies of dozens of concentration camp victims lying by the side of the road covered only by thin blankets. They had been shot by their SS guards who did not wish to undergo the "indignity" of being captured by the advancing Allies in charge of prisoners of war.

I had always feared that my fellow marching companions in those first few days after the evacuation of Dautmergen had perished in the same way. After the war was over, I tried unsuccessfully to make contact with them. Little did I know that in a few hours after my return visit to Schomberg, the twenty years of worrying and wondering was to come to an end in a most dramatic way.

Soon it was dawn and time to prepare for our visit to the cemetery. After a hurried breakfast, we were about to set off on this short sentimental journey when my wife reminded me that we needed some water. I returned quickly to the inn where I was confronted with a question from the landlord's daughter: "Have you come to attend the trial of the SS officers who were in charge of the Schomberg camp," she asked. "What trial?" I retorted after a puzzled pause. "The trial at Hechingen. It has been going on for many weeks," she said.

My German, I believe, is adequate, but she had obviously detected a foreign accent and assumed that any foreigner in Schomberg at that time must be involved with the trial. I could hardly believe my ears. But it was true. At Hechingen, the county town some 30 miles from Schomberg, four former Nazi officers were being tried for their part in the war and witnesses had been arriving from all over the world. I, too, would have been called officially, but all attempts to trace me had failed. It is because of this that people have said so often since that fate must have guided me back to Schomberg in that unforgettable summer of 1965. As soon as I had recovered from the initial shock, the happy thought crossed my mind that perhaps some friends, or maybe even relatives, had been called as witnesses, and were even at that moment only a short distance away.

My immediate reaction was to postpone the visit to the cemetery and go instead to the courtroom at Hechingen, but after a little further reflection I realized that this would have been totally illogical. It would have been quite absurd to have traveled to Schomberg for a specific purpose and then to abandon the idea when I was so close. The trial at Hechingen, after all, had been proceeding for several weeks, and another few hours would make little or no difference.

Nonetheless, as I walked between the plots of the 1,755 victims who had died between 1944 and 1945, my mind kept projecting itself momentarily to the trial. Who would be there in the dock? Would I see any familiar faces? What evidence would be brought to light? The questions came thick and fast.

The suspense became unbearable and, after paying my respects at the cemetery, I drove to Hechingen and made my way to the courthouse. The proceedings were well underway and I paused at the door of the courtroom, insatiably curious but a little apprehensive of what might lie on the other side of the door.

A moment or so later I was inside. At first, I was bewildered and, I suppose, overawed by the galaxy of faces, but quickly I began to orientate myself and take stock of my surroundings. I looked at the defendants' bench, and immediately recognized three of the four accused: Franz Hofmann, Stefan

Kruth and Helmut Schnabel. Time had aged but not mellowed them. This was my first thought, and it transpired to be correct. The same cold eyes were still blinking without emotion. The same transfixed expressions looked as brutal as I remembered them 20 years earlier.

Franz Hofmann and Stefan Kruth
(Photos: Courtesy of Yad Vashem)

There is theory that men and women who have been snatched from the jaws of death have, in those crucial moments between this world and the next, seen their entire life unfold before their eyes. It may or may not be true, and it is ironic that having been so perilously close to the brink myself on so many occasions, I do not know the answer. All I know is that the sight of those three faces in the court released in my mind the most graphic panorama of my sufferings in Nazi captivity.

It is almost impossible to express just how I felt coming once again face to face with the murderers of relatives and friends after a lapse of 20 years. I can only recall that after the initial bombardment of imagery and memories, a feeling of numbness enveloped me for some considerable time. When I finally came back to my senses and realized where I was and what was happening to me, I saw that a man in the witness box was weeping, and that one of the accused was laughing – laughing at him.

I could not suppress my emotions. I stood up at the back of the courtroom and tried to speak. But my unplanned outburst succeeded only in provoking a sharp order from the Chairman of the Bench that I should leave the courtroom forthwith. I walked out into the corridor seething with rage and thinking that if only I had been allowed to go into the witness box I could have permanently wiped the smiles off the faces of the accused.

As I decided what to do next, a court official approached me and demanded to know if I had any business in the building or if I knew anything of the proceedings. I told him simply that I had been a prisoner at Dautmergen, and that I had worked for a time in the camp office as interpreter and messenger. He seemed impressed by my answer and said: "I think it would be advisable for you to see the State Prosecutor." I agreed at once.

At 2:00 p.m. that same day I was shown into the Prosecutor's office. When the usual preliminaries and formalities were completed, I explained that, because of the nature of my work in the camp office, I could shed a great deal of light on some of the darker, and often totally unlit, episodes of Dautmergen's existence. He, too, was obviously impressed, and he asked me if I would be prepared to go into the witness box that same day because one of the scheduled witnesses had not arrived from Israel. I discovered later that this witness was a pre-war friend and neighbor of the family.

I was taken into court and my name was announced together with the fact that I was a "chance" witness who happened to be passing through Schomberg, and had heard that the trial was taking place. On hearing my name, one of the accused – Hofmann – jumped to his feet and conferred with his defending counsel. A few moments later the lawyer raised an objection to my being called, as my name had not been entered on the official list of witnesses. The Chairman, after trying to convince the defense counsel to hear what I had to say, had to concede the fact that on a point of law he was perfectly within his rights and asked me to return to the court at some later date to present my evidence. I immediately agreed to do so.

I was taken from the courtroom to the police headquarters where I was interviewed informally about my experiences in the Dautmergen camp, and about my ability to present new and pertinent evidence to the trial. I was able to identify three of the four accused from old photographs and, after a short break for a meal, I returned to the police headquarters where a stenographer was ready to take down my statement and compile a complete dossier. With the help of regular cups of black coffee and a packet of cigarettes, I worked through without a break until 2:00 a.m.

The following day, after making the necessary arrangements for my official attendance at the Hechingen court, I was ready to leave Schomberg with my family and to complete the remainder of our interrupted journey back to England. Just as I was about to depart, a man I had seen in the court the previous day came up to me and said that he remembered me from my days at Dautmergen. In the course of our conversation I discovered that after escaping from the marching party in April 1945, the remaining prisoners were abandoned in a field in the middle of nowhere and their SS guards had fled from the advancing Allies to save their own skins.

By sheer coincidence the man also knew the whereabouts of one of my closest school friends – they had been liberated together and now lived in the same town in Israel. He gave me his address and we have been corresponding with each other ever since. For that reason, if for no other, my return to Schomberg was worthwhile.

Two months later, on October 12, 1965, I was back in the courtroom once again face to face with my tormentors. I took a long, hard look at them and pondered on the injustices of the world in which we live; that innocent, young people of many nationalities should have been so cruelly tortured and murdered and that the perpetrators of these most despicable acts should still be alive, looking affluent, healthy and not showing or expressing the slightest sign on remorse.

Because of my rather lengthy deposition the court assembled at 8.30 a.m. and for the whole of that day no other witnesses were to be heard.

After the usual preliminaries had been completed, the Prosecutor read certain passages of my statement and asked me to confirm that I had in fact dictated those words. Having confirmed that this was the case, the defense counsel then began their cross-examination, endeavoring to discredit everything that I had said. At one point in the proceedings, concerning the cold-blooded shooting of a close friend of mine by one of the accused, the defense lawyer asked me to describe the way in which his body was lying after the "alleged incident".

I felt so utterly incensed at this insensitive and irrelevant question that I broke down in the witness box. Try as I did I could not utter another word and the proceedings had to be adjourned for two hours to allow me to recover my composure. My emotional breakdown was reported in both the German and the British Press, and possibly elsewhere, too. The British 'Daily Telegraph' reported on October 13:

"A British witness burst into tears here today after telling a war crimes trial how an accused former SS man had beaten to death six inmates of the Narva death camp in Estonia on Christmas Eve, 1943.

The trial of four former SS men for complicity in the murder of inmates at several death camps was interrupted for several hours until Mr. Alan Weiler, 37, of Manchester had recovered.

Mr. Weiler accused former SS Sgt. Helmut Schnabel, 53, of having taken five or six sick inmates to the parade ground of the camp on stretchers with the camp Commandant, where he both beat and kicked them to death 'in front of us all'.

When the defense lawyer challenged the statement Mr. Weiler, who was taken to the camp from the Vilna Ghetto, started crying."

During the adjournment, I regained my composure and realized that I had a duty to the dead martyrs to give a worthy account of myself in the witness box. On returning to court after the recess, I miraculously managed to control my temper and emotions in spite of repeated attempts by the defense counsel to upset and discredit me.

I was the 138th witness at the Hechingen trial. Volumes and volumes of evidence had been prepared and read out in court, and on both my visits I saw spectators crying like babies as they listened to the horrifying facts that emerged. Even the Police Inspector who sat with me until the early hours taking my deposition, although a hardened investigator, admitted that he had never heard such harrowing stories.

In fact, the morning after I had made my statement, he was taken to hospital after collapsing with a heart attack and I will always be convinced that its onset was brought about by having to listen to the grim recollections of the inhumanities of the death camp. After taking ill, he survived for just one day.

Subsequently, three of the four accused were found guilty. No evidence was offered against the fourth, Eigen Wurth, because none of the witnesses knew him or had even heard of him. At Hechingen on March 10, 1965 the following sentences were passed: Hofmann 13 years. Kruth 12 years, Schnabel 10 years. (*The case against Hofmann was complicated by the fact that he received a 12-year sentence in 1961 at the Munich Court of Appeal as well as two life sentences at Munich and Frankfurt for other war crimes. At Hechingen, he was given as further one year sentence but, because the tribunal judge became ill, the hearing was later resumed at Ulm where the additional year was endorsed but no further action was taken because of the two life sentences imposed at the earlier court hearing. The additional year's sentence related to the execution of two fugitive prisoners from the Neckarelz concentration camp, near Mosbach in Germany. In effect, Hofmann did not receive any new sentence at Hechingen. Hofmann died in prison in Straubing on August 14, 1973)*

CHAPTER 1

My Childhood Years

The world was a cossetting, peaceful gentle place when I first came into it in a private nursing home in Vilna on July 12, 1928.

My father, Szolem Weiler, was a young, successful and respected merchant in the town and his substantial, although not inflated income, made it possible for him to afford a private bed for my mother's confinement. In the summer, he used to run a wholesale fruit merchants business but throughout the cold winter months, when fruit became far too expensive for the ordinary Polish housewife to buy, he sold raw fur instead to the major wholesale furriers in Vilna. As a profitable sideline, he also used to sell wild boars hair which at the time was widely used as bristles in the manufacture of brushes.

He and my dear mother, Eta Weiler, who was born into one of the more revered families in Vilna, the Matlowskis, lived at the time I was born in a comfortable, tastefully appointed flat in Kasztanowa Street (Chestnut Street), an avenue appropriately lined with chestnut trees, in one of the most fashionable and desirable neighborhoods in Vilna. Our avenue was only a few minutes walk from Mickiewicz Street, an imposing, majestic shopping thoroughfare named after the famous Polish national poet, and which in many ways was not unlike the Champs Ėlysées in Paris. Since Vilna because part of the Soviet Union it has been renamed, Lenin Avenue.

The quiet avenue on which we lived in those previously peaceful days was also close to the town's open-air market which every Friday hummed with the chatter and jostling of eager stallholders and bargain hunting shoppers.

Like all street trading throughout the world, I have little doubt that among the disorderly, colorful array of goods there were both genuine bargains as well as inevitable catchpennies, but as a child I saw it not so much as a place of business but as a sort of fairground, often complete with sideshows.

As a young boy with a few groszy "spends" in my trouser pockets I often used to dart excitedly between the stalls looking for a toy or trinket I could afford. Sometimes there was a pat on the head and an understanding wink from a kindly stall keeper who let me have my toy in spite of the fact I was a few coppers short, but at other times I would find myself shooed-off with a menacing gesture by a less sympathetic stallholder who thought I had spent too long looking soulfully at goods I could not afford.

At other times, whenever the mood took me, I used to wind my way from our flat to the town center along a devious, backstreet route which took me along a small, but one of the best-known streets in the whole of Vilna – the Third of May Street. It was named after the day on which Poland was granted its Constitution, but even now I have never discovered why such a seemingly insignificant cobbled street should have been nominated for this national honor.

My grandfather – on my mother's side – Sascha Matlowski lived in the street and I don't think that I ever passed without calling to see him and listen to some of his fascinating stories about our town and the people he had known who lived in it. He was always delighted to see me and I never left without a pocketful of hardboiled sweets which he gave to me "for being a good boy." Needless to say, my visits to his home were frequent to say the least.

Vilna in those days was a commercially orientated, cosmopolitan city with a population of almost a quarter of a million people – of which about 35 per cent were Jewish, 45 per cent Polish Catholics and the remaining 20 per cent a pot-pourri of Lithuanian, Russian, a small number of Germans and a handful of Karaaites, an ethnic people from southern Russia. Although numerically the population was predominately Catholic, Vilna was always regarded as the "Jerusalem of Lithuania" in view of its reputation as one of the most important and significant seats of Jewish learning and teaching in the world.

There were people in Vilna, ordinary men and women, who could recite the texts of the Old Testament from memory and it is only a slight exaggeration to say that there were almost as many synagogues in Vilna as there were shops.

It was quite usual for a group of 10 or more people, perhaps from the same family or the same street, to form their own synagogue and each and every trade in the town had its particular place of worship – rather like religious trade union headquarters. The butchers, the bakers, the candlestick makers – they all literally had their own synagogues.

There was, nonetheless, only one Great Shul, one Great Synagogue, which stood somewhat paternally over its smaller offsprings in its own precinct. When I was about eight years old I used to sing in the Great Shul choir for a short time, but for regular worship my parents and I attended the local synagogue in Portowa Street (Port Street) which was only a short walk from our flat.

In those idyllically happy days in Vilna I was a pupil at the Hebrew Religious School which, I suppose, was about half-an-hour's walk away from home. I was there at my desk every morning at 8 a.m. and I can even now hear the one o'clock bell which signaled the end of class for the day.

During the winter months, from November to March, when there was an 18-inch-thick layer of ice on the roads and the countryside was permanently under snow, I used to make my way to and from school on skates.

I gave have many memories of the short time I spent at that religious school, but probably the most vivid amongst them is the time I walked in the school procession at the funeral of Josef Pilsudski, the Polish national leader. Pilsudski was a military dictator but he had always, for personal reasons, been sympathetic to the Jews. At one time, they had saved his life and I believe that his second wife, who died not long before in Britain in her 90s, was in fact Jewish. His mother was buried in the Rossa Cemetery at Vilna and in his last will and testament he requested that his body should be divided into three parts. One part was to be buried in Cracow, another in Warsaw and his heart in Vilna at this mother's feet.

A national day of mourning was declared throughout Poland for his funeral and we all had a day off school to take part in the procession. It was the first funeral that I had attended and, not unnaturally, I was overawed by the solemnity of the occasion

Little did I know then, however, that death in all its ugliest, most macabre forms was to loom so largely for me in the future and that its shadow was to follow me everywhere until I was a young man – and I believed the only surviving Jew in Europe.

Unfortunately, my days at the Hebrew School came to an end all too quickly. My father came up against serious financial difficulties in his business and, after struggling for a while, he found the high school fees too prohibitive. With great reluctance, he was forced to take me away and in 1937 I moved to a co-educational Council School in another part of Vilna. He had speculated on what would have been a highly profitable business coup involving the transportation by rail of an enormous consignment of perishable foodstuffs. But there was some kind of hitch and almost all the goods went rotten before reaching Vilna and my father's hopes of making a small fortune perished in the bargain

My parents had to give up our luxury flat in Kasztanowa Street and move into less expensive accommodation in Sadowa Street, in a pleasant but less fashionable area of Vilna. The new flat cost only about 35 zloty a month (about

£1.7s) compared with the 120 zloty he had been paying previously. My father also found new business premises in the Market Hall which was just around the corner from our new home. In this new setting, my father's business prospered once again, enabling him to move to a larger and more comfortable flat in Kwaszelna Street.

On reflection, I feel sure the move to the Council school was beneficial in that it served to widen my educational horizons. My native tongue was Yiddish; I had learned Hebrew at the religious school and in my new school I was beginning to learn Polish – although it seemed strange being taught it as a foreign language when I was actually living in Poland.

I was a good scholar and. in spite of the fact that we were living in a less salubrious part of Vilna and my father was not as well-off financially, they were happy days for me. My younger brother Lejzer, who was born in May 1934, and I never knew what it was to go short of anything. We had a closely-knit family who were always ready to assist each other when necessary, and as far as I was concerned there were no real hardships to bear.

Every Pesach both my brother and I were rigged from head to toe in new clothes and even if my parents could not afford to buy them for us themselves, there was always a number of willing aunts and uncles who ensured that, materialistically, we wanted for nothing.

Nonetheless, my first report from the Council school must have presented by father with acute frustration and unhappiness. I understand that it indicated that I had made excellent progress, showed considerable promise and recommended my father to ensure I had all the necessary private tuition.

It hurt him desperately, because he could just not afford it. Shortly after he had read it, he took me on one side and said: "Abram, your teachers are very pleased with you. They say you are a clever boy and that it would help you if you had a private tutor. I know they are right but tutors are expensive and for the time having a tutor will not be possible. Still if you have the brains I am sure you will not need any help from anyone."

I had always had great confidence and faith in my father and I will never forget those encouraging words he said to me on that occasion.

With them still echoing in my ears, I returned happily to school. Systematically I overcame all the hurdles of my class examinations and in 1941 I was fortunate enough to pass with high marks for the Lenin High School, which my mother had attended during the First World War at the time of the Czars, but was then known under a different name.

My parents were overjoyed. Ever since I had started school they had hoped, like so many other Jewish parents, that I would have the ability and desire to become a doctor and my success in gaining a place at the High School gave them renewed encouragement. There was no reason why I could not have gone to Vilna University, one of the oldest in Europe, and qualified as a doctor in my hometown.

But it was not to be. The simmering hostilities in Europe began to boil over and all hope of taking my place at the Lenin High School permanently slipped away to the bitter disappointment of my parents and myself.

During my years at the Council school I used to spend my summer holidays in the countryside with some business acquaintances of my father, at a place called Slobodka, near Troki, about 30 miles from home. I used to stay there for between four and six weeks. During the summer of 1939 war broke out between Germany and Poland and Vilna became a part of the Soviet Union. Later, due to a treaty between the Soviet Union and the Lithuanian Republic, Vilna became, for a time, the capital of Lithuania. This lasted until 1940 when Lithuania itself was annexed to the Soviet Union.

All this is relevant because as soon as the Russians took control I would have been able to go to the Lenin High School free of charge. I should have started my studies there in September 1941, when I was 13 years old, but the war broke out between Russia and Germany on June 22 of that year, putting a permanent end to all my scholastic ambitions.

On that June day, I was at home with my family. My father, by this time, was once again in a far healthier financial position, earning some 2,000 roubles a month - around four times the wage of the average factory worker - as the head buyer for a Lithuanian foodstuffs co-operative, called Sodyba.

In the morning, he had been preparing to travel to the Lithuanian-German border to buy a large consignment of honey. As he packed, he was listening obliviously to the radio. Then at 10:30 a.m. he was suddenly transfixed by the somber voice of Molotov coming over the air in his now famous broadcast.

Molotov announced that the Fascists had attacked the Soviet Union – that war had broken out between Germany and Russia in spite of the non-aggression pact between the two countries.

My father waited for a while, naively hoping that it was all some gigantic hoax and that he would be able to catch the next train. But it was a journey he never made. Instead he was to leave Vilna on a trip which, theoretically, ended some years later with his death in a Nazi concentration camp.

CHAPTER 2

Our Flight From Vilna

Molotov's broadcast cast a cloud of ill-foreboding over the whole of Vilna. It created fear and panic in almost every Jewish home and the debate within my own family about our immediate future lasted for several hours.

No one knew exactly what the outcome of this act of aggression would be and everyone was discussing and asking one basic question: Would the hostilities escalate into a full-scale war or not?

My father's first inclination was to remain firmly entrenched in our own home and face the consequences whatever they might be, and when they arose. But we had all heard the harrowing stories of Hitler's ill-treatment of the Jews and after further reflection my parents decided that it would be wise and safer for us to pack hurriedly and leave Vilna.

We decided to try and make our way westward to Minsk, the capital of White Russia in the Soviet Union.

Having come to this decision, our first and most urgent task was to find suitable transport. Moreover, my father had to act expeditiously as there was little doubt that hundreds of other Jewish families in Vilna were of the same mind and that in only a matter of hours all available means of transport would have been commandeered.

With this thought in the forefront of his mind my father took me with him out into the streets – to meet and talk to our neighbors, to seek advice, to take stock of general morale of the people and generally to see what was happening. On almost every street corner there were small groups of people, talking excitedly and deliberating their future, or more precisely, whether they had a future at all. The expressions on their faces suggested accurately that Vilna had been devastated by an emotional earthquake.

One of the first people we met was a friend of my father, an ex-major in the Polish Army named Frucht and, without exchanging a single word, they both knew the subject of the conversation which was to ensue:

"You have heard the news, of course?" asked my father rhetorically.

"I have, I have – and I fear it's the worst," he replied.

"Well what are we to do?"

"Mr. Weiler you must take your family away from Vilna. In an hour or so the town is going to be ripped apart by the Germans. You must go, of that there is no doubt."

My father, I am sure, had already made up his mind to take his advice but, not unnaturally, he still wanted to discuss the situation with someone closer to him, a member of our own family, before reaching any final and perhaps fatal decision. In view of the far-reaching consequences the decision was almost certain to have, he needed the assurance of a second opinion.

We bade a solemn farewell to Major Frucht and set off to my uncle's flat in Nowogrodska Street, about 15 minutes walk away from our own home. We arrived to find his home in utter turmoil. My uncle, Myer Weiler, his wife and two children were all at home and almost all the people from their neighborhood seemed to be there as well. Everyone seemed upset and some were crying as though some physical disaster had already befallen them.

My father and his brother greeted each other like mourners at a funeral and almost immediately they began their deliberations. They talked soulfully and in private for some time, agreeing ultimately that only one course of action was left open to us: to leave Vilna as quickly as we could.

As all private vehicles had been requisitioned by the Red Army and there was no chance whatsoever of finding a suitable car, or cars, in view of the fact that we would have required several for all members of our large family. If we were to leave Vilna it would have to be by horse and cart.

Later that same evening my father went to see some friends who worked for a Lithuanian meat co-operative called Kaistas whom he believed might be able to provide us with this slow but vital means of transport – and our only means of escape.

He was lucky. My father's friends promised that a horse and cart would be made ready for us at first light in the morning as it was already too late for us to make a start that night.

The thought of our impending flight from the advancing Nazis made sleep quite impossible and shortly after 5 a.m. the following day (June 23) we began to prepare for our journey into the Soviet Union. We dressed hurriedly, gathered together a few small personal possessions and essential requisites, and then began our tour of Vilna to collect those other members of our family who were to accompany us. Altogether, including our immediate family, there were 15 people prepared to make the journey, among them my father's mother Guta, my Uncle Myer and their family.

Quite naturally the departure was fraught with tearful arguments and disagreements concerning what was regarded as essential luggage. Everyone wanted to take as many articles of clothing and as many personal possessions as they could carry themselves believing, not unjustifiably, that they would never see their homes or their belongings again.

My father, who together with my uncles, found himself in charge of the whole frenzied operation, had no choices but to be ruthless and insist that only those items of food, clothing and essentials, in addition to a handful of personal mementos, could be taken on the trip. Even so, he could not resist the temptation himself of taking 10 rouble gold pieces and some items of jewelry. He secreted them in a small bag which my mother stitched into the lining on the inside of his trousers.

To economize on space my father advised everyone to wear as much clothing as they could and many of the men wore one suit on top of another. In the early morning, it was not too hot but by midday, when the June sun was at its hottest, it became physically unbearable and we were forced to shed one or two layers of clothing.

We reached the outskirts of Vilna by about 7 a.m. at the start of what we knew would be a long and arduous 200 km trek to Minsk. The roads were narrow, the going tedious and shortly after we set off we realized that we would do well to reach Oszmiany that day, a small town some 30 miles from Vilna. Under normal circumstances, on a fine summer day, the journey to Oszmiany would have taken no longer than four hours, but our progress was continually interrupted by intermittent bombings by German planes along the roadside, and it was late evening before we approached Oszmiany.

The war was still only a matter of a few hours old but already German planes, droning menacingly overhead, were beginning to take their toll of human life. All along the roadside we saw the lifeless bodies of innocent people, like ourselves, who had been machine-gunned from the air. Indeed, it was simply a matter of good luck that we were not lying there among them. The whole of the road to Oszmiany was littered with vulnerable bands of refugees, tired and timid, some on foot, others on horses and carts like ourselves, and all clinging pitifully to their children and their bundles of treasured possessions. They were all travelling in the same direction and they all had the same objective – to put as many miles between the advancing Nazis and themselves as was possible.

The air attacks continued throughout that first day at approximately half-hourly intervals. First, we would hear the low humming of distant engines and seconds later the rattling of our old cart would be drowned by the penetrating rat-tat-tatting of machine-gun fire and the spluttering of bullets. The planes swept in no higher than the tops of the telegraph poles and we could even see the faces of the German pilots and hear them shouting and jeering. It seemed to be a game to them. Every time they opened fire the bands of refugees would scatter and make for cover in the woodland which lined the road for much of the journey. Some were lucky and emerged unscathed after the planes had passed overhead. Others were not so fortunate, and were mowed down before they could reach the relative safety of the trees and undergrowth. It was not possible to count all the newly slain corpses but the number must have added up to several dozen.

Perhaps the tedium, the agonies and the tragedies of that day would have been a little more bearable if we had been assured of finding a safe haven at the end of it. But throughout the journey we heard rumors that German paratroopers had already landed ahead of us and there seemed every likelihood that we were heading towards more dangerous territory than the area we had left behind. Several hundred people, in fact, abandoned their journey and decided to return home, many of them to Vilna, maintaining that it would be safer to be in their own homes and among their own people, rather than among strangers in enemy held territory. Perhaps they were right. Nevertheless, we decided to plod on and by 8 p.m. we reached the outskirts of Oszmiany.

The town was choked with Russian troops, tanks, armored vehicles and lorries and it was instantly obvious that there was not the least chance of making any further headway into the town. My father, however, refused to accept the fact that we had literally reached the end of the road. He jumped from the cart and began to walk resolutely towards the town center, saying that he hoped to return shortly. At the time, I did not know where he was going.

True to his word he rejoined us some 15 minutes later, announcing that he had found somewhere for us to stay and that we would all be allowed to pass through. At that moment, I think I believed in miracles.

By a stroke of good fortune, he had a friend in Oszmiany called Barnes – a former business acquaintance – and, in the short time that he was away, he persuaded him to put us up in his home for the night. In Oszmiany we were strangers and Mr. Barnes was frightened to take anyone into his home who did not live in the town or who was not known to the authorities. But somehow my father managed to impress upon him how important it was that we should take cover for the night and promised that we would leave his home at the first opportunity.

When we descended upon him he was obviously extremely nervous. He was worried that our presence would endanger his life and the lives of his own family and he asked us to go immediately into his cellar to hide. He said that it was in our own interests – that we would be safer in the cellar in case of an air or artillery attack, but I believe now that this was simply and excuse to ensure that we were all out of sight.

We were in no position to make demands, however, and a little reluctantly we descended one by one into the cellar. We had barely had time to take stock of our new surroundings when we were silenced by the crack of shells exploding only a very short distance away.

Although I have no doubt, on reflection, we were in the safest place in the Barnes household, my father could not resist the temptation to surface and see what was happening in the town. Quite apart from this we had eaten practically nothing all day and it was a matter of necessity that someone left our "bunker" to go on a mission for food. This, as it happened, presented no problems. Mr. Barnes kindly let us share the food from his own larder and within a few minutes my father returned to the cellar like a bird returning to a nest full of gaping, ravenous mouths. After eating with us, my father resurfaced to reconnoiter the area and make an assessment of our chances of completing our journey to Minsk. He returned long-faced and with a demoralizing story that the Russians had already left the town and that people had seen advanced columns of Germans entering Oszmiany from the west.

That night no one slept.

At first light the following morning, June 24, it was decided that we could not stay in the cellar forever and that we should make every effort to go as soon as it was safe to do so. Mr. Barnes was, if anything, more fearful than he had been on our arrival the night before and he refused to allow us upstairs. Under the Soviet system the authorities had to be notified if individuals moved from one town to another or if a householder in one town gave refuge to strangers from another area. Mr. Barnes' nervousness undoubtedly stemmed from this, coupled with the fact that by this time Oszmiany was echoing under the thud of the Nazi jackboots. Reluctantly we stayed like caged animals in our hideout wondering what was going to happen to us.

Half-an-hour or so elapsed and the answer came traumatically. There was some loud banging close by and a moment or so later the trap door leading down into the cellar was lifted and a uniformed German from the Panzer (tank) corps peered down into the darkness. Without uttering a word, he pulled the trigger on his revolver and fired a shot into our midst. Luckily, we were cowering around the walls and no one was hit.

Then he yelled just one word, several times: "Out! Out! Out!" and proceeded to threaten that he would fire again if we refused to obey his order.

We had no alternative but to emerge one by one until all 15 of us had left our place of hiding.

It was the first time that I had come face to face with a German soldier and I was struck dumb with fright. I am sure that if he had spoken to me, I would not have been able to reply.

Once we had vacated our cellar hideout we were marched at gunpoint towards the courtyard in front of the house where a German communications van had been set up. There, we were confronted by many more Germans who eagerly began to interrogate us one by one. My mother, whose German was good, acted as spokeswoman for the group and she explained honestly that we were simply trying to make our way eastwards.

"Are you Communists?" one of them demanded. Again, my mother told them the plain truth - that we had heard what Hitler does to the Jews and, while we had no personal grievances against the Germans, we were trying to save our own lives by escaping to Russia.

Her statement was received with an unexpected, hearty burst of laughter from the Germans who proceeded to pick out all the children, including myself, and treat us to bars of chocolate and hot drinks from their field kitchen. Such paradoxes were to become, in my own experience, a not infrequent feature in the Germans' attitude towards Jews.

After some deliberation, they decided to let us return to Mr. Barnes' house. There my father and my two uncles held one of their many conferences to decide what to do next – but in fact our next move was decided for us. By lunchtime Oszmiany was overrun with German troops and it was obvious that before long we would have to leave. But as the day progressed the German troops themselves began to leave in small convoys – although they seemed in no desperate hurry to pursue the Red Army eastwards. Before long only a handful of Germans, together with those who were manning the communications unit, were left in Oszmiany.

Ironically the Germans we encountered on this first, and isolated occasion, were extremely hospitable and, although we had made up our minds to leave, we did in fact stay one more night in Mr. Barnes' cellar. On Wednesday, June

25, the roads seemed much clearer. All the advanced columns had passed and there were only one or two military vehicles to be seen in the area.

So, after a sound sleep and a nourishing breakfast we thanked Mr. Barnes and his wife for their generosity, clambered back on our horse and cart and started our return journey to Vilna.

CHAPTER 3

Return To The Ghetto – And The "Yellow Star"

Our horse had not yet regained its strength after the exhaustions of the outward journey and for our return we had no choice but to walk alongside the cart.

Progress was painfully slow and I don't think that we had travelled more than a mile or so out of Oszmiany before we heard whispers of a new and distressing threat to our safety: bands of young Poles who were robbing the returning Jews of their few precious possessions.

I soon learned that war, as if it were not evil enough in itself, provided a bloodstained backcloth against which criminals of all races and religions, including the Jews themselves, could act out their immoral, unscrupulous and offensive practices. Murderers, looters, blackmailers, thieves, rapists and even as we discovered, highway robbers all exploited the war for their own equally wicked ends. I suppose it is one of the sad, irreversible facts of humanity that greed, lechery, violence are inbred characteristics of every society and that their ugliest features become visibly evident in ugly times.

All that we could do at the time by way of a practical solution to the danger which we were facing was to stop for a few minutes by the roadside, remove our best clothes from the bundles we were carrying and put them on top of the garments that we were already wearing. We hoped that if we were set upon by these young marauders, they would at least not take the clothes that we were wearing on our backs.

We then set off again towards Vilna in the hope that the luck which had been with us so far would not desert us before we reached our homes - nor afterwards come to that!

About half way we approached a small lake at the side of the road and, silhouetted against the skyline, we saw a German soldier in his swimming trunks sitting by the edge of the water. A revolver hung loosely from a belt around his waist. For a moment or so we thought that he was preoccupied with his daydreaming and that we would be able to pass by unnoticed. But we were mistaken. As we drove passed he swiveled round, fixed us with his eyes and ordered us to halt our horse and cart. After quickly looking us over he pointed at me and beckoned me over to the spot where he was standing.

My mother's protective instincts instilled her with courage and without hesitation she began to walk towards the soldier instead of me. But for some reason, which was not at all apparent to me at the time, he only wanted me and expressed his annoyance by snatching his revolver out of its holster. With its barrel, he began waving to my mother, yelling at the same time: "You go back, go back, I want the boy. I want to talk to the boy".

Reluctantly my mother had no choice but to go back to the horse and cart while, at the same time, I began to walk slowly towards him fearful of what he wanted with me.

My German in these early days was far from fluent and I could not understand what he wanted or what he was saying. But as he talked he kept pointing alternately at the pair of black leather Russian boots which I was wearing and at a barefooted shepherd boy who was tending some sheep in a nearby field.

I realized after a while that he was ordering me to take off my boots and give them to the little peasant boy. There was no point in offering any form of protest or resistance and obediently I sat down on the grass to take them off. But they seemed to be glued to my feet. After several hours of walking under a tireless sun my feet had swollen and no matter how hard I pulled and tugged I could not take them off. The soldier undoubtedly thought that I was being deliberately obstructive and eventually he impatiently grabbed the boots himself, wrenched them from my feet and then threw them to the boy.

All the time I was crying bitterly as I was parting with what, at the time, were among my most treasured possessions.

Barefooted, I ran back to our horse and cart where my mother embraced me, sobbing and with tears in her eyes. Although I had only been some 100 yards or so away from the family party I had been out of sight and they had been desperately worried about my safety. I am sure that when I did not return after a few minutes they feared that they would never see me alive again. By comparison with encounters that I was to have with the Germans in later years this was a relatively insignificant episode but it is nonetheless one that I shall never forget.

The rest of the journey back to Vilna was uneventful. Several times we exchanged experiences with other families returning to their homes but it was not until we came within 10 or 12 km of Vilna that we witnessed further evidence of the hostilities. Lying in pools of blood in ditches by the roadside we came across the bullet-ridden bodies of several members of the Maccabi football team, an amateur Jewish team which I often cheered and hero-worshipped in Vilna. Among the corpses I recognized many of my idols and it saddened and sickened beyond belief. We assumed that they, too, had been trying to make their way eastwards but it was not clear just how they had met their deaths.

By nightfall, when we arrived back in Vilna, I was limp with tiredness, frightened and utterly bewildered. The city was in a state of chaos and confusion. People were walking about the streets, distraught with worry, disorientated and, in many cases, also homeless and bereaved. As we trundled the last few hundred yards to our own home we did not know what to expect but instinctively feared the worst.

Our fears proved correct. Most of our belongings had been taken, including my mother's most treasured possession – a Singer sewing machine in a cabinet which was a present to her from my uncle. Most of our clothes had been taken, too. In fact, when we opened the wardrobe all we found were the family photographs which we had forgotten to take with us in our haste to flee to Russia. Who could have been so unkind, so cruel to rob us? We settled down to an uncomfortable night's sleep with the question unanswered.

The following day, when everyone had settled back in their own homes, my father once again decided to go out into the streets to find out what had been happening in Vilna in our absence.

It appeared that the Germans had entered Vilna on the morning of June 24 – the same day as they had stormed into Oszmiany - and had immediately bared their teeth, by arresting Jews, Catholics, Communists and even prominent people connected with trade unions and civic life. Only the Lithuanians seemed immune to these initial Nazi outrages. The Germans thought, and rightly so as it transpired, that the Lithuanians would be faithful collaborators and they would be able to rely upon them to assist in the massive extermination program they were soon to launch.

It became clear, too, that Lithuanian youths, mostly University students, had been responsible for the upheaval we found at our home on our return. After the Russians evacuated the city these young Fascists had put on white arm bands and set themselves up as a sort of police force, called the Ipatinga. In this ludicrous guise, they went on an insane rampage through the streets of Vilna, robbing Jewish homes, looting and, when anyone stood in their way, shooting and killing. These young thugs completely ransacked our home in their search for gold, jewelry and other valuables and, in their wake, virtually nothing in the house was left unturned.

A reign of terror started almost as soon as the Germans occupied the city and not many days passed after our return before the Ipatinga, or the "Human Hunters" as they became known, began molesting and kidnapping those Jews who, for one reason or another, had to venture into the streets. After all, the Jews had to leave their homes to find food and it was only natural that from time to time they should make a dash through the streets to see close friends or relatives and find out if they were alive and well.

The Ipatinga were as indiscriminate as wild animals. In gangs, they would run through the streets or lie in wait in doorways and street corners ready to snare the first unsuspecting Jew that came along. First, they would take their captives to their "headquarters" where they would give them a towel and a bar of soap and then tell them that they were going to be taken to labor camps to work for the Germans.

This, indeed, would have been bad enough but in fact we learned later that they were transported instead to Vilna's Lukiski Prison and afterwards to their deaths at Ponary, a popular peacetime picnic forest some eight km from Vilna where most of the city's Jewish community were to perish. For each Jew that the "Human Hunters" caught the Germans paid 10 marks a head and in the first few days of the occupation the Ipatinga must have earned several thousand marks by this despicable trafficking.

My own second cousin, Icik Matlowski, was, in fact one, of the first victims. Neighbors had seen him taken forcibly from his flat where lived with his wife but at the time they were not aware that he was being led away to his death. Icik, who would have been about 29 years of age at the time, was married just before the war but he and his wife had no children. His family ran a wholesale fur business in Vilna and my father had carried out many transactions with them over the years. We could only assume that the Ipatinga thought that they would be able to reap a rich harvest of valuables from his home, apart from the fee that they would receive from the Germans for his head.

Shortly after he disappeared, his family made contact with the Ipatinga and attempted to bribe them for his safe return, but without success. There were rumors that he had been herded onto a cattle train taking prisoners to a labor camp in Lithuania but we learned later the sad truth: that together with dozens of other Jews he had been shot at Ponary.

To lull the Jews into a false sense of security, the Ipatinga would every now and again take men from their homes, put them to work until nightfall and then return them safely to their families. Cases such as this were rare and were specifically engineered to illustrate the "'exemplary" behavior of the Germans. But the trust that the Germans hoped that these isolated incidents would engender was not forthcoming. When the Ipatinga came into the courtyards of the blocks of flats seeking willing hands to spend, as they would

say, "just one day" in a military unit or in the German command offices, there
were no volunteers.

**Two Jews just before their execution surrounded by German soldiers. Ponary, Poland
June-July 1941.**

Photo: courtesy of Yad Vashem

This, of course, did not prevent the Ipatinga from taking an unwilling Jew
by force and many potential victims went into hiding as a matter of routine
rather than take the risk.

Not infrequently, my father would spend all day entirely on his own in a
hiding place which he constructed in a wooden outhouse in the courtyard of
our flat in Raugiklos Street. There was a loft in the building which was used
for storing timber and logs for heating our home and, whenever the Ipatinga
were in the vicinity, he would conceal himself behind a section of timber.
Often, he would tell my mother how it made him feel like a panic-stricken rat
listening to a pack of savage dogs sniffing out their quarry and lusting for the

kill. Nature, fortunately, had not provided the Ipatinga with the same keen sense of small as a pack of hounds and they never found him.

My uncle Myer, who was with us on our abortive escape into Russia, was not as fortunate. We discovered that he had been caught by the Ipatinga in a potato field near his home in Nowogrodska Street and that he had been taken on the inevitable journey, first to Lukiszi Prison and then to Ponary. We heard this sad tale from some prisoners who for some inexplicable reason, had been released.

During the early days prior to the formation of the ghetto, the German command churned out new laws with nonsensical rapidity. All Jews, regardless of age or sex, had to wear the Star of David so that they could be more easily identified and, as a result, more frequently ridiculed, insulted and even spat upon. In garish, yellow-colored material, the stars were stitched firmly on the back and front of one's clothes and no Jews were allowed to be seen in the street unless they displayed this distinctive label of their faith. As Jews, we were proud to wear the Star of David, but emblazoned on our clothes in that way, we felt like branded cattle destined for the slaughterhouses. Indeed, for many thousands of Vilna's Jews there was just such a finale to their days under the rule of the "butchers" of the Third Reich. I am convinced that the wickedly devious Nazi mind deliberately chose the Star of David, the Jewish symbol of peace and love, to be, in effect, the sign of death for Jewry throughout Europe. Those who wore it were destined either for a quick death at Ponary or a slow one in the labor camps which were soon to scar the countryside of Estonia and Germany.

Shortly after the German occupation of Vilna, Jews were also banned from walking on the pavements being forced, instead, to walk in the gutters.

Then, just to make life even more uncomfortable, they were forbidden to walk two abreast. Instead, they were ordered to march through the gutters goose-fashion, one behind the other. About this time, too, the German Command imposed a 5 p.m. curfew on the Jews of Vilna, which made it perilously risky for any Jew to attempt to travel, either by foot or by road, during the late evening or at night. Dozens, however, tossed their common sense to the wind and successfully broke the curfew time and time again. Others, less fortunate, never returned to their homes and were never heard of or seen again.

Ponary, Poland (outside of Vilna)
Jewish victims digging a trench in which they would later be buried after being shot.
Photo: courtesy of Yad Vashem

Every German who was appointed to take charge of the civil and the military administration of Vilna - and there were several of them - brought with him a completely new batch of rules and regulations, or revised or amended those already in existence. Most of these so-called laws, however, were utterly absurd and served no purpose other than to demoralize the Jewish population even further and to try and enforce an attitude of servility and servitude to the Nazi regime.

This insane kaleidoscopic administration continued until the beginning of September when an order was made by the German Commander which led to the formation of the Vilna Ghetto. It stated clearly and categorically that all Jews from a date to be specified would have to leave their homes and move en masse into certain streets in Vilna which had been earmarked for the Jewish population. All non-Jews living in the area of Vilna set aside for the Ghetto were told that that they would have to move out and find fresh accommodation. As it transpired, the Ghetto was in the center of the city, very close to my original home and consequently I knew the area well.

The announcement by the Germans of their intention to create the Vilna Ghetto presented my father with a major dilemma: with a choice of either going into hiding in the country or remaining entrenched in our own home.

During the orgiastic outrages of the Ipatinga, a friend of my father's – I can only remember that his first name was Jan – came to Vilna and offered to hide us at his home at Slobodka, a beauty spot near Treki, where I used to spend almost all my summer holidays as a child. But even in these early days, the Germans made it abundantly clear that non-Jews who gave refuge to Jews would themselves face the death penalty and, therefore, not wishing to endanger his friend's life or the lives of his family, my father reluctantly declined his offer.

My father at the time thought that he would hear no more from him, but he was mistaken. For when, prior to the formation of the Ghetto, Jan heard that our lives were in even greater danger than before, he once again sacrificed his own safety and offered us refuge under his own roof.

By this time, the Germans were forcibly taking Polish Catholics as well as Jews to work in their labor camps and to ensure that we received his new offer of help, he sent his 70-year-old mother to deliver it to us personally. On the face of it, she seemed a strange choice for such a mission but because of her age and her inability to work, there was very little chance that she would be snatched from the streets by the Germans. Almost as soon as she came into our home, she began to plead with my father that he should pack immediately and return with her to the safety of her son's home. A horse and cart was waiting on the outskirts of Vilna to take us there, she told us. But my father stubbornly refused to leave. She went down on her knees to try and make him change his mind, but he remained adamant, reiterating time and time again that under no circumstances would he endanger the lives of another family.

Eventually she realized that all her persistence was fruitless and, with tears in her eyes and a heavy heart, she wished us good luck and good bye.

It would not have been too difficult in those pre-Ghetto days to have escaped from Vilna in spite of the fact that the city was occupied by the Germans in large numbers. There was always the possibility of running across a German patrol and, with little knowledge of their movements and of the geography of the city, the chances of being apprehended were high. What is more, there was little doubt that most other families, given the same opportunity to escape as we were given, would not have turned it down. They would have packed and fled.

My father's motives for refusing were morally sound but there were times later when we found ourselves in Nazi concentration camps, stretched to the limits of human endurance, when I found it hard to forgive him for turning down this offer of a place to hide. It is possible, of course, that had he accepted, I might have perished and other members of my family, now dead, may have survived.

Nonetheless, I will always believe that on this occasion he made the wrong decision.

CHAPTER 4

Life In The Ghetto

It is a futile exercise to suppose what might have happened to our family had we fled from Vilna to Slobodka before the iron rule of the Ghetto administration clamped down around us. But we were soon made starkly aware of the consequences of our decision to stay.

On Sunday, August 31, 1941, a day that will go down as one of the blackest in the history of Vilna Jewry, dozens of German soldiers began to congregate in the streets, parks and public squares. Then, just before noon, a group of them firing pistols, stormed into Saklanna Street from Vielka Street. At the same time, they were shouting and bawling that they had been fired upon by Jews secreted in hideouts along the street. There was not one word of truth in their allegations but it provided them with an excuse to start scouring the area for suspects and, in so doing, beating up old and young alike of both sexes, and wrecking as much Jewish property as they could. By this time, it did not take a great deal to frighten the Jewish population and like professional boxers pounding persistently at an open cut, the Germans ensured that none of the wounds that they inflicted ever healed.

As a reprisal for the alleged shootings, the Germans encircled the area in which they claimed the culprits were hiding and, during a night of typical Nazi ruthlessness, they arrested all Jewish inhabitants in the surrounding streets: Saklanna Street, Sydowska Street, Gaona Street and Jatkowa Street.

The German overlords ordered the Jews to pack whatever meagre belongings they had left after the ravages of the Ipatinga and then, in droves, they were led away to the bulging cells at Lukiszi Prison.

By then we had grown accustomed to the fact that young Jews disappeared almost every day, ostensibly taken to labor camps for just a few hours work, but until that Sunday we never anticipated that the Germans would indulge in such wholesale removals of men, women and children. But the gluttony of those few hours did not satisfy their appetites for blood and they were to return to gorge themselves still further.

Just 24 hours later, on Monday, September 1, the Germans, with the willing help of their Lithuanian lackeys, surrounded several more streets in the vicinity of Niemicka Street, where almost all the inhabitants were Jewish, and began to repeat their performance of the previous night.

Over two nights it was estimated that at least 10,000 people, young, old and sick, were dragged, sometimes screaming, from their homes, beaten mercilessly and, as we learned later, transported to Ponary, where their suffering ended with a bullet through the brain.

Almost every Jew in Vilna lost a close relative or friend in those two days and, for me personally it turned out to be one of the most tragic episodes of all. My beloved grandmother, Chaya Bracha Matlowski, who would then have been approaching 70, was arrested at her home at 7 SW. Nikolaja Street (St. Nicholas Street) during the second of the two actions and, together with my favorite aunt, uncle and cousin, she was taken to Ponary and executed. She was a pious, gentle and harmless woman, a devoted mother and grandmother, and there was not one member of our large family who did not genuinely love her dearly. Even in the last years of her life, when she was nearly blind, she would sit up half the night knitting socks, scarves and earmuffs for her many grandchildren to make sure that they would be warm during the long, bitter Polish winter. It was unthinkable that a woman such as this should have perished like a criminal at the hands of spineless monsters.

Corpses hanging on the gallows at Ponary
Photo: Courtesy of Yad Vashem

I can only hope that she did not suffer too greatly and that she was comforted during her last and most horrible journey by my aunt, Pesia Szneider, my mother's youngest sister, who went with her to her death at Ponary. I doubt if ever a young boy had a better, kinder aunt than my Aunt Pesia. She used to live about halfway between my school and our house and several times each week I used to call at her home for a hot or cold drink, depending upon the time of year, and some sweets or chocolate.

In Poland, it was always the custom among Jewish families to buy new clothes for the Feast of the Passover and if my own parents found that they could not afford them for my young brother and me, Aunt Pesia would always buy them for us.

To me, as a young boy, my grandmother and my aunt were two of the most wonderful women in the world and even now, as an adult, I still believe that they were. Nonetheless, they were murdered together with my beautiful nine-year-old cousin Zenia and my Uncle Samuel for no reason other than that they were Jews.

The atrocities during the first week in September shook Vilna Jewry to the roots, dispelling any illusions that lingered on in some optimistic quarters that we would soon awaken from a nightmare. The tragic episodes of those two days engraved an indelible impression on my mind that I shall carry with me to my grave. In those two days, I not only lost my grandmother, aunt, cousin and uncle, but nearly all my closest school friends as well. They were unfortunate to live within the area surrounded by the Nazis and, together with their parents, they were led away to Ponary and shot in cold blood and without ceremony.

There were 13 of my classmates in all and even now I can remember and picture every one of them. The six whom I knew best were Josele Lewin, Chatzke Szwarc, Leib Grobsztein, Zalmen Szteinfeld and two girls Ester Weinsztein and Rachel Kovner.

I could not believe that we would never again sit together in the classroom, act in school plays, kick a football about the school playground or pinch apples from neighbors' orchards. Somehow, I thought that they were too young to die and that they would all be there at their desks when next I returned to school.

A mass murder site of Jews at Ponary
Photo: Courtesy of Yad Vashem

But two days later, when the numbness thawed and I realized the full painful truth for the first time, I became hysterical with grief. My mother, who was crying all the time herself, tried unsuccessfully to pacify me but in desperation she had to take me to my father's sister's home in Nowogrodska Street to see if she could console me and persuade me to eat. By that time, I had not eaten a morsel for three days and my health was beginning to deteriorate.

I had hardly had time to settle into my aunt's house when rumors began to circulate through Vilna that the Germans were about to form the Jewish Ghetto. My aunt, who had four children of her own, was loath to have the responsibility of a fifth child not her own and, almost as soon as she heard the news, she persuaded a Christian neighbor, with whom she was friendly, to escort me back to my own home.

I arrived only a few minutes before the 3 p.m. curfew to find my mother and father anxious and distressed. They had been discussing our future as a family and had come to the inevitable conclusion that there was absolutely nothing we could do but wait for fate to take its course.

CHAPTER 5

Under The Nazi Jackboot

Ever since the first German soldiers marched into Vilna, the Jews had scurried neurotically about the streets like frenzied ants disturbed in their nest. Their community had been savagely emasculated. Homes had been ransacked, families fragmented beyond redemption and Jews in every strata of society systematically oppressed, mocked and persecuted.

Virtually all that remained was a rapidly evaporating fighting spirit, a dogged determination to survive even in the face of the harshest adversity and a naive belief, still held by a few, that the worst was over. But how wrong the optimists were.

On September 6, 1941, blindly oblivious of the suffering that they had caused already, the Germans clinically carried out the promise we had all hoped and prayed they would never keep: their promise to form the Vilna Ghetto. It was the beginning of the end for the Jews of Vilna. As long as they were able to pursue their ant-like behavior pattern there was always the hope that a sufficient number of them would survive to refurbish the Jewish community within its natural setting. But with the formation of the ghetto the Nazi jackboot slowly began to descend to crush and rub the remaining Jews slowly into the dust.

It is a date engraved on the heart of Vilna. For on that black day every Jew was to be uprooted from his or her home and driven into a ghetto where, to all intents and purposes, one ceased to be a human being. Individuals were ciphers. I was No. 5714.

The day started for our own family with a knock on the door of our flat at 6 a.m. My father answered it and was confronted with our janitor, a man by the name of Boleslaw. His face was long and grey with worry.

"Mr. Weiler," he said, like a man about to pass a sentence of death, "In view of our long friendship I have come to warn you to prepare yourself and your family to leave your home. A few minutes ago, I heard that the Jews are about to go into a ghetto."

He advised my father to pack whatever we could carry and offered to take care of any valuables, promising that he would always be prepared to return them to us once we had settled in our ghetto home. But we had already experienced an example of his "kindness". On our return from Oszmiany, my mother saw Boleslaw's wife wearing one of her dresses, and we had reason to believe they had taken other articles too. After thanking him for his kindness my father came back inside and he and my mother began to pack at once, although most of our belongings had been taken during our abortive attempt to escape to Russia. Nevertheless, they collected together all our remaining bedding and clothing and, with very little thought of the consequences, walked vacantly out into the courtyard where all our neighbors were already assembled.

Everyone was wondering what was going to happen next and precisely where we were to be resettled, when at about 9:30 a.m. a group of Lithuanian police, accompanied by a German soldier, walked into Kwaszelna Street and unceremoniously ordered us to march in the direction of Rudnicka Street. We obeyed without protest.

At the top of Rudnicka Street we could see the hastily erected ghetto wall and gate just a few yards beyond the Church of All Saints. We had assumed that the ghetto would be a long way from our flat but as it turned out our new home was barely five minutes walk away. Had we known that our ghetto home would be so close we would almost certainly have taken many more of our personal possessions with us. In the mistaken belief that we would be taken on a long trek, perhaps for a few miles, we deliberately left the heavier and bulkier items behind. It grieved us to think that although the contents of our flat were such a short distance away it was highly improbable that we would ever see them, or the flat, again.

As we approached the ghetto gate the other Jews, in groups of all sizes, converged on Rudnicka Street from Zawalna Street, Stefanska Street and Konska Street. We were to become a captive, subservient community within our own home town.

On the inside of the gates thousands of people - men, women and children - were sitting or standing beside their belongings waiting to be told what they had to do and where they had to go next.

We were more fortunate. My mother's brother, Fayvel Matlowski, lived with his family in a flat above his chemist's shop at 14 Rudnicka Street, which was inside the ghetto, and we were allowed to stay with him. My uncle, I remember, was not at home when we arrived but, in spite of this, his flat was bursting at the seams with people, all pushing and sometimes even coming to blows over their rights to a little floor space. It was a two-bedroomed flat with a kitchen which at most could only have accommodated eight to 10 people. But there seemed to be twice that number. For several hours, the place was in complete chaos but my parents, brother and I firmly stood our ground, refusing to be moved by anyone. After all it was my uncle's flat and we were determined to stay. We did at least have some right to be there, whereas many of those jostling for position seemed to be complete strangers.

When my uncle eventually returned in the afternoon with his wife Sonia and their small son Sascha, he was also accompanied by a man who claimed that he was in charge of the building and, making it quite clear, decreed that pre-ghetto inhabitants had priority to occupy the premises. My uncle Fayvel immediately took possession of the bedroom for his wife and son, as well as my mother, father, brother and myself. The living room was shared by friends of my uncle, a man called Szymon Keidan and his wife and baby, and another friend by the name of Kushiel Probe.

Three days later, on Tuesday, September 9, people were still arriving in the ghetto and, with every hour, the accommodation problem became more and more acute, until ultimately the Germans were forced to plan a second ghetto to absorb, the overflow - if only for a short time.

There was, of course, a less troublesome solution to the accommodation problem which had a special appeal to the Germans and which they employed on innumerable occasions – extermination. Indeed, several of the closest members of my own family perished, including my paternal grandmother, my father's sister and her husband and their four children, as well as Uncle Myer's wife and their two children. They had all lived in the Nowogrodka Street area and, together with all the other Jewish inhabitants of the street, they were directed into the ghetto through Lidka Street. When they arrived, they found that the street was full of people who had not been accommodated, they too waited. But instead of being resettled in the ghetto they were surrounded by Germans and Lithuanian police who marched them away to Lukiszki Prison and then, in small groups, to their deaths in Ponary.

At least 6,000 Jews from the Nowogrodka Street area lost their lives at this time and there is no doubt that I too would have been among them had it not been for the foresight of my aunt Cheyna in returning me to my parents as soon as she heard rumors that the Germans were to form the ghetto.

In the years to come I was to come perilously close to death on several occasions but, in retrospect, I will always regard this instance as my first, and one of my luckiest escapes.

The deaths of so many close members of our family in such a short space of time made my father dreadfully ill. In just one night of horror he had lost his mother, sister, brother-in-law, sister-in-law as well as six nieces and nephews – in fact all the relatives from his side of the family who were living in Vilna at the time. There was nothing we could do to console him, quite apart from the fact that my mother and myself had hardly regained our senses after the loss, only a few days earlier, of my maternal grandmother, Aunt Pesia, Uncle Samuel and cousin Zenia. Only my younger brother, who was too young to understand such tragedies, remained unaffected during those first few days in our ghetto home.

Our family had been torn into miserable shreds, and was beyond repair. After just one week only my Uncle Fayvel, and his family, as well as my parents, brother and myself remained. The rest had gone forever and we could not help thinking that it was simply a matter of time before we, too, fell foul of the German murder machine.

Man, nonetheless, is a creature who tries to survive under all circumstances and after a few days my father recovered some of his sanity and strength and was lucky enough to obtain work at the Vilna railway station. It was considered a good job, mainly because it afforded him with the opportunity to secure a little extra food to supplement the meagre rations on which we tried to survive. The soup cooked for the Germans passing through the station was so vile that the Nazis did not mind if the Jews took some of it home to their families in the ghetto. It was barely palatable but contained a little nourishment and I am sure that it helped to maintain a reasonable standard of health within our family.

As time went on, a full administration was established within the ghetto with departments to control all the essential services such as housing, labor, the distribution of food, sanitation and even schooling, although the latter was functional only on an underground, unofficial basis.

The new ghetto administration formulated a system under which homes were allocated according to the place in which one worked. We had to move into a block of flats in Straszuna 15, the neighborhood designated to railway workers and their families. But at the same time the Germans maintained their iron rule overall and continued to pursue their heartless and haphazard policy of removing people from our ghetto to a second one. If they had simply expanded the ghetto to alleviate the overcrowding that undoubtedly existed then there would have been few critics but we soon discovered their motives were nothing like as humane as this.

Ghetto No. 2 was formed virtually as an afterthought by the Germans because they soon realized that it was physically impossible to house all the Jews in Vilna in the six streets originally earmarked for our new homes. But instead of absorbing this overspill population and allowing them to establish their own ghetto community, the Nazis simply used it as a "transit camp" for Jews on their way to their deaths at Ponary. Ghetto No. 2 lasted only 41 days.

On Yom Kippur day, October 1, 1941, in keeping with the Nazis' unrivalled flair for the macabre, the Germans started to liquidate the second ghetto and, in a matter of a few days, only the original ghetto, with its depleted population, was left. Even so, the German authorities still held the view that too many Jews remained among the living and they took immediate steps to reduce the number of Jewish employees to a minimum.

Their first and most important move was the introduction of a Yellow Permit which was only issued to those Jews who were either employed by or who were useful to the German cause. Those privileged few, fortunate enough to receive what in fact amounted to a passport-to-live, were also allowed to have three dependents (a wife and two children under the age of 16 years). By simple mathematics the Germans handed out only 3,000 Yellow Permits to the selected Jews so that they could be sure that the population of the ghetto – at least the legally existent population – did not exceed 12,000.

On this occasion, my father was not among the chosen few. During the pruning process, he lost his job at the railway station and with it the right to live in the railway workers' block.

Our legal existence in the ghetto had come abruptly to an end. We now not only had to carry on our desperate struggle for survival but a struggle made even more desperate because we would have to go into hiding.

CHAPTER 6

Going Into Hiding

For four months my parents, younger brother and I had lived a tightrope existence balanced precariously over the cavernous jaws of the Nazis. Every few weeks a fresh strand would be severed by the Germans and on October 23, 1941 they began to gnaw away at the last – and most vital.

We felt as helpless as a sacrificial lamb about to have its throat slit by a sadistic Priest of Satan.

We were informed that the following day, October 24, all those Jews who were in possession of the coveted Yellow Permits were to leave the ghetto, together with their dependents, and make their way to their places of work. This could only mean one thing; that the Germans were planning to make a raid on the ghetto and seek all the illegal inhabitants and massacre them at Ponary.

Once again, we found ourselves hovering on the brink of disaster. Not only had my father failed to secure a permit but, by virtue of the fact that he had lost his job at the railway station, we were being ousted by the ghetto authorities from our railway workers' accommodation at Straszuna 15.

To help us out of this fearful predicament my mother went to see my Uncle Fayvel, her brother, with a proposition which was to cause considerable acrimony within our family circle. Under the Nazis' regulations it was permissible for a Yellow Permit holder to have children, apart from his wife, as legally protected dependents. Uncle Fayvel had a permit and only one son. My mother, therefore, asked him if he would be prepared to adopt me temporarily – being the oldest son – so that I would be able to leave the ghetto in safety with my Uncle and his family while the Germans secured the ghetto for illegal inhabitants.

My Uncle Fayvel was not a hard, unfeeling man but my mother, nonetheless, had a difficult time trying to impress upon him the importance of saving my life. Quite apart from any personal reluctance he might have had, counterforces were at work, too, making her task even more difficult. Considerable pressure was, at the same time, being put on him by his own wife to adopt her 18-year-old sister, Nehama, who had just finished high school, and so save her life instead mine. This disagreement between my mother and my aunt developed into a heated and emotionally charged quarrel which lasted for several hours, until the matter finally resolved itself with an alternative which no-one had thought of previously.

Nehama's boyfriend, a young ghetto policeman by the name of Lewin, like other ghetto administrators, including the police, had been issued with a permit which provided the same protection rights for his family as the permit held by Uncle Fayvel. This young man, whose first name I cannot remember, decided to "marry" Nehama right away so that she would automatically be registered as his dependent and be safe during the action planned for the ghetto.

Synagogue marriages by the Jewish religious leaders, or indeed any official marriage between Jews, were forbidden by the Nazis but, as an effective means of saving lives, dozens, possibly hundreds, of "paper" marriages were arranged during the Yellow Permit regime.

Nehama's marriage to her ghetto policeman solved, for the time being, all our immediate problems and restored, at the same time, the equilibrium within our family. My Uncle Fayvel was able to adopt me with the disapproving consent of his wife, who, in a sudden surge of generosity, decided to invite my parents and younger brother to stay with them, too. For a while, under the protective umbrella of my Uncle's Yellow Permit I would be safe but my parents and younger brother were illegal inhabitants and were desperately in need of somewhere to hide during the Nazi action which was to follow.

Although my uncle was strictly supposed to live with his family at Strazuna 15, as he too worked at the railway station, his close acquaintance with the ghetto elite enabled him to live in more spacious accommodation elsewhere. Number 13 Szpitalna Street – the pre-war home of his in-laws - was to become our home for the remainder of our stay in Vilna.

Szpitalna 13 was the home of Uncle Fayvel's father-in-law, Nehemia Zilber, a ghetto VIP. He was a baker by trade and he had succeeded in securing a Yellow Permit and, with it, the right to bake bread for the ghetto population and distribute it on ration cards. His bakery was situated just below the flat. Under the circumstances, the offer of this accommodation provided the solution to all our immediate problems. First of all, we had a roof over our heads, I would be safe to move outside the ghetto and my parents and brother were in a "safe" house by virtue of the fact that Mr. Zilber was useful to the ghetto administration and my uncle's sister-in-law was "married" to a policeman.

What is more, there was a brilliantly constructed hiding place for about 30 people underneath the bakery which was made available to us should all our other advantages suddenly disappear or in the event of an unexpected raid by the Germans. The hideout had been constructed by a Vilna builder during the first few weeks of the ghetto's existence. During those early weeks, Jewish families, anxious to take whatever steps they could to preserve themselves, had inundated him with requests for hideouts and his services had been at a premium.

Mr. Zilber's hideout consisted of a sliding trap-door built into the floor at the rear of the water pipes and meter which served our block of flats. On the other side of the door was a staircase which led down to two small rooms, one of them about 12 ft. by 10 ft. There were mattresses on the floor which could be used for sleeping, shelves stacked with black bread and other emergency food supplies and, in another corner, there were buckets which could be used as latrines should anyone be forced to spend a long spell in the hideout. Sometime later, another similar hideout in the same building was discovered by the Germans. One of its occupants was dragged out into the courtyard and shot and the rest were taken away and executed at Ponary.

On the morning of October 24, before I left the ghetto with my uncle, I said a tearful farewell to my parents and brother as they prepared to descend into their cellar hideout, together with other illegal inhabitants. The hiding place was exceedingly well camouflage and the fact that I knew the ghetto police would almost certainly lead the Germans away from the hideout was reassuring – but I nevertheless could not suppress very real fears that I would never see my family again when I returned. I lingered on while saying goodbye as though I was saying it for the last time and eventually Uncle Fayvel had to pull me away forcibly.

We walked sorrowfully out of the ghetto together with thousands of other Jews, all of them wracked with the same feelings of doubt about what they would find in the ghetto on their return – or for that matter, whether they would return at all.

About midday we arrived at my uncle's place of employment and were immediately herded into a small building. There were at least 600 people in our group and, by the early evening, as the last of them arrived, our reception and inspection center had become so overcrowded, the German employers decided to move several dozens of us into another building. My Uncle Fayvel and I were among them.

Our new accommodation made life physically more comfortable but, no matter how luxurious the surroundings had been, my acute melancholia remained. I could think of nothing apart from my parents and brother back home in the ghetto and, to make matters worse, my Aunt Sonia made it clear she was not favorably disposed towards me. Although Nehama "married" her ghetto policeman, my aunt still maintained that she would have been safer had Uncle Fayvel adopted her temporarily as one of his legal dependents. Knowing she regarded me as an interloper made me feel decidedly uncomfortable and thoroughly miserable.

Somehow, however, those two days of misery and anxiety went by and I returned with a thumping heart in my chest to see what awaited me back home in the ghetto.

It is almost impossible to describe the joy that overcame me when I entered our flat and there found my mother, father and brother safe and sound. I knew at once that their hiding place had not been found by the Germans, almost certainly because of the many influential friends that Mr. Zilber had among the ghetto police.

But, 5,000 other Jews, illegal but innocent ghetto dwellers like my parents, had not been so fortunate. They had gambled on not being found and had lost.

The sudden disappearance of such vast numbers of men, women and children left a void in the ghetto which for many months afterwards was still being filled by the tears of those they left behind. Almost everyone lost either a close relative or a dear friend during my short absence and the pained, pathetic expressions on their faces on my return told the horrific story of that two-day action more poignantly than words could ever tell.

It was evident, too, that what little fight had been lingering among the Jews of the ghetto had been knocked out of them. Most of them had been turned into rag-doll puppets, limp and listless, and forced to dance to the unending Teutonic tunes of their Nazi oppressors. Everyone seemed apathetic about their personal fate and resigned to the fact that it was simply a matter of time before the Germans found an excuse to liquidate the remaining ghetto population.

What is more, the events of the forthcoming weeks seemed to prove them right. Several more actions were mounted by the Germans and in each several hundred more Jews were uprooted from their homes and taken to their deaths. The last action took place only a few days before Christmas Eve, 1942 and, on several occasions during those dangerous weeks, we had to make use of our ghetto hideout.

A new year, however, brings with it new hope and, with the dawning of 1942, life in the ghetto seemed slowly to return to an even keel and our chances of survival seemed revitalized.

CHAPTER 7

Becoming A Blackmarketeer

New Year, 1942, with its welcome and ephemeral respite from the persistent body blows from the Nazis, provided an opportunity to take stock of the carnage which had destroyed nearly three-quarters of the Jewish population of Vilna.

Of the original 75,000 Jews only between 18,000 and 20,000 were still alive in the ghetto at the beginning of the New Year. Some 10,000 had been put to death during the sham reprisals, a further 6,000 had been taken away and shot on entry into the first ghetto, 9,000 had been liquidated in the short-lived second ghetto and at least 5,000 perished following the introduction of the Yellow Permit. Some 20,000 had perished during the other "minor actions" and during the "Human Hunters" era.

In just a few months of Nazi rule, 50,000 people, whose only "crime" was their religion, had been put to death in the name of Hitlerism.

Approximately 20,000 Jews, however, survived and, what is perhaps even more remarkable, were the vast number of illegal inhabitants who were among them – including ourselves. For a very short time I am sure we began to believe that we were chosen people among the Chosen People and that no harm could come to us.

Future events, however, were soon to illustrate the asininity of this belief.

Those who remained alive, whether protected by the Yellow Permit or not, had still to carry on living, despite what had happened in the past or what was likely to happen in the future. Towards this objective, there was one common problem which tested their insecurity and inventiveness to the full – the provision of adequate supplies of food.

Even in the summer, the food rations allocated to the ghetto population by the German overlords would have been hopelessly inadequate, but against the ravages of the bitter Polish winter, they could not have sustained human life for very long. It was obvious to all that ways and means, however devious or hazardous, had to be found to supplement our abysmally meager rations. While there was, unfortunately, very little we could do to thwart the might of the Third Reich, we could at least attempt to fight the pangs of hunger.

Food rapidly became the most precious commodity in the ghetto and, to obtain whatever extra nourishment they could for the ghetto population, the Jewish foremen at the various workplaces pulled off some quite staggering black market and unofficial deals with their German and Polish employers. Such transactions, as one might have expected, involved considerable sums of money and, in several instances where hard cash was not always readily available, bargains were struck with diamonds, other precious stones and even American dollars. In Poland at one time, there was very little confidence in the stability of the Zloty and, occasionally, the banks themselves went bankrupt. There were, however, vast numbers of Jews in Vilna who had wealthy relatives in the United States and, as a result, there was a regular influx of dollars coming into Vilna. People soon began to realize that these dollars, unlike other currencies in Europe, were unlikely to be devalued and for this reason above all they were much prized in the big food deals.

The Ghetto Police, although far from blameless in the treatment of the Jews of Vilna, displayed a great deal of mental agility in obtaining the urgently needed extra food supplies as well as a considerable flair for distributing it fairly.

The so-called Police Co-operative was instrumental in obtaining by far the largest amounts of food and, at the same time, they managed to distribute it through the official channels as "extras" added to the authorized ration cards. To make these lifesaving purchases, the Police obtained their money in many ways, including the imposition of a tax on every ghetto family, the amount being determined by their income, and by confiscating gold, diamonds and jewelry from the wealthier Jews. It may be argued that it was morally wrong to dispossess people of their hard-earned treasures in this way but when one considers that their actions indirectly saved the lives of hundreds of children and infirm adults, albeit for a short time, I believe their methods can be wholly condoned. Had the Jewish Police not confiscated these valuables and exchanged them for additional food, there is little doubt that the Nazis would have stolen them in any event without their owners or their dependents deriving any benefit whatsoever.

For a short time, too, workers returning from their jobs outside the ghetto would arrive home with various foodstuffs which they had obtained by either trading their personal clothing or simply by buying it at grossly inflated prices from friendly Christian people whom they knew. Very occasionally, an individual would find he had more food than he required. Under those circumstances the surplus food was sold almost immediately on the black market and those who profited out of it would use the additional money to improve their general standard of living, buy a few luxuries for their families or use it to finance future food transactions.

Black marketeering of this kind, however, could only continue in the ghetto as long as the Germans were prepared to condone it - and that was not always the case. There were long periods when the control of the ghetto was so strict that it was practically impossible to smuggle in even a slice of bread without being detected.

On scores of occasions those who tried and failed to pass the guards were taken to the former Glasers sausage shop which stood alongside the ghetto's gates, searched, beaten brutally and sometimes even taken away and executed. One such victim was a much-loved opera singer named Luba Lewicka who, on reaching the ghetto gates, was stopped and searched by Frans Murer, a member of the SA in charge of Jewish affairs in the Vilna area, and he found a small quantity of peas on the inside of her clothing. She was instantly beaten up by Murer and subsequently taken to Lukiszi Prison prior to her execution at Ponary.

When the outside supply channels were blocked, the black-market prices for food in the ghetto would rise to an unprecedented height and the administration had to use its fullest powers of ingenuity to prevent mass starvation among the population.

Several small food factories also existed in the ghetto, including a flour mill and two small sweet factories. One of them was in the room in which we lived and was run by a Mr. Widecki. There were also two cafeterias which served thousands of cups of coffee and sandwiches to people who could not afford to purchase food to eat in their own homes.

Life in the ghetto, particularly for those forced to live an illegal existence was fraught with a multitude of hazards. In many ways, it was like living in the middle of a minefield in which one false step could mean instant death. One could never be sure of anything – least of all surviving from one day to the next. For this reason, people lived for the moment, dismissing from their minds any thought for their future, either in the long or the short terms. Even so as long as one was alive there was a constant need to earn additional money to buy the extra rations which invariably meant the difference between a satisfied stomach and virtual starvation.

Ghetto workers employed by the Germans were paid a mere pittance for their labors. In fact, after various compulsory deductions, there was not really sufficient money left to buy even the paltry food rations allocated to us.

Not everyone, however, was cunning, or perhaps fool hardy enough, to become a black marketeer. It was unquestionably a decidedly risky profession and many of those who chose to undertake it, lived to regret it. Both the Nazis and the Ghetto Police showed no mercy for them whatsoever and those who were unlucky enough to be caught, normally paid for their sins with their lives. The Ghetto Police looked upon it unfavorably for two basic reasons; firstly, because they wanted to discourage others encroaching on their territory and secondly, because a black-market trade presented problems of security. They argued that had the Germans ferreted out a flourishing black-market trade during one of their surprise raids on the ghetto, there would have been little doubt that large numbers of innocent people would have been made to suffer.

Despite all these risks I decided to become a black marketeer. The lose by my father of his job at the Vilna railway station had left us as a family without any form of income and to enable us to buy food we had even reached the stage of selling our own clothing. Quite obviously, a situation of that kind could not be tolerated for very long.

Black marketeering seemed to be the only satisfactory solution. So, with money my father loaned to me I set myself up in a small business.

My shop consisted simply of a sideboard drawer with leather straps attached in such a way that it enabled me to carry it like an usherette supports her tray of ice-cream and soft drink at the cinema or theatre. At first, I sold sweets which I bought from Mr. Widecki but, when it became clear that this was unprofitable, my father advised me to change to the more lucrative business of selling cigarettes, tobacco and saccharin.

This instantly proved financially rewarding and, in no time at all, I began to learn the finer points in the art of black marketeering. The first lessons I learned were to find a reasonably regular supplier whom I could trust and who did not overcharge, to establish a regular clientele and, above all, find a safe pitch out of sight of the Ghetto Police.

I discovered, too, that the people who worked on the railway were the best source of supply for my kind of merchandise. Every so often, former workmates of my father would bring me supplies. I found a pitch on the corner of Jatkowa Street and Szpitalna Street across the road from our flat and, in a matter of only a few days I had a large number of regular customers. Among them were several members of the ghetto elite including Herr Oberhardt, who was second in command of the Ghetto Police under a man named Jacob Gens, a former administrator in the Jewish hospital in Vilna. Every morning at 6:30 a.m. I used to call at his flat at Strassuna 1, and deliver his favorite brand of cigarettes in yellow packets of 25.

Jacob Gens
Photo: Courtesy of Yad Vashem

By virtue of his job, Oberhardt, who would have been about 35 years old at the time, was not the most revered figure in the ghetto but, for one very good reason, I have an untarnished regard for him - he saved my life.

During my days as a black marketeer I had many uncomfortable encounters with the Ghetto Police but somehow, I managed to wriggle out of trouble on each occasion and continue my illegal, but remunerative trade. Then one day the Germans came into the ghetto unannounced and caught several dealers red-handed with their merchandise. The Jewish police had no alternative but to arrest four black marketeers, including myself and march us away to the ghetto prison at Lidska Street.

As soon as we were safe behind bars, the Germans departed and said that they would return the following day and escort us personally to our executions, stressing that we had committed the crime of dealing in merchandise forbidden in the ghetto.

Death seemed inevitable and we resigned ourselves to the fact that we only had a few hours to live.

As the day of our execution dawned, Herr Oberhardt, unaware of my predicament, waited impatiently at his flat for his daily cigarette ration. When it failed to arrive, he flew into a rage and in his anger, began to look for me, discovering from fellow dealers that, together with three other young men, I had been arrested and was awaiting execution.

Oberhardt immediately made his way to the prison, and after just a few minutes conversation with the guards I was released. I never saw my three fellow prisoners again and to this day I do not know for certain what became of them. But I believe that shortly after I left my cell they were taken out and shot.

Sometime later I saw Oberhardt, thanked him for saving my life at that eleventh hour, and asked him just how he had achieved what appeared to be impossible. I never discovered the answer. All he would say was:

"You are a lucky boy and you do not need to know how I did it - just be thankful and keep me supplied with cigarettes."

Needless to say, I did.

CHAPTER 8

Survival In The Ghetto

Within a very short time the ghetto became a melting pot of human experience. Jews from every social strata, who before the war were unlikely to ever have met, were suddenly tossed traumatically into the ghetto cauldron and forced to live under the one roof, often under the most trying conditions.

A great number of people adapted themselves surprisingly painlessly to their new and strange environment but, not unexpectedly, there were equally large numbers who could not, or would not, integrate amicably with their new neighbors.

Some of them were even positively hostile to this type of co-existence and demonstrated their distaste and dissatisfaction in the most aggressive ways.

Our flat at Szpitalna 13 provided a model example of the sort of conflicts that manifested themselves among the Jews throughout the ghetto. It comprised a small entrance hall, an equally small kitchen and two rooms approximately four yards square, one behind the other. The occupants of the rear room were Mr. and Mrs. Nehemiah Zilber and their two daughters Raya and Hehama; my Uncle Fayvel, his wife Sonya and their son, Sascha, and a Mr. and Mrs. Golomb.

In the other room were Sarah and Meilach Widecki, their son, Moissele, and daughter, Sonia; Mr. and Mrs. Tomin and their daughter, Helga, Mr. Miron Abelovitz, his wife, Anna, and nephew, Liova, as well as my parents, brother and myself.

I remember it was so overcrowded that the Wideckis and Weiler families had to sleep at two different levels in an attempt to conserve as much space as possible. Even so, when everyone made up their beds it was still practically impossible to walk through the room without stepping on someone or without hurting one's legs on a protruding piece of furniture. Under these cramped, claustrophobic living conditions, in which privacy and solitude were unknown luxuries, our nerves and tempers soon began to fray at the edges.

Some people, even today, assume that because, as fellow Jews, we were facing one common oppressor, we behaved as blood brothers within one closely knit family. They believed that all Jews were bound inseparably together with the bonds of kinship and faith. There were indeed those Jews who unquestionably would have sacrificed their own lives rather than betray the trust of a fellow Jew but, for the most part, the ghetto population exhibited the same human strengths and weaknesses as people almost anywhere in the world. In the confined space of the ghetto, however, their relationships and their behavior was accentuated and, in the even more constricted confines of our flat, the conflicts were magnified to even greater proportions. We were living at a time of great stress, when even the most trivial disagreement could shatter our fragile composure and make us lose our tempers.

Although there was no significant difference in the financial standing of the families who shared the flat with us, a number of our neighbors tried permanently to create the impression that they were socially superior. This class consciousness led to continual skirmishes between the occupants and, in one extreme instance, to what amounted to a bitter feud. In fact, our room was split into two hostile camps with piles of old blankets used to divide the warring parties- the Abelovitz and Tomin families on one side and Widecki and Weiler families on the other.

Before the war, Mr. Abelovitz was perhaps the most popular and successful optician in Vilna. In many ways, he was a well liked and kindly man. But he could not reconcile himself with the thought that Hitler had been responsible for forcing him to cohabit with people he regarded as his social inferiors. What is more, he actively demonstrated his resentment by completely ignoring Mr. and Mrs. Widecki as well as my mother and father. He also looked upon the Widecki and Weiler children - of which I of course was one - as though they were the result of the unnecessary folly of ignorant people, and consequently he used to brush us aside like dirt whenever he passed us.

Quite apart from this he and his wife, like other snobs in Vilna, used to speak Russian to each other, forgetting that most of us could understand the language in varying degrees and could follow the gist of their conversation. They even forbade their nephew Liova to talk to Mr. Widecki's daughter or to myself.

I was only 13 or 14 years old at the time and so it did not matter a great deal to me whether they spoke or not but, as I grew older, I became increasingly conscious of the futility of Abelovitz's resentment and of the imaginary barriers of class distinction that existed in our flat.

There is little doubt that it would have given the Nazis a great deal of perverse pleasure had they known – and probably they did know – how capable the Jews became at hating one another during their confinement in the ghetto.

The Tomin family were a complete enigma. Apart from rare exchanges of conversation with the Abelovitz family, they spoke to no-one, except when they thought their territorial rights were being abused or that someone else was encroaching on their lebensraum (living space). Mr. Tomin was an analytical chemist who came to Vilna in 1940 from Kovno, the old capital of Lithuania, about 100 km from our town. During the whole of his stay in Vilna, he worked at the same hospital, and when the Germans occupied the city he became a "nutzliche Jude" – a useful Jew. He was allowed to retain his post at the hospital and he was privileged to be among the handful of Jews who had permission from the German authorities to leave and enter the ghetto at any time, also to walk freely outside the ghetto unaccompanied by a guard. The Germans treated him well and he always seemed to be able to return from work laden with food.

When food was exceptionally scarce in the ghetto, as it was on innumerable occasions, the Tomins never seemed to want for anything. Never, however, did they offer one morsel to anyone else.

Had they occasionally shared their plentiful rations, I would never, for one moment, have dreamed of taking any of their food without their knowledge but the fact that they hoarded it in such a mean and miserly way made me resort to mean tactics of my own. For whenever Mrs. Tomin left the flat, I used to make a point of raiding her larder.

On one specific occasion, my mother asked Mrs. Tomin to sell her some of the egg powder that she used for making omelettes, but she refused, making the excuse that she only had a small quantity left and that, in any event, we were not used to such luxuries and would not appreciate it. When I heard this, I was so incensed that I made up my mind to steal the egg powder from her – so that we could get used to "such luxuries".

Of course, Mrs.Tomin knew full well who was responsible for the disappearance of her precious egg powder, but there was very little that she could do about it. Had she informed the ghetto police, they would simply have confiscated it and, with it, her other supplementary rations. I was utterly brazen faced about the whole matter. As she made omelettes on a tiny primus stove, concealed behind a curtain, I would frequently poke my head inside and pull my tongue out at her.

Her 17-year-old daughter, Helga was also predictably toffee-nosed, maintaining that it was beneath her to speak to anyone in what she regarded as a lower social class. During the two years that we were forced to be neighbors, we never once said a civil word to each other.

The Wideckis, on the other hand, were the complete antithesis of all that was objectionable in the Abelovitz and Tomin families. By Polish standards,

Meilach and Sarah Widecki were quite wealthy. Mr. Widecki used to own a sizeable sweet and jam factory, which ensured that he was never in financial difficulties. But he never upheld the principle of social distinctions of any kind or that a rich man was in any way superior to a poor one. He was a sweet natured and devoted family man to whom the philosophies of Messrs. Abelovitz and Tomin were utterly obnoxious.

Before the war, Mr. Widecki and my father were trusting business acquaintances and during our stay at Szpitalna 13, they became the closest of friends. My mother and Mrs. Widecki also developed a close affection for each other and quite naturally the children of the two families soon became friendly, too. Our reciprocal friendship also had its practical benefits: during the frequent disagreements, we had in the two years, the Wideckis were always our allies and we, of course, used to help them fight their battles.

Life in the other room was infinitely more peaceful and placid – although I never really discovered what it was really like. Mr. Zilber never once quarreled with his wife or daughter in public, reserving personal matters of this kind for the privacy of the bakery.

Similarly, Mr. and Mrs. Golomb, the only "outsiders" in what was, in effect, a family room, kept themselves to themselves. Mr. Golomb was the foreman of the group working at the Spanish Military Hospital and a pharmacist by profession. His wife was an extremely intelligent, kindly young woman who spent much of her time helping my Aunt Sonia cope with the child.

The Golombs did not have the same supercilious airs and graces of the Tomins and Abelovitzs although, if anything, they were their intellectual superiors. They treated everyone with respect and humility. During my father's period of unemployment, Mr. Golomb even invited me to join his working party so that I could go with him to the Spanish Hospital where it was comparatively easy to make contacts and purchase food.

I have no doubt that my Uncle Fayvel, who was a placid and amiable man, and who had no special aspirations as far as I was aware, helped to maintain the friendly atmosphere in his part of the flat.

On reflection, it can reasonably be said that those who lived in the room next to ours enjoyed a happy and peaceful coexistence, whereas in our room I do not think one hour elapsed without a quarrel of one kind or another. In between there were long periods of uncomfortable silence which, in many ways, were more unbearable than the frequent outbursts of harsh words.

It was sad that as Jews struggling for survival against a common oppressor, we could not always exist harmoniously side by side with our new neighbors.

CHAPTER 9

Living And Dying By Bread Alone

There were times in the ghetto when men, women, and children were literally compelled to live by bread alone – and there were times when they died by it, too

The perpetual problem was that we never really knew for certain whether the Germans wanted us to starve to death or whether they wanted us to receive sufficient nourishment to sustain us for the ordeals of the labor camps in later months. Sometimes, for example, they would send in truck-loads of food for the manual workers in the ghetto and then, a few days or even hours later, shoot a man simply for attempting to smuggle a measly slice of bread.

We never knew from one moment to the next what the Germans intended should become of us and, consequently, the ghetto population could not depend for its survival on the official food allocation, as meagre as it was. Officially, each man, woman, and child in the ghetto should have received between 650 grams and 1,300 grams of bread each week, according to its general availability. Sometimes we received the full allocation, sometimes a good deal less and, not infrequently, none at all. The food situation was always predictably unpredictable.

On exceptionally rare occasions, we managed to obtain such luxury foodstuffs as sugar, fats, oats, and during the lull of activity in the first half of 1942, each ghetto inhabitant even received several allocations of fresh meat (200 grams) and sugar (100 grams) on their official ration cards. No eggs were issued until June when, for some inexplicable reason, we each received one egg apiece.

Food was obtained by all manner of means when and where it was available but, for the most part, it was supplied by the Jewish Police co-operative. They were instrumental in obtaining fresh green groceries and, on one occasion, during the summer of 1942, they were successful in getting hold of 10,000 liters of milk each month which they allocated to all the ghetto children.

The food situation was at its best in June of that year. At that time, there were some 18,500-people living in the ghetto, and from sources both legal and illegal, everyone received an average of six kilograms of bread, 550 grams of meat, 350 grams of sugar as well as other items of food for that month.

Sadly, but predictably, this healthy state of affairs, both from the supply and medical points of view, did not last. The relative food glut of that June soon reverted to a scarcity and to avoid starvation or malnutrition, most people were forced to barter their clothes for food. One could, for instance, exchange a silk shirt in good condition for a kilogram of pig fat. This in turn presented the pious, orthodox Jew with an obvious religious quandary. He could not eat the pig fat as it would have offended against the strict Jewish dietary laws, but there was nothing which prevented him from trading it yet again for several kilograms of potatoes or some other food which was permissible for him to eat.

There were, quite naturally, many devout Jews who would rather have starved to death than contravene any of the dietary observances of their faith, but, by and large, the vast majority of the ghetto population gave themselves a dispensation, temporarily abandoning their observance of all dietary laws for the duration of the war. Perhaps, at no time in the history of the Jewish people did their religion play a lesser part or its leaders have a lesser voice in Jewish life than they did during the oppressions of the Nazi era.

The rabbis of Vilna, and Torah students who lived among us in the ghetto, were quite content to be left in peace to pray. The Ghetto police rarely interfered with them – although praying or any form of any authorized assembly were strictly forbidden by the Germans. Nonetheless, two Yeshivot Talmudical colleges existed for a short time and there were also a number of minyanim (Jewish religious quorums of 10 or more people), dispersed throughout the ghetto streets. Most of the people, however, were too preoccupied with the hour-by-hour battle for survival to take any active part in organized religion, and instead prayed alone, each in his or her own manner.

The religious doctrines of Judaism stood for very little during the years in the ghetto – partly due to the fact that it was almost impossible to reconcile the dietary laws with the food which was available. But, on the other hand, the interest in cultural activities never at any stage showed any sign of waning. In spite of the persistent internal and external strife in all its most sinister forms, a theatre, a library, and several schools of all kinds flourished in the ghetto.

The library, which functioned from its original premises at 6 Straszuna Street and which, before the war, contained some 60 000 books written in seven languages, was the most frequently patronized. The number of books borrowed seemed to be in direct proportion to the degree of suffering which the ghetto population had to endure at any one time. The more the Germans persecuted us, the more avidly we read, or so it would have appeared.

In October 1941, after one of the most brutal massacres had taken place, the library had in excess of 1,000 members on its list, but by December of that year, the number had risen to 2,500. After every major action by the Germans, the library was inundated with people hoping somehow to find some unsullied area of sanity and solace between the covers of a book – and by so doing find some temporary refuge from the realities of the latest Nazi outrage or atrocity.

Thousands of volumes, written in English, French, Polish, and several other languages, which the Germans considered were hostile to their cause, had been removed from the shelves and burned. But in spite of this wanton destruction many thousands of Yiddish and Hebrew books remained, from light fiction to the greatest works of Jewish literature. All of them were eagerly devoured by the same literary-conscious community which was responsible for the formation of the Jewish Scientific Institute in 1928. Indeed, throughout its history, Vilna has produced many famous writers and is even today regarded by many scholars as the cradle of Yiddish literature.

The theatre, on the other hand, had a somewhat stormy passage during the ghetto years. Whenever there was a lull in the hostilities, it was patronized by the ghetto elite, including the Police, but at times when Jews were being murdered in their hundreds, large numbers of ghetto inhabitants held the view that stage shows, even of a serious, non-frivolous character, were in the poorest possible taste and, as a result, thousands of potential patrons stayed away. Not infrequently, an actor or actress would lose his or her life at the hands of the Germans during the period set aside for rehearsals but the old adage 'the show must go on' was applied to the ghetto theatre as elsewhere, much to the consternation of those who thought it was sacrilegious to present plays including comedies, figuratively speaking on the fresh graves of members of the cast. Yet, despite all this opposition, the theatre managed to survive and give thousands of people a great deal of pleasure practically to the end of the ghetto's existence.

Educational facilities for Jewish children were decreed illegal by the Germans but several schools did exist within the ghetto, many of them functioning almost from the inception of the ghetto, due largely to the devotion of a nucleus of the best-known teachers in Vilna. With no regard for their own personal safety, they organized the cleaning and decorating of derelict buildings and, with the help of their pupils, converted them into bright, cheerful classrooms. By mid winter 1942, there were only 1,500 school children left in the Vilna ghetto, just half the number who entered it on its formation.

To cater for those who remained, there were two kindergartens, three primary schools, a high school, technical, music and art departments, as well as some specialized courses complete with examinations, boards of examiners and certificates for those who were successful. My younger brother, Lejzer, attended primary school from the very beginning, but his education was frequently interrupted by the necessity, on innumerable occasions, to go with the rest of the family into the cellar hideout. This, of course, applied to many of the children attending the illegal ghetto schools, and it is a great credit to them and their teachers that under such appalling conditions that they managed to learn anything at all.

Indeed, some of Vilna children who survived, among them those who attended the ghetto school and also those who did not, went on to become nationally known figures and experts in their own fields: such as Alex Wolkovsky (now Alexander Tamir) the pianist and composer, and Shmuel Bak, who has achieved international recognition as an artist. (see footnote).

Professor Alexander Tamir

As a complete contrast to these cultural and educational facilities provided within the ghetto, there were also two brothels where Jewish girls hired their bodies to satisfy the sexual desires of those who could afford their rates, and a night club which was patronized by high ranking police officers who, at extortionate prices, could obtain the rare luxury of French cognac. If for nothing else, the brothels and the clubs made it abundantly clear that no regime in the world, however harsh, can suppress man's innate desire for enjoyment, even in its more bizarre forms.

(*Alexander Tamir became one of the pivotal figures in the world of music in Israel. At the time, this memoir went to print, at the age of 86, he was professor of piano and head of the Hephzibah Menuhin Piano Chair and the Eden-Tamir two-piano Chair at the Jerusalem Academy of Music and Dance and president of the Chopin Society in Israel. When he was only 11 he composed "Shtilar, Shtilar" (Quiet, Quiet), a Yiddish lullaby that was sung in the ghetto in order to avoid punishment from the Nazis. He formed a piano duo with the late Bracha Eden that became world renowned and remained active until Eden's death in 2006. He and Eden recorded the works of many of the world's greatest composers including Johannes Brahms, Felix Mendelssohn and Sergei Rachmaninoff. They were also the first to perform and record the two-piano version of Stravinsky's "The Rite of Spring".*

Shmuel (Samuel) Bak, who was born in Vilna on August 12, 1933, is one of the world's most celebrated conceptual artists who since 1959 has had solo exhibitions in galleries in New York, Boston, London, Paris, Berlin, Munich, Tel Aviv, Jerusalem, Zurich, Rome and many other major cities. Samuel Bak never painted direct scenes of mass death but much of his work was influenced and informed by his personal experiences during the Holocaust. His talent was first recognized at an exhibition of work in the Vilna Ghetto when he was only nine years of age. He and his mother survived but his father and four grandparents all perished at the hands of the Nazis. In 1948, he and his mother emigrated to Israel where Samuel studied at the Bezalel Art School in Jerusalem and completed his mandatory service in the Israeli army. In 2001, he returned to his hometown of Vilna for the first time and has since visited on many other occasions. In 1993 he moved to Weston, Massachusetts).

Chapter 10

Civil Administration Under Hingst and Murer

In August 1941, there was a change in Vilna from a military to a civil administration and for the first time the Jewish community heard the names of Hingst and Murer, names which they were soon to associate with the familiar rattle of death. Physically, they were indistinguishable from human beings, but they behaved more like horror comic characters produced as a result of some fiendish genetic mutation.

To the Jewish population of Vilna, they appeared as vampires sent to suck the last drops of blood from their bodies, and that in fact proved to be their single-minded mission. Almost as soon as they took over, they began to impose monstrous new laws that served no other purpose than to devalue the already near-worthless lives of the Vilna ghetto Jews. Attempts in recent years have been made in several quarters to absolve such torturer-executioners of their crimes on the grounds that they acted under orders, but there is little doubt that both Hingst and Murer (and others to follow them), derived a great deal of sadistic satisfaction from their work and carried out their duties with relish.

Hans Hingst, who would have been in his early thirties at the time, held the rank of Gobietakommissar der Stadt Vilna while Franz Murer, who would have been about 23, was his assistant for dealing with Jewish affairs. Hingst must have been especially proud of his deputy. If he chose him for his ability to instill widespread fear among the Jews, and for his ability to kill and torture dispassionately, then he succeeded admirably. The mere mention of Murer's name was enough to send shivers down the spines of even the bravest Jew.

Murer, who was unquestionably the most feared and hated of all the German overlords, had on favorite "sport." Without warning, he and his underlings would storm into the ghetto at a time when the working parties were returning from the city, and meticulously search everyone for smuggled foodstuffs and other goods before they were allowed to pass through the ghetto gates. There were nearly always a small number of workers who had taken the risk of bringing home a few crumbs of food for their hungry families and, if they were caught, they invariably paid with their lives. Murer would beat them insensible with his own hands, and then order their removal, first to Lukiszki Prison, and then to their deaths at Ponary.

די צוויי מאסן-מערדער מורער און הינגסט (פון לינקס אייף רעבטס).

Franz Murer (lef) and Hans Hingst
Photo: Courtesy of Yad Vashem

The Nazis, one cannot deny, had a great natural talent for selecting the right men for the job. One such hand-picked individual was Martin Weiss, a gaunt, monkey-featured Nazi, who very quickly made it transparently clear that he, too, derived ecstatic enjoyment from murdering innocent people, especially children. Weiss was so fond of his work, he even went to the lengths of building himself a summer villa in the center of his murder kingdom at Ponary. Like the devoted exponent of the "art" of murder that he was, he even practiced the techniques of killing before the ghetto was formed!

In the middle of July 1941, together with the help of his underlings - the Lithuanian Ipatinga - Weiss organized the pogrom on the Jews of Nowogrodzka Street, in which more than 500 people were shot and killed. Some time later, on the day that the ghetto was being formed, he was seen leading an 11-year-old schoolgirl to the ghetto gates where he put her against the wall and shot her simply because she was not wearing the prescribed yellow star on her clothing.

Martin Weiss
Photo: Courtesy of Yad Vashem

A young woman who was one of the very few who managed to escape from Ponary witnessed another of his "achievements" when an 18-year-old girl named Morgensztern was walking hypnotically towards her grave, half naked. She recalled later how Weiss ran up to the girl, led her away, and began telling her that he wanted to save her life. The girl tried to run away from him, appealing pathetically that all she wanted was to be left to die with the rest of her family who had just been shot. But Weiss refused to grant her this one small wish. He persisted in telling her how beautiful she looked in the moonlight, and started talking to her philosophically about the beauty of life and of living. To Weiss it was simply a macabre game. After toying mercilessly with her life, he pulled out his revolver and shot her. Then, with a burst of insane laughter, he dragged her limp body to the grave.

Weiss, it has to be said, did not reserve his torments, or his bullets, for the Jews alone. On one occasion, for example, he ordered the arrest of some 500 Polish Catholic nuns, priests and theology students. They were taken to Lukiszki Prison at gunpoint where they were told to undress and don the clothing of recently murdered Jews. With the yellow stars on their chests, Weiss then led them away to Ponary where he gave the order for their mass execution.

It is hardly surprising that his prestige rose astronomically among the Nazi hierarchy. In a very short space of time he was promoted from the humble rank of feldwebel to sturmfuhrer and his uniform gleamed and bristled with medals presented to him by his superiors as tokens of their gratitude.

There are well documented stories of Nazi leaders who, in the luxury of their drawing rooms, could be overcome with emotion listening to chamber music, but who at the same time could stare with stony hearts out of their windows at the palls of black smoke rising above the gas ovens in the extermination camps. Weiss, as far as I am aware, was not a musician or a lover of music, but in many ways, he did exemplify this inexplicable schizoid trait in his character.

In the Gestapo gardens at Rossa Street, a clean and pleasant area of the city that the Germans chose to billet some of their troops, he began to cultivate flowers. No one could ever hope to fathom the depths of such a brain. One minute Weiss would slaughter a child in cold blood, and the next, so to speak, handle the petals of a rose with the tenderness of a lover's caress.

Then there was Bruno Kittel, a late arrival on the scene. He appeared as a replacement for Murer in the summer of 1943 for the purpose of pummeling the last anguished breaths from the crippled Jewish community. It was a job he was well equipped to do. Several weeks before the actual liquidation of the ghetto, Kittel began to make his presence felt by regularly demanding workers for the Estonian concentration camps. He showed no favor or mercy, and he was probably responsible for the murder of police chief Jacob Gens.

Bruno Kittel
Photo: courtesy of Yad Vashem

Kittel was also in charge of the "final selection" made at Rossa Street on September 23 and 24, 1943 and, as such, it was he who decided who should go on living and suffering in the concentration camps, and who should perish in the crematoria of Majdanek, an extermination camp near Lublin in mid Poland. But, in particular, I will always remember Kittel as the brute who, with a mere wave of his hand, decreed that my own dear mother and brother should go to their deaths.

Chapter 11

The "Lides Affair"

Every now and again, in spite of the persistent goading from Hingst, Murer and Weiss, some internal trauma would shake the rickety foundations of the ghetto and temporarily we would forget the presence of the Nazis. The "Lides Affair" was a case in point.

My father's cousin Herel Lides was a quiet, unassuming man who was incapable of hurting anyone, either mentally or physically. He was a hat maker with a large shop on Ostrobramska Street and, by pre-war Polish standards, his pocket was financially well lined, a fact which indirectly was responsible for his gory and untimely death. When he and his family were forced - like other Vilna Jews - to move into the ghetto, he could not, quite obviously, take the entire stock of his shop with him. Instead, he took all the gold that he could lay his hands on and, almost as soon as he settled in his new ghetto home, he became a dealer and black marketeer in gold and foreign currency. This fact did not escape the attention of the ghetto underworld. Yes, we even had an underworld in the ghetto and, like criminals elsewhere, they were always looking out for ways and means of making some easy money.

Herel Lides became an easy and obvious target for them. By some foul trickery, they lured him away from his flat at Straszuna 10, to a cellar across the road, robbed him of all his gold, and then savagely murdered him, cutting up his body into small pieces presumably in the hope he would be unrecognizable, and that they could dispose of it more easily. It was the first case of murder in the ghetto and, needless to say, its discovery came as a sickening blow to the law abiding Jewish population.

Murder and violence had of course become a dominant, regular pattern woven into the fabric of our life in the ghetto, but until the Lides Affair, the Germans or the Lithuanians had always been the culpable parties. But with the gruesome murder of Herel Lides, the Jews became fearful of a new threat to their lives from within their own community. Jews killing Jews: the idea was nauseating, unthinkable, but it had happened, and there were widespread fears that it would happen again.

People became more nervous than ever, but fortunately the ghetto police quickly and efficiently alleviated their anxiety. In the course of investigating the Lides murder, they discovered another body, a theology student named Gerstein, who had been reported missing by a friend. It was on the information supplied by this friend that on June 3, 1942, the police were able to arrest five members of the ghetto underworld: L. Grodzenski, J. Polikanski, H. Wituchowski, and the brothers J. and E. Gajwusz.

Police Chief Gens set up a court comprising five lawyers and members of the ghetto council and, at the same time, he also took advantage of the opportunity to bring to justice a ruffian named Avidon, who some weeks earlier had attempted to murder a policeman by stabbing. Avidon was unquestionably a dangerous man. He had on several occasions denounced the Jewish Council of Lida (a town some 90km from Vilna) to the Gestapo, and as a result several thousand-people lost their lives. In effect, he was a mass murderer.

The court did not take long to reach its verdict. It decreed that all six men should be hanged. Only the formalities remained. The verdict was endorsed officially by the ghetto council, and preparations were put in hand immediately for the sentences to be carried out at the earliest possible opportunity.

On June 4, the day after the arrests were made, Police Chief Gens ordered all the ghetto inhabitants to assemble, and he made the following announcement: "Out of the 75,000 Jews in Vilna, there now remain 16,000. All those remaining must be good, honest and work-loving people. Anyone who does not conform can expect an end similar to those sentenced today. In every case we will try those concerned, and with our own hands destroy them. Today, we will execute six Jewish murderers who killed fellow Jews. The Jewish police will carry out the executions, and carry on protecting the ghetto as before. The police will carry out the executions as part of their duty."

No sooner had his words been absorbed by the sea of stunned grey faces than the preliminaries for the executions were begun.

Accompanied by a strong police guard the six criminals were taken to the former Vilna meat market in Jatkowa Street and unceremoniously hanged from ropes suspended from empty meat hooks in the market courtyard – each rope joined together so that the police hangmen would not know which of the six he personally executed. It was a grisly, ghoulish sight to see human "carcasses" hanging from hooks used only a few months earlier for sides of beef and lamb but, from a peace keeping point of view, the macabre spectacle fulfilled a useful function. For after the executions had taken place the ghetto inhabitants were ordered to file slowly passed the lifeless corpses as a grim warning of what would happen to them if they had any similar ideas of murder for gain, or indeed of killing for any other reason.

Although a number of people managed to keep away from the market hall on the June day, I was not one of them. Together with a crowd of other ghetto dwellers I was pushed to form a queue and ordered to file beside the makeshift meat hook gallows. I did not want to look but somehow, I could not help gazing with a pale, transfixed stare at the six dead criminals. It was the first time in my life that I had seen dead men hanging and it was a horrible experience which I never forgot. When I came out of the Jatkowa Street exit I vomited and for weeks afterwards I could not sleep at night as each time that I tried to close my eyes I could still see the hanging men's purply-black faces with the expressions of wild fear and pain upon them.

The Nazis had succeeded once again; this time in turning the Jews into murderers and executioners. But by far the most tragic aspect of this whole sordid episode was the fact that the ghetto police received dozens of applications from would-be executioners all offering their services – free. It seemed that people whose palates had once only sampled the sweetness of life had, or were acquiring, a taste for death.

For several days after the executions the ghetto was in a state of turmoil, split in effect into two rival camps over the way in which the trial and the sentences had been carried out. On the one hand, there were those who felt greatly relieved that six evil men had been removed permanently from our midst, but on the other hand there were those who protested that the ghetto police had overstepped the mark by setting themselves up as judge, jury and executioners. They maintained, too, that the market hangings set a precedent in which every ghetto inhabitant's life would, thereafter, not only be at the mercy of Murer and company but at the mercy of Gens and company, too.

The controversy was a major talking point in the ghetto for several weeks but soon the whole Lides Affair, like every other homespun tragedy in the ghetto was forgotten and dismissed from people's minds. After all the loss of eight lives, be they innocent or guilty ones, was merely a drop in the ocean compared with the deaths of countless thousands at the hands of the Germans.

CHAPTER 12

My First Teenage Sweetheart

Once the tremors caused by the market place hangings had subsided, life in the ghetto returned once again to an even keel. Hingst, Murer and the other German henchmen continued to make frequent, unwelcome visits to the ghetto but for the rest of the summer of 1942 we all seemed to be able to breathe a little easier.

As always, however, one question loomed ominously in front of every single one of us: How long could this relative peace and calm last? Everyone knew, if they were honest with themselves, that it could not last forever. They knew that the Nazis would not tolerate a situation in which smiles were beginning to light up the gloomy faces of the Vilna ghetto Jews. Maybe it would last a few days, even a few weeks or at best a month or so – no-one knew for certain. But before long we all knew that the Nazis would take some dastardly step to ensure that our budding happiness never blossomed and that despair and misery would once again become the dominant features of life in the ghetto.

Until that happened everyone at Szpitalna 13, as elsewhere, made a determined bid to make our day-to-day existence as comfortable and as pleasurable as was possible under the circumstances, although to achieve this ephemeral happiness we often had to endure minor, self-inflicted discomforts. There were many nights, for example, when we were all kept awake by the noise of Mr. Widecki and his family busy manufacturing sweets to supplement their budget. Sometimes, there were complaints but I never found any cause to object. In fact, I frequently used to help by wrapping the sweets and thereby benefit from the small but welcome financial rewards which accrued from this nocturnal venture. The only complainants, as far as I am aware, were the Tomins: probably because they were jealous that they did not have anything that they could do which would bring in a little extra income. Even Mr. Abelovitz used to do a little eye-testing on the side.

Our own financial position, at this time, was also fairly healthy. Because of the more stable situation and the need for more working hands, the Germans relaxed their Yellow Permit laws and the illegal ghetto inhabitants were legalized on condition that they sweated and toiled for the Third Reich and so became 'Useful Jews'.

My father returned to his old job at the Vilna railway station. This helped a great deal. He was fortunate enough to secure a job in the station canteen for

German troops where he could eat as much as he wanted during the day and in the evening, he would invariably return home with soup and sometimes some bread which his employers had given to him. This, together with my black marketeering exploits, gave us a reasonable standard of living compared with other families living in the ghetto. Every so often, too, I would venture outside the ghetto and, almost always, I would succeed in returning with additional items of food for our family "larder". Only on one or two occasions were the trophies of my sorties confiscated – usually by policemen who did not know me. Had I met Murer on one of his many raids that, of course, would have been an entirely different matter – but fortunately my luck held and I never did come face to face with him.

I must not, however, convey the impression that we did nothing apart from work, quarrel and scavenge for food. There were times during the long sultry summer evenings when Mr. Widecki's sweet "factory" was not functioning and all was quiet, when I would bury myself for hour after hour in the pages of a good book. I read all sorts of books during my years in the ghetto, from classics to comedy, travel to fiction. One which I remember in particular was "Tevye der Milchiker", the Yiddish classic which has since been adapted and become an international success as "Fiddler on the Roof".

I used to sit in the corner of the room and every so often I would glance up from the pages and gaze longingly through the windows over the courtyard and beyond to the barricaded gate at Rudnicka 27. My vision came to an abrupt halt at the gate but my mind's eye went far, far beyond it. I would imagine that it was wide open and that I was walking though it at the beginning of a journey which would take me unhindered to the wondrous, exotic places that I had read about in the books. Time and time again when dear little Sonia Widecki saw me sitting there deep in thought and gazing into my world of make-believe she would come over and join me and tell me of her dreams and hopes for the future.

She was a beautiful, intelligent girl about two years younger than I and I will always remember her as my first teenage sweetheart and a very dear friend.

Using the endearment for Abram she would say: "Abrascha, how I wish that these terrible gates would open so that we would once again be free like we used to be before the war..." And she would recall affectionately how her parents used to take her for long walks by the River Wilija or on fine summer days go to the Zakrety Forest where the air was as cool and clear as crystal.

As she spoke the tears would well up in her eyes, her voice falter with emotion and I would have to do my best to console her and bring the smile back to her lovely face. "Sonia" I used to say, "When that miracle happens and the gate opens I will go straight to America and become a millionaire. Then I will send for you so that we can be married". "You silly boy Abrascha," she would answer, her smile returning. "If that miracle does happen you will not need to go to America, you will have 'America' right here in Vilna."

Although my father and Sonia's father had known each other before the ghetto was formed, she and I met for the first time at Szpitalna 13. When we were not gazing into our crystal-ball of dreams, we would simply talk about our mutual school friends who had been snatched cruelly away from us by the Germans and also about her experiences at the ghetto high school where she was a pupil. But our favorite topic of conversation used to be the blissfully happy trips we used to have on the River Wilija by steamboat before the war. Somehow the sun always seemed to shine on those trips or, at least, if it rained, we never seemed to notice. It did not really matter anyway. All we remembered were the happy times – how we would run on and off the boats at popular holiday stops such as Pospieszki, Wolokumpje and Werki and how we would buy an ice cream at each port of call as well as an ice-cold orangeade, and how we would romp in the nearby forests to our hearts' content.

What ecstatically joyful times they were. Would we ever know such happiness again? Would anyone know such happiness again? Had the sun been snuffed out for good by the black cloud of Nazism? Thoughts like this brought us back with a jolt to the prison-like existence we were forced to lead in the ghetto, and we felt miserable again. Nevertheless, we were determined not to remain morose for long and time and time again we would sit quietly together reliving the happy times we had known and exchanging our dreams for the future.

Sonia and I became close friends at a time when we needed each other most of all, just after we had lost all our classmates, and the hours that I spent talking to her are without doubt the only really pleasant memories I have of my years of ghetto life in Vilna.

CHAPTER 13

The "Colonia Toz" Mass Murder

As far as the Germans were concerned the old Jews living in the ghetto were merely expendable pawns who could be sacrificed at will in the glorification of the Third Reich or who could be used as part of some venomous ploy to confuse and demoralize the Jewish population.

The removal during the summer of 1942 of some 80 old and infirm people to a rest home at Pospieszki – a former holiday camp called Colonia Toz – was a supreme illustration of these wicked manipulative tactics. For the Nazis, it served a dual purpose: to lull the old people's families and friends into a sense of false security and equally to provide additional fuel for the German propaganda machine.

It was a heartless, miserable trick – but by this time we had grown to expect no more.

For a short time, we really did think that the icy hearts of the Nazis were at last beginning to thaw just a little – that for the first time they were showing that they were capable of a genuine act of kindness and compassion. A few weeks or so after the old folk arrived at Colonia Toz photographs were taken by Nazis Press photographers showing them looking happy and fit and tucking into their first hearty meals in many months. There was always the possibility that the pictures had been rigged and that as soon as the shutter had been pressed the plates of food were devoured by some greedy pig of a German officer. But before long those who had doubts about the authenticity of the photographs began to accept the fact that they could well have been genuine. Their original suspicions were allayed by letters which began to trickle back to the ghetto from the old people which apparently had not been written under duress and which in general stated how well they were being treated by the Germans in the rest home.

Indeed, we discovered later that the hospitality was genuine enough. But sadly, like almost all the more pleasurable aspects of life in the ghetto, it was short lived. The Germans cleverly realized that unsolicited testimonials of their kindnesses would create a good deal more impact than any forced smiles or forced words could ever do. So, for some weeks they gave the old folk all the warmth, comfort and food that they required and led them to believe that this new milk and honey existence would continue indefinitely. It didn't. As soon as the Germans had harvested the last grain of propaganda their "warm" hearts suddenly became icy again and their bogus kindness transformed rapidly into cruelty.

After a mere six weeks in heaven the 80 old men and women woke up one morning to find that they were to be dragged away to the hell of Ponary where, having served their purpose, they were put to death with no more dignity than turkeys which had been fattened up for Christmas and then slaughtered.

The Colonia Toz mass murder, like the Lides Affair, created reverberations of anger within the ghetto but soon they, too, died away and for the rest of that summer life, for most of us, remained comparatively quiet and uneventful.

There were, however, strong rumors of actions by the Nazis in the Vilna Province. The Jewish festivals were approaching and as Hingst, Murer, and Weiss had in the past deliberately chosen these holy times to perpetrate some of their unforgivable atrocities, everyone was naturally fearful of what was to be unleashed upon us this time.

All we could do was wait, hope and pray.

The days went by and nothing happened and then on the eve of Yom Kippur – the Day of Atonement – Police Chief Gens received an order from Weiss stating that all ghetto inhabitants would have to report for work as usual on the following day – on Yom Kippur. This, of course, meant that all those Jews employed outside the ghetto had no choice but to go to work, whereas those who worked inside the ghetto reported to their places employment but did absolutely nothing all day. In the late afternoon, when the outside working parties which had been laboring under the surveillance of the Germans began to return to the ghetto, the ghetto police allowed us to assemble for prayers.

Much to the surprise of everyone, in view of the massacres which followed the liquidation of the second ghetto on the previous Yom Kippur, the day passed without incident and without interference from the Germans, and we all went to bed that night breathing a sigh of relief.

In mid-October, however, the ghetto population once again found itself being placed on the rack of Hitlerism. The German top brass visited the ghetto on several occasions, implanting by their mere presence new fears in our minds and, at the same time, new rumors began to circulate that Jewish settlements on the outskirts of Vilna were being wiped out systematically and that thousands of Jews were being shot in nearby forests.

Paradoxically, there were signs of an entirely different kind which indicated to the more optimistic ghetto dwellers that, in fact, our future was more secure than at any time since the German occupation of our city. The Jewish Police were issued with uniforms by the German authorities and the optimists maintained that they would not have done so if they were proposing to liquidate the remaining Vilna ghetto Jews in the near future. It transpired to be a false assumption.

We began to realize their real intentions when Lewin, the ghetto policeman who entered into a paper marriage with my Aunt Sonia's sister Nehama, came to our flat and told us that he had been chosen, together with 29 other policemen and some officers, to go to Oszmiany to distribute permits similar to those which we had been given in October of the previous year. He and the other policemen had been issued with black leather coats, Russian boots and military hats bearing the Star of David. The officers were also issued with revolvers.

When they returned from their enforced visit to Oszmiany, Lewin came to our flat again and related the full horror of their mission: how they had been used by Martin Weiss to help exterminate hundreds of fellow Jews. He explained how he and the other policemen had been transported by lorry to Oszmiany where, on arrival, they found that Jews from the nearby towns of Smorgony, Sol, and Sofrany, were already herded into the ghetto together with the Jews of Oszmiany. There were some 3,000 Jews all in all in Oszmiany at the time and when they discovered that the Jewish police were to be put in charge of them there was what amounted to an inaudible cry of elation – and immense relief. As always it was merely momentary joy.

We listened in silence and trepidation as Lewin continued to unfold his story.

It seemed that Gens' second-in-command, a man called Sala Desler, the son of a rich textile merchant who had been in charge of one of the three police precincts of the Vilna ghetto, had been to the Jewish Council in Oszmiany to demand 1,500 Jews for extermination – and had been refused. Desler, a man in his early thirties, had then returned to Vilna where he supposedly had succeeded in persuading Hingst to agree, on behalf of the German Authorities, to accept instead 600 old, sick and crippled people.

Lewis went to report that Desler then returned to Oszmainy where he presented the new demands to the Jewish Council. But again, they refused to enter into such despicable bargaining in human flesh and blood, be they young or old, healthy or infirm, men or women.

The following day the Jewish police ordered all Jews to assemble in the town's main square. No one suspected that any harm would come to them on this occasion because the order had come, not from the Germans, but from the Jews, albeit policemen.

Lewin continued his story and, by the expression on his face, we knew we would be both saddened and sickened by its ending.

No sooner had the Jews gathered in the main square, than a process of segregation was begun. All the old, sick and infirm were pushed to the left, while those who were young and reasonably fit, were pushed to the right. It was instantly obvious to everyone what was happening and immediately those ordered to the left, and so earmarked for extermination, tried frantically to bribe the Jewish police with gold and jewels in a bid to be moved to the other side – and live.

Several policemen accepted the bribes willingly but did nothing to help the victims. On the other hand, there were also even greater numbers of policemen who wept like babies as they carried out their orders under the unflinching eye of the German overseers.

All in all, they selected 410 old and crippled Jews and those among them who could not walk unaided were placed in waiting carts like hulks of useless meat.

Unceremoniously, they were then wheeled off to oblivion – into a nearby forest where they were all shot by eight Lithuanian policemen in the presence of several Jewish police officers, including Desler and Mischa Levas, the infamous commander of the Vilna ghetto known as Torwache – "The Gatekeeper".

After the executions, the Jewish policemen returned to Vilna where in traditional German military style, they paraded in front of Gens in their full uniformed splendor, all of them carrying hefty wooden truncheons.

Lewin's story distressed us unconsolably. Not only were we saddened by the fate which had befallen our Jewish neighbors, but also because we were now more certain than ever before that our own future was perilously insecure. Lewin himself was also physically disturbed by the wholesale butchery in which he had been compelled to play a leading and distasteful role.

He predicted gloomily that is was simply a matter of time, and very little time at that, before we all perished in the same way and that our only chance of saving our lives, albeit slim, was to join the Partisans in the forests, like many young Jews from the Vilna Province had done already. He vowed there and then that he would soon be joining the resistance movement.

Lewin kept his word. Within a month he disappeared from the ghetto and, with a group of policemen, he made his way through to the natural cover of the Rudnicka Forest to join the Partisans. Nehama, his so-called wife, frequently received messages asking her to join him but, as far as I can recall, she never left the ghetto of her own accord. On several occasions, too, he begged me to join him as well as his younger brother, Abraham, a former school friend of mine. I was willing, indeed keen, to go but my parents would not hear of a separation in view of the worsening situation in the ghetto.

My father believed that whatever we did as a family, we should stay together and he often would say: "Whatever the fate of all Israel, will be our fate also."

CHAPTER 14

Joining The Partisans

After the slaughter of the Jews of Oszmiany, life in the Vilna Ghetto became increasingly more uncertain and unbearable. The population lost what little faith it still had left in German promises, although the optimists among us still believed that because of our usefulness as slave labor to the German war effort our lives, at least, would be saved.

Sadly, it was a promise which all too often in the past had proved to be worthless. Time and time again, the Nazis had promised us life and given us death and, to the pessimists among us – or more correctly the realists – there seemed no valid reason to suggest that their motives or their intentions had changed. By this time almost every Jew in the ghetto had lost at least one close member of his family or a dear friend and there seemed every likelihood that we would all ultimately perish in the same way as soon as we had expended our last useful breath in the Nazis cause.

With this ominous threat of genocide hanging over us like a Teutonic Sword of Damocles, the trickle of people who decided to try and escape to join the Partisans in the nearby forests, soon swelled into a torrent. Active resistance, even if it only dented the German armor, was better, more noble, they felt than the life of passive submission we were being forced to lead in the ghetto. The young people of the ghetto felt that if they had to die then they could at least make an heroic attempt to take a Nazi to the grave with them, and, indeed, many of them did just that.

Most of the old folk in the ghetto understood the forces of anger, love and fear which drove so many young men and women from their homes, from the bosoms of their family, to become guerilla fighters in the forests. To most of us who, for one reason or another, had to remain in the ghetto, they were heroes and patriots and, had we been given a chance, we would have been only too ready to join them and fight for our survival. But when we heard that Joseph Glasman, the former assistant to Police Chief Gens had joined the Partisans, too, a wave of despair spread into every ghetto home. With the exception perhaps of Gens himself, and some of his close associates, no one in the ghetto could have felt or have been more safe than Glasman and when he had obviously come to the conclusion that he, too, was not safe, we all realized just how serious the threat to our lives had become. His escape demoralized everyone.

After Glasman's escape, the building of hideouts in the ghetto was greatly intensified. Those who already had a hiding place improved it and went to great lengths to make it more difficult to detect, and those who had no hideouts began to construct them rapidly.

About this time, too, a new and worrying rumor began to circulate in the ghetto to the effect that Himmler, the head of the Gestapo, had ordered the extermination of all European Jews by January,1943. There had been rumors of one kind or another before and each time we tried, with immense fortitude and strength of mind, to dismiss them from our thoughts until such time as we had some positive proof that they contained some substance. We tried on this occasion, too, but just before Christmas 1942 the proof came.

A group of 10 women were arrested for smuggling food into the ghetto and executed. (Not long afterwards cart loads of food entered the ghetto illegally and ironically the Nazis chose to ignore it completely). Then, not many days after this execution, 23 Jewish workers were, for no apparent reason, taken to Lukiszi Prison and, after some days there, they were transferred to the ghetto prison pending an investigation by the Germans. Everyone breathed a sigh of relief in the belief that the ghetto prison was a good deal safer than Lukiszi. But once again the optimists were wrong. The following day, 19 of the 23 were removed by the Gestapo and shot at Ponary for their non-existent crimes.

These two acts of cold-blooded butchery confirmed in our minds that the rumors of Himmler's proposed mass extermination program were correct.

Contrary to what we had expected, however, the first few days of New Year 1943 were without incident. In mid-January, we were all issued with numbers – mine was 5/714 – and there were also rumors that we were also to be issued with passports similar to those which had already been handed out to Christians outside the ghetto, apart from the fact that ours would bear the inevitable label – "Jude".

Our fortunes seemed to be like pendulums swinging menacingly between life and death on a clock which was ticking away uncontrollably towards zero hour. One moment we seemed close to death; the next life was full of hope. But always we felt that the end was inevitable – that soon the pendulum would stop swinging in an unholy blood bath which would permanently obliterate the ghetto and its surviving Jews.

Speculation about our communal fate was rife when, towards the of January, a new Gestapo Chief for Vilna was appointed – a Nazis by the name of Neugebauer. We hoped, naively, that the new administration would be less tyrannical, less intolerant but, after merely a few days in his new office, Neugebauer made it abundantly clear that there would be no relaxation of the iron rule. He was a pitiless, bullying despot of the first order. Almost as soon as he arrived he called on Gens and made it clear that should the Germans lose the war all European Jews would be liquidated. In truth, we had every reason to believe that the same fate would have befallen us had the Germans emerged victorious.

Under Neugebauer's rule, Franz Murer became a more regular visitor to the ghetto and, at every opportunity, he beat and flogged Jews for the most trivial reasons or for no reason at all. Murer was also aware of the fact that illegal supplies of food were hidden in the ghetto dwellings and, in what was obviously a renaissance of Nazi stringency, he made numerous forays in which he scoured every corner for unauthorized crumbs of food. Where he found them the "culprits" were, without exception, taken from their homes and executed.

For a time Murer enjoyed his regular sorties into the ghetto in search of illegal food supplies but, after a short time, he grew bored with the chore and gave orders for the foraging expeditions to be continued instead by the ghetto police. Gens and his assistants carried out the orders to the letter, realizing that should Murer decide to make a spot check, they too would be made to suffer should he have found illegal foodstuffs secreted anywhere in the ghetto. To ensure that this never happened they searched all the living quarters from top to bottom and confiscated every item of food which had not been obtained on the official ration cards.

Our flat came under vigorous scrutiny, too, and when the ghetto police left they took with them Mrs. Tomins' precious supply of egg powder – but, at least, our lives were preserved.

Murer's frequent raids on the ghetto and the blitz on illegal foodstuffs by the ghetto police made it practically impossible, for the first time since the creation of the ghetto, to bring in unauthorized supplies of food to supplement the meagre ration. As a result, food prices rose astronomically and the black-market trade flourished.

It looked as though we were entering a fateful phase and that the rumors of our liquidation were shortly to prove accurate.

Towards the end of March 1943 more than 700 cart loads of people, all of them with bedding and plentiful provisions, started to pour into adjoining premises. Over a period of three days, Jews from Michaliszki, Swieciany, Swir, and Oszmiany, and surrounding villages, converged like Gypsy tribes on Vilna laden with all their worldly possessions. Some of the families had as many as five 100 cwt bags of flour and cereals and, although the excessive amounts were confiscated by the ghetto police at the gates, most of the new arrivals were allowed to take their supplies of food into the ghetto with them.

Murer, for some reason known only to himself, never even bothered to search them. This we regarded as an omen of the worst kind. Our immediate interpretation of his temporary indulgence was that he had already made up his mind that both the new provincial Jews and those of us already entrenched in the ghetto were to be exterminated.

Like condemned criminals awaiting execution we were being allowed one last feast – or so it appeared.

As the provincials arrived, however, it was the food itself, and not our immediate future, which created the most serious threat to our general stability in the ghetto. They came with chickens, alive and cooked, honey, fats, jams, sugar, and certain varieties of cereals which we had not been able to obtain in Vilna since before the war. The thought of these newcomers, interlopers as we thought of them, temporarily filling their stomachs with such abundant luxuries, while we struggled for survival on comparative pig swill, made us madly jealous and there were near riots on the day they arrived. The ghetto police had to intervene. To put a stop to the food thefts and the disturbances, they ordered everyone off the streets during the arrival of the newcomers so that, although we knew that large supplies of food were being brought in, we would not be able to see it with our own eyes.

In due course, the inevitable happened – a flourishing black market was established when the provincials' superfluous food was made available by them for sale. It was an unsavory business but, at least, what we had lost through Murers' raids, we regained from our new neighbors. After all is just as nourishing.

A few days after the provincial Jews arrived, and after all the excitement had settled down, Szpitalna 13 lost its first inhabitant since the ghetto was formed. On reflection, I doubt whether any other dwelling in the whole of the ghetto could have made the same claim at that particular time – and even then, our loss was not at the hands of the Nazis.

After living for 18 months in conditions and with people he regarded as completely alien to him and his way of life, Mr. Abelovitz died after a heart attack. For reasons which I have already explained, I had no reason to be especially fond of him, but nonetheless, I felt sad when I learned that he had passed away in the ghetto hospital. Mr. Abelovitz was so well liked by his fellow Christian workers at the optical co-operative that they came to the ghetto gates to accompany him to his last resting place – the Jewish cemetery which was situated outside the ghetto.

CHAPTER 15

"Legal" And "Illegal" Diseases

It has always been a constant source of amazement to me that among the 14 people who lived in our room, there was no serious sickness and that Mr. Abelovitz was in fact the only one of our group admitted to the ghetto hospital.

Elsewhere, other families were not so fortunate, although illness, generally speaking, was no more evident during the war years than before and there was no indication that those living a life of deprivation in the ghetto tended to be sick more frequently than those living in more salubrious circumstances outside it.

The health problem was not so much one of the prevention and the treatment of disease, but rather its concealment from the German authorities who decreed that there should be two clearly defined categories of disease in the ghetto – legal and illegal.

A patient suffering from a "legal" disease or illness could be treated at the ghetto hospital without interference from the Germans but if, on the other hand, anyone contracted a so-called illegal disease, they were shot as a matter of course and those who attempted to administer treatment were invariably shot with them.

Scarlet fever, influenza and diphtheria were permitted illnesses, for example, but typhus fever, yellow fever, and cholera were verboten. Those unfortunate enough to contract a forbidden illness had a minimal chance of survival. Not only were the conditions themselves more potentially lethal, but also because were they discovered by the Germans, their suffering would have ended abruptly with a bullet through the brain.

Incredibly, there were no major outbreaks or epidemics of the forbidden "killer" diseases in the Vilna ghetto, but sporadic cases did occur and, in each instance, elaborate measures had to be taken to conceal them from the Nazis. One method was to draw up a false set of card case notes which could be substituted at short notice for the genuine records cards whenever the Germans decided to make an impromptu inspection of the wards.

Murer, Hingst, and German doctors who visited the ghetto threatened on several occasions to burn the hospital to the ground, together with patients and staff, if they discovered that even one case of typhoid fever, or some other highly infectious illegal disease, had been concealed by the Jewish staff. It was certainly no idle threat. The general hospital at Kivno, a town 102 km from Vilna, suffered precisely that fate when the Germans found out that a patient with typhus was being treated in one of the wards. Its 150 staff and patients perished when the Nazis gave orders for the building to be sealed off and then razed to the ground by fire.

By a combination of good luck and good management, the ghetto hospital in Vilna avoided such a disastrous and ghastly end but there were times when it sailed very close to the wind. Altogether, some 200 nurses, doctors, orderlies and other medical staff were employed at the hospital and each and every one of them risked their lives daily by saving and protecting the lives of illegal patients.

All the health and sanitary matters in the ghetto were administered by a special department of the Jewish Council. By modern standards, and for that matter by pre-war standards, the facilities were grossly inadequate. But the Council's task was, to a large degree, eased by the fact that the former Jewish Hospital fell within the confines of the ghetto and, as such, became known to us all as simply the ghetto hospital. All its former medical staff had, as if by some merciful quirk of fate, managed to escape the pre-ghetto actions and, throughout the two years that the hospital functioned, they continued to work there healing the sick, oblivious of the considerable personal risks that they were taking in treating illegal illnesses.

Apart from the hospital, there was also a first aid station, a clinic and a sanitary department but by far the most significant contributions to the general health and welfare of the Jewish population was made by the hospital itself. Its director, Dr. Brodski, was a veritable miracle worker. Despite a serious shortage of all the essential drugs and medicines throughout the whole existence of the ghetto, he always seemed to be able to obtain all the necessary medical requirements for use in the hospital and, as far as I am aware, no patient ever died because the right drug was not available at the right time.

Most of these essential medical supplies were obtained by the working parties employed by the Germans at various military hospitals. There were Jewish workers at the military hospitals in Antokolska Street and at the Spanish Military Hospital, as well as at a number of chemist establishments throughout Vilna. The foremen of these working parties established contacts with friendly Germans or civilians at their places of employment and, in return for substantial payments, they supplied the Jews with medicines for the ghetto hospital. With these coveted black-market drugs, the 35 doctors who were employed there continued their work of mercy with devotion and dedication throughout the entire existence of the ghetto and, by so doing, saved hundreds of lives – albeit in many cases for a short time.

All too often a doctor would discover that a patient whose life he had been able to save and who had been discharged from the hospital had been arrested by the Nazis and executed at Ponary or some other pernicious place of annihilation. How desperately unrewarding it must have been for them.

In only one respect were the medical services better than they had been before the German occupation of our city - the doctor-patient ratio. In Vilna before the war there were just sufficient doctors to care for all the health needs of the Jewish population of 75,000 people. It follows, therefore, that when the Nazis systematically reduced the number to 20,000 there became a surfeit of doctors. As a result, a number of them doubled-up in other non-medical roles, including jobs in the sanitary department.

Vilna's medical practitioners had always had a high reputation throughout their profession and among their numbers were many of the most notable surgeons in the country. These included an eye specialist named Dr. Rucznik and ear, nose, and throat consultant, Dr. Wolkowyski. There was even an abortion unit in the ghetto hospital which operated on an underground basis under the directorship of Dr. Michal Romm.

During 1942 there were 530 patients with infectious diseases treated in the ghetto hospital – almost 18 per cent of the total number of patients seen at the hospital for the whole of that year. Of those with infectious diseases, 113 had paratyphoid, 89 scarlet fever, 113 influenza and 112 diphtheria. In the same year 264 people died in the hospital, representing 8.2% of the total number of patients. Fifty-two died from degenerative heart disease, 23 from kidney diseases, 29 from pneumonia and other lung conditions, 12 from appendicitis, 49 from tuberculosis and 99 from a variety of other less common infections and diseases.

In the same year, 420 women were treated at the ghetto hospital for a variety of gynecological and obstetric problems, including the termination of pregnancy. (See Table Below).

Month	Bleeding	Abortions	Miscarriages in 2nd Pregnancy	Other gynecological operations	Total
Jan	23	6	0	5	34
Feb	24	17	3	0	44
Mar	17	14	1	0	32
Apr	12	20	7	2	44
May	10	18	2	6	36
Jun	1	28	3	7	39
Jul	3	21	3	5	32
Aug	6	20	4	6	36
Sep	8	13	3	5	29
Oct	4	20	2	1	27
Nov	5	27	2	6	40
Dec	4	20	1	5	30
Totals	117	224	31	48	420

The first aid station, which was run by a Dr. Szapiro, and the clinic made their own equally important contributions to the general standard of health in the ghetto. Their staffs were on the whole pre-occupied with the less serious complaints, minor ills such as headaches, toothache, cough, colds in addition to rendering first aid to accidents cases.

In the field of preventative medicine, the ghetto's sanitary department achieved the most remarkable success. Originally, it was conceived as a sanitary "police force" but because it did not possess any professional experience in dealing with matters of this kind, it was remodeled with the addition of medically trained personnel along the lines of an Anti Epidemics Department with the same powers as the ghetto police.

On several occasions, the Germans threatened to obliterate the ghetto if an epidemic were to spread among its population and, in the interests of our own survival, it was, therefore, of paramount importance to prevent such a disastrous outcome.

It was a task which they had to undertake in the face of severe adversity. The ghetto was unquestionably overcrowded, the hygiene facilities were desperately inadequate, sometimes non-existent, and the population was weak and undernourished. Widespread disease in conditions such as this would have seemed inevitable but, in spite of these unfavorable odds, there was not one single epidemic during the whole two-year existence of the Vilna ghetto. Isolated cases of typhoid did occur but they were rapidly contained, the contacts systematically traced and the disease was never allowed to reach epidemic proportions.

By means of persistent propaganda and some enlightened methods, the Sanitary Department officials successfully mobilized the complete co-operation of the ghetto inhabitants in persuading them to keep their own living quarters absolutely spotless. This they achieved by delegating authority to the janitors who were each made responsible for the cleanliness of their own block of flats and in the instruction and supervision of the necessary cleaning and disinfection work. Floors, walls, windows were all kept scrupulously clean in every building in the ghetto and it was rare even to see a scrap of paper in the street.

Great emphasis was also placed upon the importance of hygiene in public buildings, especially in those where food was handled, such as bakeries, kitchens and cafes. In fact, there is little doubt that the strict rules concerning hygiene were almost entirely responsible for minimizing the incidence of sickness and in preventing an epidemic.

A public bath, run by the Sanitary Department, was always well attended and organized so that each day in the week was allocated to the people housed in certain streets in the ghetto. What is more those who could not give the Sanitary Department a good reason for their non-attendance at the baths on the prescribed day were liable to a fine.

In fact, after a second public bathhouse was erected, it became compulsory for every ghetto dweller to have a bath at least once a month. Those who did not were refused their ration books. Some people, who came from homes where they had been in contact with infectious disease cases, had to attend them more frequently but, under these circumstances, they were exempted from payment.

The problems of refuse disposal in the ghetto were solved in a most satisfactory way, in that the horse and cart drivers who used to enter the ghetto to remove the piles of garbage, invariably "smuggled" in fresh supplies of food. They made a handsome profit for themselves but, at the same time, the ghetto benefited considerably in the tangible shape of extra foodstuffs.

CHAPTER 16

Making The Vilna Province "Judenrein" – Clear Of Jews

In the spring of 1943, as new life was beginning to erupt in the countryside and forests after the bleak and barren winter, the Nazis made it abundantly clear that their interest lay in the realm of death. They made no secret of the fact that they intended to make the Vilna Province 'Judenrein' – clear of Jews.

By this time, only a bemused handful of Jews were left alive in the Province and the Germans, in pursuit of their objective, embarked upon their removal with no more compassion than a pest controller ridding a sewer of vermin.

The Vilna Memorial
Photo: Courtesy of Safira Rapoport

The only remaining Jewish communities of any size were at Oszmiany, Michaliszki, Swir and Swieciany and, to solve what to the Nazis was an undesirable state of affairs, Gens was notified by the Gestapo that he, Desler, and a group of 50 ghetto policemen, should make their way to these towns, assemble all the Jews, and escort them to Kovno.

For their mission, the Jewish policemen were once again ordered to dress in Nazi-style black leather coats and jack boots and, brandishing truncheons, they set off, first of all, for Oszmiany and Swieciany. Gens and Desler split up, one of them heading towards Oszmiany, the other to Swieciany. On arrival, the two police chiefs and their strong-arm men uprooted, without notice, the 5,000 Jews living in each of the two towns, assembled them hurriedly at the local railways stations and, on two separate trains, brought them to Vilna on what they assumed was the first leg of their journey to Kovno.

The first train load of Provincial Jews arrived at the Vilna railway station on Sunday, April 4, late in the evening. It was met by Franz Murer himself, who told Gens and the police who accompanied them to report immediately to the Gestapo headquarters. There, Weiss informed Gens that the Kovno Ghetto had refused to accept the new arrivals and that, as a result, the Germans had no choice but to send the Provincials to their deaths at Ponary.

Once again, the ghetto police had been made stooges, foully betrayed and duped by the Nazis.

Gens and his policemen spent the night at the Gestapo headquarters, but early the following morning they returned to the Vilna railway station to await the arrival of the second trainload of Jews, with Desler in charge. As he waited on the platform, a dejected-looking group of Jews, who had originally come from Kovno, arrived at the station under a Jewish police guard, having been told that there they could join the Provincials and return to their home town.

Gens, whom I still believe was much maligned by the Jewish population of Vilna, realized that there was only one humane course of action for him. Knowing, as he did, that instead of going home to Kovno, the Vilna Jews - among them some of his own relatives - would have gone instead to their deaths at Ponary, he hastily sent them back to the ghetto explaining briefly that it was in their own best interest and they would soon know why.

Alone with his thoughts, he then continued to wait for the other train to arrive. When it came, he greeted Desler and told him at once to assemble all his police assistants and go immediately to the Gestapo HQ, where they were kept until midday.

When the two of them returned to the ghetto, we guessed from the expressions on their faces that they had a sorry tale to tell, and we were right. All at once, like the sun when it is masked by a black cloud, everyone looked as though they were in mourning, predicting correctly by past experience that such ill-tidings could only mean that more Jews had fallen foul of the Nazis.

It was not long before everybody in the ghetto heard how at least 10,000 Provincial Jews perished at Ponary.

Three days after the news broke, Martin Weiss stormed unexpectedly into the ghetto and "kidnapped" 20 policemen, and the morale among the Jews reached an even lower, more wretched ebb. No one thought at the time that the policemen would ever be seen or heard of again but that same evening they all returned, safe, sound, yet heartily sickened. In their short absence from the ghetto, they had seen for themselves the horrors of Ponary.

Weiss had forcibly taken the policemen to Ponary to "tidy-up" the ghastly aftermath of the carnage. Nothing was hidden or withheld from them. It was as though Satan had opened the gates of Hell for God-fearing day visitors.

It seemed that under German guard the two train loads of Jews had been taken to Ponary where, on arrival, they had been surrounded by Lithuanians armed with machine guns. The railway wagons were opened one by one and when the frightened Jews saw the scene around them they had panicked and started to run in all directions. Few of them ran more than a few yards. As they tried to escape, their legs were cut from beneath them by a sheet of bullets fired at them by the Lithuanian troops.

When other Jews in the unopened wagons heard the shouting and the anguished screams of those who had been shot and wounded, they made super-human efforts to save themselves from the same fate. With their bare hands, they ripped up the wooden floors of the wagons and as quickly as they could, they dropped onto the track below and started to run like timid hares for the relative safety of the forests.

It was a futile act by desperate people. For, in fact, only nine or ten of those who attempted to avoid the rain of bullets survived that night and day of horror. The rest lay dead and dying only a few yards from the track.

In their short, enforced visit to Ponary, the Jewish police had, for the first time, seen with their own eyes evidence of the Nazis' atrocities in the unforgettable form of pile upon pile of newly-slain men, women and children. It had been their unenviable task to clear and clean up the bloodbath of Ponary – and, indeed, as they went about their whitewash operation, they fully expected that, having completed the job, that they, too, would be murdered and their bodies stacked neatly alongside those which already lay rotting. Strangely, they were wrong. After, so to speak, saw-dusting the arena for the next consignment of innocent victims, they were surprisingly released by the Germans and allowed to return to their homes.

This surprised us all. Not only had the Germans, for the first time, openly admitted the existence of Ponary, but they had allowed the Jews to see it for themselves – and return to tell the tale. Previously the Gestapo had always tried to camouflage its existence and the location.

While we were all too aware of the fact that thousands of our loved ones had been ripped from the bosoms of their families and were never seen or heard of again, few of us in the ghetto ever observed their executions or witnessed the immediate results.

The fact that the Jewish police had been to and returned from Ponary was interpreted by everyone in the ghetto as an omen of the worst kind. It was generally accepted that the Germans were poised to "solve the Jewish problem" finally and that, having set themselves upon this course of action, were no longer making any attempt to hide their intentions from our eyes. It was as though they had bared their blade from the scabbard and, having shown us the knife-edge, were about to cut our throats.

The prospect of our imminent extermination left us stunned and for several days there were large numbers of people in the ghetto who did not even make the effort to go to work, preferring to remain with their families for what they feared could have been their last few hours.

When the Germans saw the disruptive effects of this mass absenteeism, Murer himself called upon Gens and assured him that, contrary to our fears, the Vilna ghetto was safe as long as the Jews continued to work honestly and diligently. No one had any faith any more in such German promises but, nonetheless, after a short time, more and more people slowly began to return to their work in the city.

Again, about this time, the building of hideouts was intensified to provide just that little additional insurance against the likely eventuality of a sudden German action, contrary to their assurances. The religious Jews began to pray even harder, both for their dead martyrs and for an early end to our suffering. Apart from this, life in the ghetto returned to normal.

A Vilna Ghetto work document
Photo: courtesy of Yad Vashem

Some short time later, there was another unexpected development which created a moral rift among the Jews themselves. After Murer and Weiss, and their henchmen, had finished sorting through the clothing of the Ponary victims, and had taken everything of value for themselves, they "generously" sent the remaining clothes and possessions to the ghetto to be distributed by an organization known as Winter Aid. It ignited a major controversy. On the one hand, there were those who thought that, no matter what the circumstances, it was morally wrong to accept and make use of the belongings of fellow Jews who had died in this way. But, on the other hand, there were others who contended that if it improved the living standard of just one person or made just one person a little happier, the acceptance was morally justified. Gens himself encouraged us to accept them on the basis that a refusal would not only offend Nazi sensitivities, but also give the Gestapo the impression that the ghetto was an affluent place which could manage without charity.

The shooting of the Provincial Jews at Ponary brought to an end to all illusions about the Germans' final intention. The Jews of Vilna had always tended to think of themselves as the chosen among the Chosen. They were renowned for their optimism in the face of hunger, pain and poverty, believing even when their spirits were at their lowest, that events would take a turn for the better. But the Ponary massacre, coupled with the news which reached the ghetto of the tragedy of Warsaw, put paid to all our feelings of optimism for good.

מצבת הזכרון ב"פונרי" שהושמדה בשנת
1952 בגלל שלוח המצבה היה כתוב ביידיש
ועברית ל-1410/100

The Memorial to the Jews who died at Ponary
Photo: Courtesy of Yad Vashem

The Jewish population of Warsaw, the biggest in terms of numbers in Europe, had been fighting heroically against all odds and, when we learned that they were fading fast under the ceaseless Nazis onslaught, we shed a long tear for them and for our own bleak future. The dying heroes of Warsaw in their crumbling cellar hideouts and shell-battered buildings, fired, however, even greater patriotism in the young Jews of Vilna and support for the underground movement, the U.P.O., reached unprecedented proportions.

By its very nature, the U.P.O. had to be a secret organization but, despite this, it was not difficult to join its ranks of guerilla fighters. Essentially, the U.P.O. was engaged with the recruitment and training of young men and women to join the Partisan groups operating in the forests of the Vilna Province but, at the same time, they also stole – and on occasion even bought – arms from the Germans, which they would be able to use in the likely event of the final liquidation of the ghetto.

In pursuit of these objectives, they were hindered by several factors, not least among them the constant threat of exposure by the Jewish police, who took the view that the very existence of the Partisans was an ever-present danger to the safety of the ghetto. Orthodox Jews sermonized that Jews should rely on their faith in God, and that they would achieve a great deal more by praying than fighting. But despite this opposition, the U.P.O.'s numbers grew steadily as the situation became more and more serious.

News from other parts of Europe concerning the plight and progress of our fellow Jews filtered through to Vilna in a number of devious, circuitous ways, but, almost always, along the recognized underground channels. Most of what we knew of the Jews elsewhere was gleaned through the columns of the two major underground newspapers – The Free Lithuanian and Independence. They were both written and printed outside the ghetto but, from time to time, they were smuggled in and avidly devoured by the ghetto population. They contained a great deal of obvious propaganda but, by sifting it mentally, it was possible to unearth a few grains of fact about the world outside the ghetto.

But for the most part, the Vilna ghetto dwellers, including ourselves, were preoccupied with the day-to-day task of simply staying alive.

CHAPTER 17

Icik Witenberg And The United Partisans Organization

The organizer of the United Partisan Organization in the Vilna ghetto was Yitzhak Wittenberg *(sometimes seen as Icik Wittenberg)*. He was born in Vilna in 1907 and, as a very young man, he entered the trade union movement and was liked by all his associates. In 1940, he became chairman of the leather-workers' union. He was also a prominent member of the Communist party and, as such, he had to live a completely illegal existence from the first day that the ghetto was formed.

Yitzhak Wittenberg
Photo: Courtesy of Yad Vashem

He was an idealist, preoccupied with only one thought and one objective: to prepare an armed opposition against the Nazis. Wittenberg held the view that the role of the U.P.O. should be to defend the ghetto population within the ghetto. In the event of a final showdown with the Germans, they would be equipped with sufficient arms to keep our aggressors at bay, until such time as large numbers of Jews could flee to the relative safety of the forests.

It was an ideal which he never realized.

On July 9, 1943, several members of the Vilna underground Communist Party were arrested and the next day Kittel, one of the Gestapo hierarchy, came unannounced into the ghetto and demanded Wittenberg for interrogation.

Interrogation, as far as the ghetto was concerned, meant only one thing – death. From past experience, we knew that anyone removed from their home for interrogation by the Nazis never returned and we could see no reason to believe that Wittenberg's fate would have been any different from those who had gone before him.

Kittel, realizing that there was not the remotest chance that Wittenberg would be handed over on demand, attempted what, for a wily Nazi, was a surprisingly naive and futile exercise in subterfuge. In an effort to convince the ghetto that Wittenberg was wanted only for questioning and that he would be allowed to return unharmed to the ghetto, he arrested a man by the name of Averbuch and, after questioning him for some time, released him immediately.

The example, he hoped, would convince the ghetto population and, in particular, those who were hiding and protecting Wittenberg that he, too, would be released in the same way. But Kittel's trickery fooled no one. Wittenberg remained in hiding in the ghetto.

But for how long? Wittenberg's protectors knew that before long, Kittel would run out of patience, and that he would return. They knew, too, that he would not be fobbed off permanently. After some thought, they came to the conclusion that if he, Kittel, had assumed the ghetto would fall for his trickery, then there was a chance that he would fall for theirs.

For some days, there was a discreet silence. Then, it was suddenly announced that Wittenberg had died and a forged death certificate was shown to Kittel. Everyone hoped that Kittel would believe the story, without demanding to see the body, and that, thereafter, life in the ghetto would be a little more peaceful. We were wrong. Kittel was not so easily fooled and, on reflection, it was perhaps absurd of us to believe for one instant that he would have swallowed a ruse of this kind.

Our attempt at deception ruffled Kittel's temper and, as a direct result, he became even more determined to "interrogate" Wittenberg. With this single-minded objective, he made a move with his most valued and versatile "piece" – Sala Desler, his secret agent in the ghetto.

I know nothing of the conversations which took place between them, but the outcome of their encounters remains vivid in my mind. On July 15, 1943 at about 1 a.m., at a meeting of the Jewish Council, which was attended by Wittenberg, the police broke in and arrested and manacled this most wanted man. His kidnappers then bundled him off towards the ghetto gate but, just as his captors were about to take him through on his journey to Gestapo headquarters, they were waylaid by a group of Partisans, who overpowered them and freed Wittenberg.

A mobilization of all Partisans in the ghetto was decreed and on July 16, soon after daybreak, the ghetto received an ultimatum. It stated: that if Wittenberg was not handed over by 6 p.m. that day, planes from Kovno, with their bellies bulging with incendiary bombs, would burn the ghetto to the ground.

At the same time, as if to make us feel guilty at ever doubting his word, Kittel repeated his statement that Wittenberg would be released as soon as he had been interrogated.

Once again, as had happened so frequently in the past, the ghetto population was divided in its view about the most desirable course of action. Some thought Wittenberg should be hidden and defended at all costs but there were others who contended that the life of one man was inconsequential compared with the lives of thousands of Jews, and that he should be handed over to the Germans forthwith.

As these arguments continued, the ghetto underworld, under the leadership of police chief Desler, searched the ghetto in an attempt to find Wittenberg's hideout for themselves. He was entrenched the whole time at a house at Oszmianska Street 3, where the Partisans were assembling machine guns and other arms, and drawing up their plans for an armed resistance. The search went on day and night but his whereabouts were never discovered.

Wittenberg himself believed that Kittel's threat to bomb the ghetto was sheer bluff in spite of the fact that we had irrefutable evidence that the ghettos at Glebokie, Wolozyn and Warsaw had been virtually reduced to ashes by German bombs when the Jewish population had mounted an uprising.

With the sand in our "hour glass" rapidly running out, the Vilna ghetto population began to panic and the U.P.O. decided that, for his own safety as much as anything else, Wittenberg should be moved secretly to a hideout which was known to only a few of his closest allies. He was duly moved and, almost immediately afterwards, a meeting of the U.P.O. Command Council was held. The majority view was that it was morally wrong to fight against one's own brothers, no matter what the circumstances, and that the demand by the Nazis for Wittenberg, with the accompanying threats, was simply a way of making it easier for the Germans to destroy the Vilna Ghetto. Wittenberg maintained that Kittel and the Nazis should not be appeased and that the ghetto should not give way under their threats. But at the same time, he made it clear that if the U.P.O. did not support him, he was even prepared to make the supreme sacrifice and take his own life.

Even this, however, would not have solved the situation. Kittel demanded him alive.

Wittenberg realized then that there was only one noble course of action for him to take. He decided to leave his hideout and give himself up.

He said goodbye to his comrades, appointed his successor and, without looking back or pausing, he walked bravely out of the ghetto gates. There, totally unmoved by his actions, Kittel, who had been waiting for him, bundled him immediately into his car and took him to Gestapo HQ.

There in the cellar, he was roughly handed over to Max Gross, the Nazi's special investigator of Partisan affairs. His long and tortuous interrogation began.

The next day his bleeding, broken body was found in the corridors of the Gestapo HQ. by one of the Jews who worked there as a cleaner. Through this man, who was obviously intended to discover the dead Wittenberg, we learned what the Nazis had really meant by interrogation. Wittenberg had died in misery and pain. His hair was burned off, his eyes spiked out and his hands, still tied, were broken and lacerated.

After that, July 16, which went down in the history of the Vilna Ghetto as "Wittenberg Day", the U.P.O. command decided that the ghetto streets were not the best battleground for their fight against the Germans and they resolved, once more, to sink back into the obscurity of the forests.

Groups of Partisans gradually began to move out into the province, and the first of them, under the command of police chief Glazman, left on July 22, less than a week after Wittenberg's death. They were issued with arms and left the ghetto in a group that went to work in the city still wearing the Star of David on their chests. Within the following week, more and more groups slipped quietly out of the ghetto to join the Partisan forces but not all of them reached their destinations.

Some – the unlucky ones – were spotted by German patrols and mowed down by machine gun fire before they even reached the outskirts of the city.

In almost all cases, the groups left the ghetto on the pretext that they were going to work in the city outside the ghetto gates. It came, therefore, as a major blow to more than 100 such working party groups when, on August 1, they were dismissed by their employers, losing their right to leave the ghetto legally.

Then, quite illogically, the Germans announced that they wanted men for two working parties – one at the airport at Porubanek, and the other at the goods depot at the railways. Altogether, they wanted more than 4,000 people. The jobs seemed no worse than those we had been doing previously, and most people accepted.

Several days later, however, they were all surrounded at their workplaces by the Gestapo and the police, and they forced them to enter the wagons of goods trains.

At least 300 Jews put up some resistance but they were shot dead at the Porubanek airfield as they tried to escape.

The remainder, seeing what would happen to them if they tried to flee, had no option but to board the trains waiting for them. On August 16, they were taken to a concentration camp in Estonia and, as if it were some privilege to suffer and die with them, their relations were "invited" by the Germans to join them.

When Neugebauer realized that no volunteers were going to step forward he threatened to take all the relatives of those already in captivity in Estonia. His threat had its desired effect and, in a very short space of time, a large transportation of Jews was assembled and again sent under guard to Estonia.

The liquidation of the Vilna Ghetto, it seemed, had begun in earnest.

In sheer desperation, my Uncle Fayvel left the ghetto to make arrangements to hide all our family in a bakery in the suburbs that was owned before the war by Mr. Zilber. On September 1, just two days after he left, the ghetto gates were closed and the Germans announced that no-one was allowed to leave for any reason. Those with jobs outside the ghetto had, under the new regulations, to work inside it instead.

As far as the Germans were concerned, the 16,000 Jews who remained in the Vilna Ghetto at this time were 16,000 too many and shortly after they closed the ghetto gates, virtually entombing us in our own homes, they wanted a further 6,000 Jews for Estonia where they said that workers were urgently needed. But again, there were no volunteers. Instead everyone scurried to their hideouts in the hope that, by some miracle, they would be missed by the Germans when they began to make their selection.

The U.P.O., realizing that it was only a matter of time before the Germans entered the ghetto to take their 6,000 workers by force, ordered an immediate and total mobilization of its remaining forces. For the most part, the preparation was formalized and uneventful except for one group of Partisans who were preparing to defend a building at Strasguna 23 and who were disturbed by German troops and police.

The defenders opened fire at the Germans, killing a few, wounding others. But it was a short-lived triumph. Reinforcements were summoned by the Germans who placed charges of dynamite beneath the Partisans' building and blew it to the ground. In the explosion more than 100 people, including the Partisans, lost their lives under the piles of rubble and masonry.

After this incident, every building in which Partisans barricaded themselves was dynamited and destroyed. At the same time, the Lithuanian police and the Gestapo continued to search – and to find – Jews cowering in their hideouts. Those who were discovered in this way were assembled and, under heavy guard, escorted to Rossa Street for transportation to Estonia, on a one-way ticket.

The dynamiting of buildings and the transportation of Jews continued incessantly. Scores of Jews died with each fresh explosion and in all 8,000 Jews were removed to Estonia. It seemed as though it would only be a matter of a few days before the whole of the Vilna ghetto fell on its knees, never to rise again.

But somehow the old dog wouldn't lie down and die. On September 5, Kittel called off the hunt and announced: "The Vilna Ghetto continues to exist as before."

CHAPTER 18

The Liquidation Of The Ghetto

Kittel had announced that the ghetto continued to exist as before. It was not entirely true to say the least. He chose to ignore the fact that only 8,000 Jews remained of the original 40,000 or more who lived or passed through the two ghettos.

Nonetheless, it existed and in this respect, he was correct. Only by that time those who remained existed with no hope, or with so little it made no difference. Some desperate groups of U.P.O. fighters managed to break through the German lines and scuttle into the surrounding forests but for most of us there was nothing we could do but wait as we had done so often in the past – and pray for some miracle to save us. Some miracle we knew in our hearts that would not come.

One morning Nehama's husband, the ex-policeman Lewin, appeared unexpectedly in the ghetto with a group of Partisans. They had been sent on a special mission: to recruit a number of doctors in the ghetto and take them back into the forests to tend to the wounded and the sick among the guerilla fighters. When Lewin arrived at our flat he was wearing a Red Army uniform with a large pistol slung at this side. His appearance temporarily revived our hope. We quickly came to the conclusion that if it were possible for Partisans to walk into the ghetto unhindered by the Germans then, by the same rule, it might be possible to leave without being noticed.

I asked my father once again if I could go back with Lewin to join the Partisans but again he refused, maintaining that if the Partisans could walk into the ghetto with such ease it could only mean that the Red Army and our liberation were not far away.

Lewin realized that, even by this time, my father would not relent and with his comrades and the doctors they had recruited, he said goodbye to the ghetto and returned to fight in the forests.

I felt that with his departure went my last chance of escaping from the ghetto – and survival.

On September 13, 1945, a rumor spread through the ghetto to the effect that Gens had been taken to the Gestapo Headquarters. It created a tidal wave of panic. Throughout the entire existence of the ghetto Gens was probably the only person who could claim any immunity to the trials, torments and tribulations suffered by those of us with no rank or title. He seemed impervious, almost immortal.

His sudden removal to the Gestapo HQ, therefore, was not surprisingly interpreted as a sign that the tottering ghetto was about to crumble.

The following day Kittel arrived in the ghetto, called a meeting of the police and announced that Gens had been shot for failing to carry out the orders of the Gestapo. He then proceeded to say that Sala Desler was to be appointed in his place.

While he was alive, Gens had encountered a marked degree of mistrust among the ghetto Jews. They had interpreted his privileges as a sign that he had betrayed his fellow Jews and collaborated with the Germans. I had always maintained that he was faithful to the Jewish cause and contended that, the fact that he was executed by the Nazis, proved that I was right, or at least gave greater credibility to my argument. With his death many of the skeptics, the Doubting Thomases, belatedly realized that, although there were times when Gens appeared unsympathetic, he had for the most part endeavored to improve the lot of the Vilna Jews.

It was a well-known fact that Gens had been tipped off about his impending arrest and execution by a leading member of the Gestapo and that he could easily have escaped had he wanted. He had numerous Christian friends and contacts outside the ghetto – his wife, who lived outside the ghetto with their teenage daughter, was a Christian – yet Gens chose to stay in the ghetto like a captain refusing to abandon his sinking ship.

At first, when Kittel brought the news to the ghetto, the same skeptics who had doubted his loyalty suggested that the story of his death was merely a Nazi hoax: that Gens was alive and being well-protected by the Germans and being groomed for some new task elsewhere. But the unpleasant reality of his execution soon became evident when a Jew who worked in the Gestapo HQ, and we all knew to be trustworthy, returned to the ghetto and informed us that he had seen his lifeless body.

Desler did not keep his new post for very long. Just a few days after his appointment both he and Levas fled from the ghetto only a matter of hours before it was encircled by Ukrainian troops.

My Uncle Fayvel, who had left earlier in an attempt to find a safe hiding place for us, could not return or even pass a message to us.

We were utterly despondent. We knew that the ghetto was coming to an end but the rapidity took us all by surprise. It was impossible to come by any bread and those whose stocks of food were exhausted had to manage on whatever foodstuffs they could lay their hands on, or exist on water and fresh air.

In those frenetic hours, we at Szpitalna 13, as elsewhere, began to speculate on our immediate future and ultimate fate. Neither prospect gave us the remotest glimmer of hope. Would it be Ponary for us, like the tens of thousands before us, or would we be taken to a labor camp in Estonia to work ourselves to death?

We did not have to wait long before we knew the answer.

On September 23, 1943 at about 6 a.m. a Mr. Grinberg, who lived in the next flat to ours, looked through the cracks in the gate of Rudnicka 27 and saw scores of Ukrainian troops, armed with heavy machine guns, and as far as he could see, the weapons were pointing towards the ghetto. He also saw dozens of armored cars driving past the Church of All Saints towards Konska Street.

When he told us what he had seen, we were at first reluctant to believe him. We did not want to believe him. But soon the truth dawned. Each of us in turn peered through the gap in the gate for ourselves and one by one we came away with faces grim and grey with fear and worry.

Mr. Widecki, Mr. Tomin and my father returned to the flat and everyone gathered round a table to try and concoct some miraculous solution for our salvation – some magic carpet which, like in a fantasy fairytale, could transport us to a land of dreams where everything was sweetness and light. But for us there was no such carpet. Mr. Golomb suggested that we should first go to Rudnicka 6, where the ghetto police and council were situated, to see if there was any more positive information about this final threat to our safety and to decide upon some course of action on the strength of what we heard there. It was agreed and all male members of our house set off for Rudnicka 6. There, they found a huge, confused crowd, most of them there for the same reasons as themselves. They listened but heard nothing which roused their hopes. Even the police did not know what was happening. It was a case of the blind leading the blind.

At 9 a.m., Kittel appeared again in the ghetto accompanied by a man named Lakner, a member of the gebietskommissariat and together with the newly-appointed police chief, Bieniakonski, they came out onto a balcony and read an announcement through a loud-hailer.

It read: "In the name of the Reichskommisar for the Ostgebisten I order that the Vilna Ghetto which has existed for more than two years should be liquidated. All inhabitants must today be transported partly to Estonia and partly to Lithuania. It is in the interest of the population to comply calmly with the order, pack their belongings and in an orderly manner leave the ghetto by 12 noon."

Bieniakonski repeated the order in Yiddish and Kittel then added: "Everyone must leave the ghetto according to the order just given. If anyone remains we will blow up their houses with dynamite."

At first everyone remained in their places as if physically stunned, but slowly they began to disperse. We returned to Szpitalna 13. What else could we do? Where else could we go? Mr. Widecki, Mr. Golomb and my father decided that it was suicidal to go down to our hiding place in view of the Germans' threat to blow up the buildings – a threat which we had no doubt they were quite prepared to carry out.

Understandably, my Aunt Sonia, her parents and sisters, wanted to stay on for as long as they could in case, by some means, my Uncle Fayvel found some way of returning to the ghetto and his family.

Mr. Tomin joined in the discussion, later maintaining that it would be prudent to wait until we could see clearly how the "liquidation" was developing before we made any move from which we could not retreat.

My father disagreed with him. He felt that the time for discussion had long since passed and that it was a time for positive action. He said to my mother: "Eta, there is no point in staying any longer. The ghetto is being liquidated without a doubt, so we may as well go now rather than be blown up or shot for not complying with the German orders. You had better pack as many things as we can carry and we will make our way to the ghetto gates."

Mr. Widecki then walked up to my father and said: "My family and I are joining you. We may as well all stick together."

Mr. and Mrs. Golomb, who had already gathered their belongings together and were packed ready to go, came up to say goodbye. They only carried one suitcase each and as they walked through the door into the street, they turned and said: "If we don't happen to see you all again, we wish you all the best."

That was the last time that I saw the Golombs.

My mother persuaded Aunt Sonia that there was no point in staying. She convinced her that if my uncle could have come back to the ghetto he would have done so long before then and that under the liquidation order there was not the remotest chance that he would find a way to return.

In a very short time our family was joined by the Videckis, the Zilbers and their daughters, Aunt Sonia and Cousin Sascha and, together, we turned our backs on our home for the last time and made our way towards the ghetto gates. The Tomins and Mrs. Abelovitz were undecided as to what they should do for the best and we left them still making up their minds.

Like the Golombs, we never saw them again.

The ghetto streets were seething with people, burdened with bundles, suitcases and small children, all of them heading towards the gates as though beckoned by some Pied Piper. We were dancing to the tune of Nazism. Our group from Szpitalna 13 walked together, subconsciously subscribing to the theory that there is some security in numbers, although we knew, in truth, that our vulnerability was equally great.

With each step one question drummed increasingly louder in our heads: Would we ever see our beloved Vilna again? Somehow, too, we knew the answer. But there was no turning back. No matter what faced us we had reached a point from which we could not return.

Soon, we reached the ghetto gates – the threshold between a kind of freedom we had known for two years and an unknown captivity. How differently I had imagined it would be in those cherished hours I had dreamed my time away with Sonia Widecki. As I approached the gate I recalled sadly how I had talked with her about walking through them to a new life in America where I would make my fortune and then take her with me as my wife.

All such idyllic thoughts were driven rudely from my mind when instead of the New World beyond the gate, we were surrounded immediately by Ukrainian SS troops who, at bayonet point, escorted us towards the monastery at Rossa Street.

There, a scene of utter horror unfolded itself before us. Groups of people who had arrived before us were being beaten with rifle butts and the Germans appeared to be systematically separating the men, the women and the children. Everything happened so fast we had no time to orientate ourselves. A few minutes later we were approached by a group of Gestapo which included Weiss and Kittel. My father and I were pushed to the right and my mother and young brother were pushed towards the monastery gate. We did not even have a chance to say goodbye.

My father and I stopped momentarily to catch a glimpse of my mother and brother and a Ukrainian SS man butted us in the back with his rifle, shouting: "Move on, move on – quickly."

All day long groups kept arriving from the ghetto and the same procedure took place each time. Young men were pushed forward and old men, women and children were herded into the monastery grounds. As night fell, and the last group for that day had walked through the ghetto gate, my father and I managed to find a place to sit near the monastery wall. It was far too cold and uncomfortable to go to sleep but even had it been warm and comfortable between clean sheets and blankets, sleep would not have come to us that night. The thought of what was happening to my mother and brother kept running through our minds and, although we were exhausted, we could not sleep.

My father, with tears in his eyes, and a voice broken with distress, said: "Abrascha, why oh why did we not save ourselves when we had the chance to go to Janinas."

I could not think of a suitable reply. I just sat there and cried. To add to our misery, it was bitterly cold and during the night it also began to rain. The tears and the raindrops mingled and trickled down my cheeks.

The street in which we were sitting was sealed at each end and there must have been at least two companies of heavily armed Ukrainian troops guarding us. I took a short walk around to see if there were any gaps through which we might have been able to escape but there was none.

Throughout that first night in Nazi captivity, the Ukrainians wandered among the crowd of Jews and, under the threat of violence and even death, took away their valuables, such as gold watches, jewelry and even clothing. One Ukrainian guard took some gold roubles and money from my father, saying: "You won't need these where you're going." Then he added: "Count yourself lucky that I'm letting you keep your fur-lined coat." My father also had in his possession a gold pocket watch – which the guard would undoubtedly have stolen had he seen it – but he managed to hide it in a false pocket which my mother had sewn into the lining of his clothing.

Jews who refused to part with their belongings were beaten brutally – and then dispossessed – and throughout the night, the unmistakable noise of the beatings and their accompanying screams continued, making it impossible to rest peacefully, let alone sleep.

For my father and I the dawn could not come quickly enough. In the interminable darkness, the shouting of frightened people was so much more terrifying and our own fears were so much more vivid. At first light, it was still wet and cold and, as we tried to rouse ourselves back to life, the first little bands of Jews from the ghetto were beginning once again to filter dejectedly through the ghetto gates into the hands of the Germans.

Kittel, Weiss and their entourage, who had no doubt slept soundly in warm beds and who looked eager to pursue their work, arrived early. They remained in the area supervising the selections, yelling orders and stalking about like the villains in a macabre pantomime. Then, about 11 a.m. our attention was distracted by a group of workmen who were hastily erecting a gallows near the entrance to the monastery. My father and I were only a few yards away.

No sooner was it completed than three figures were led towards it. They were Partisans who, earlier that morning had left the ghetto along the sewers but who had miscalculated their distances and had emerged outside the Kasino Cinema in full view of some high-ranking German officers who were talking among themselves.

The three young heroes, Jakob Kaplan, a lawyer named Abrascha Chwoinik and a 20-year-old girl named Asia Big, pulled out their pistols and fired on the Germans, killing Max Gross, the Vilna Gestapo investigator, and an officer from the Kovno Gestapo. The alarm was raised and within a matter of a few seconds they were arrested and sentenced to death.

The three Partisans were hanged first, followed by a man called Grischa Lewin, a well-known watchmaker in Vilna, and another man whom we did not know.

Grischa Lewin's rope broke twice and each time he pleaded with Kittel for his life. But he might as well have screamed for mercy at a stone statue. Kittel, unmoved by his pleading, walked away with a sadistic leer on his face, and Martin Weiss stepped forward and emptied his revolver into Lewin's head.

Lewin's wife, who with her face contorted in agony against the railings of the monastery gate, had watched her husband's savage execution, lost all self control. For several minutes after the shots were fired she screamed wildly and uncontrollably, until a German soldier walked into the monastery grounds and, beating her insensible, dragged her away from the gate.

After the rumpus of this sordid interlude had subsided, Kittel shouted: "This will be the fate of anyone who dares to lift a finger against the Germans".

After this pretty little speech Kittel and his henchmen gave orders to the Jews to form columns of 10 and march towards the railway lines, where two empty trains were waiting to receive us.

Seventy people, crouching shoulder to shoulder and with very little breathing space above our heads, were packed into each wagon until both trains were full. At the same time, a selection took place in the monastery ground where some 6,500 were assembled.

The Germans selected 1,400 young women and sent them to a concentration camp at Kaiserwald (The Kaiser Forest) in Latvia. The rest, old, sick and infirm men, and all the older women and children, were transported to the gas chamber at Maidenek.

This transportation included my dear mother and brother.

From the German point of view transportations of this kind were a time consuming, troublesome and expensive exercise. In effect, they were simply taking entire populations from certain death in one location to precisely the same fate in another. Why then, one might ask, didn't the Germans simply short-circuit their extermination program by blowing the ghetto and their inhabitants to smithereens? There are two basic but equally important answers: self-preservation and money. If those Germans controlling the ghettos had destroyed them in this way their immediate role in the war would have come abruptly to an end and they would almost certainly have been ordered by their own hierarchy to join the bloody fighting on the Russian front. In this way, the Jews served as useful pawns to block any attempt to drag them into the firing lines.

Quite apart from this, the Jews were also a useful source of "beer" money to the Germans. Some Jews were allowed to leave the ghettos to work for the Germans. For this they received about 65pf. an hour, of which the Germans reclaimed 50pf in "taxes" for the war effort.

My father and I settled down as best we could on the draughty, wooden floor of our wagon, resigned to the fact that there was nothing we could do to steer the course of our immediate future. Life or death – the choice was not ours.

It was quite impossible to lie down but there were many in our group who had not slept the previous night and who, from sheer exhaustion, fell asleep on the shoulders of those around them. Before long most of our travelling companions accepted the fact that we were heading for a work camp in Estonia and the thought that our lives at least would be spared, considerably eased the tension and even brought faint smiles to some faces.

It was promoted by the fact that certain of the men among us were ordered out of the wagons to select food supplies for the long journey into the north of Estonia. This was seen as a good omen. Had we been destined for Ponary, a mere eight kilometers away, we would not have needed supplies of food. In any event we almost certainly would have been taken by lorry and not train.

Imagine our surprise when the men returned carrying plentiful supplies of food and soda water. We were given two loaves of bread each, 10 bottles of soda water, some sausage and margarine. Only a short time before we had expected to end up like Grischa Lewin with bullets pumped into our heads but instead we were given almost luxury foods. One needed to be a philosopher or a psychiatrist to fathom the eccentric ambivalence of the German mind.

As soon as all the supplies had been loaded aboard, the wagons were bolted from the outside and we continued our journey northwards. Almost without exception, not least my father and I, were sick with worry about our families but, for a short time, the hunger pains in our stomachs obliterated our heartache and we eat until we could eat no more, forgetting briefly the agonies of the past two days.

In each wagon, there was only one tiny window, divided by metal bars, laced with barbed-wire. Those of us near to it kept a constant check on our whereabouts and we all breathed a sigh of relief when one observer announced that we had passed the intersection leading to Ponary. After that the journey became as pleasant as was possible under the circumstances.

Throughout the rest of that day and all through the night the train cut its way through the Lithuanian countryside and when we were not sleeping, or commiserating with one another, we talked or thought about the life that was awaiting us in Estonia.

The next morning, after what was one of the longest nights of my life, we arrived at Siauliai, a small town in northern Lithuania. There we remained for what seemed an eternity while a train carrying German troops was given priority and passed through the station. While we waited, our German guards let us get out of the train two by two to attend to our personal needs and eventually we were back on the move again – but not for long.

Every few miles we seemed to stop for one reason or another and at Riga we were kept at the railway sidings for most of the day. Eventually, after 410 miles and five days in a filthy cattle truck, we arrived in the early hours of the morning at Vaivara, a characterless railway stop in the middle of nowhere.

Near the railway lines we saw working parties and even recognized the faces of some of the Jews who had been taken from their homes in Vilna several months previously. It encouraged us to see the faces of people we had long since feared dead.

Our train sighed to a halt and one by one the wagons were opened by German soldiers. Our bones ached after the rigors of the journey and we hardly had the strength to pick ourselves off the floor of the wagon. But the Germans showed no sympathy. As we left the train we were immediately assembled and told to leave our belongings in a pile.

Some 850 of us – those in the first wagons opened – were marched off under a heavy guard and the remainder were ordered to board the wagons that they had just left. Some years later I discovered that 750 men from our transport had been taken to the Klooga concentration camp and that many of them had perished, if not all.

After a short march, our group arrived at the Vaivara 1 camp, the headquarters of all the concentration camps in Estonia. There, on arrival, we met hundreds of Jews who had been taken from the ghetto during the last action prior to liquidation.

From the first moment, we walked into the campground and heard the click of the gate behind us we knew we were fully-fledged 'Haftlingen' – prisoners of the Third Reich.

The Vaivara Memorial
Photo: Courtesy of Yad Vashem

Chapter 19

Our Arrival At Vaivara

The sun, I am sure, never shone on Vaivara. It was a bleak, brutal, hideous place, created in a hurry from nothing but a few sticks of wood and barbed wire and laid down in the middle of nowhere.

Vaivara was a scar on the earth which turned quickly into a septic, festering sore. All around the camp, the terrain was flat, expressionless and as unfriendly as the faces of the Nazis who became our new tormentors and torturers.

As we marched towards the camp gates, the ugliness of Vaivara struck me like a blow to the stomach. It was etched in black, demonic colors and shapes - by the gun towers, casting long shadows over the sandy soil of the parade square and by the miles of the barbed wire which seemed to lacerate the skyline, defacing all that was remotely beautiful.

It never ceases to amaze me that man, even those insane or proud enough to wear a Swastika on their breasts, could have expended so much mental and physical energy on the creation of such a monstrous place as Vaivara, although it was, of course, far from unique.

We had hardly had time to exchange a few brief words with the old inmates, when we were given the order to assemble on the appelplatz - a word which we all knew to mean the parade square but which was to take on new and sinister meaning for us all in terms of pain and suffering.

It had taken five days and nights, cooped up in a stinking cattle wagon, to reach Vaivara but the fact failed to engender one iota of sympathy from the Germans. They allowed us no time at all in which to regain a little of our lost strength and, within a few minutes of our arrival, the camp elite, that is the Lager Altester (a prisoner who acted as camp elder) and the Block Altester (prisoner in charge of an individual barrack block) ordered us to form blocks of five so that we could be counted like real haflingen.

After we had been counted, three SS officers walked towards the Lager Altester. As they approached he gave the command: "Prisoners, attention! Mitzen ap!" We stood to attention and removed our hats.

The SS officers then spoke to the Lager Altester who began to read from some notes which he carried in his hand. I found out later that this was the normal procedure during the appels - the roll call. Each Lager Altester had to report to the SS Lager Fuhrer the number of prisoners present, absent or on official work (commandeered slave-labor) or, God forbid, missing from the camp.

We were still standing to attention when we heard the Lager Fuhrer's voice bellowing through the loud-speaker. He announced: "You are now prisoners. You will be treated well and according to the regulations. As long as you work well, you will be fed. You will at all times carry out the orders given by the camp administration. All those who do not comply will be severely punished. Anyone who tries to escape will be shot."

He then turned, said something to the Lager Altester and, together with his two companions, walked towards the gates. As soon as they were on the outside the Lager Altester gave the command: "Mitzen auf, wektretten." Those of us who had hats put them back on their heads and we broke up our ranks.

My father, who was standing next to me, said: "Abrascha, this is not so terrible after all. If we do as we are told, maybe we will survive this horrible nightmare." After a short pause, I replied: "Maybe, Papa, maybe." What more could I have said.

As soon as we had been dismissed everyone began to look longingly for familiar faces among those Jews who were already old hands at Vaivara and, similarly, the old hands themselves scoured the newcomers in the hope of recognizing a relative or close friends, even a father, a son or a brother.

There were, indeed, many who came across people dear to them who had been presumed dead several months earlier and my own father found several old friends who he never thought he would ever see again. After embracing and renewing their friendship, my father began to ask them questions about the sort of life we could expect to lead at Vaivara. He shielded me from the truth of their answers but I could see clearly from his expression on his face that their stories were not happy ones. In any event I was soon to discover for myself the raw truth about Vaivara.

As new arrivals, we were allocated four of the unfinished barrack blocks - altogether there were 30 - and ordered to take a bath in groups of 25. We were taken to the barracks, told to undress and enter a room bristling with showers where we were given just 10 minutes in which to wash and have all our hair shaved off by the camp barbers. At the same time, our clothes were being disinfected in an oven at the other end of the barracks. Then, after collecting our deloused clothes, we dressed hurriedly and ran to our new and uncomfortable home.

After the delousing session, which continued all through the afternoon, we were again told to assemble on the appelplatz and we were subjected to the same ritual as on our arrival but without the charming little speech of welcome from the Lager Fuhrer. We then returned to our barracks where we were each given a crust of stale black bread, weighing approximately 13 ounces, and half an ounce of margarine. We devoured the food and, with our hunger pains appeased temporarily, we went to sleep on the cold, damp earth.

The following day should have been one of joy and rejoicing among the Jews. It was September 30, 1943, Rosh Hashanah – the Jewish New Year. Instead we were rudely awakened at the uncivilized hour of 4.30 a.m. by the sounding of a gong, and a few minutes later, as we began to stretch our aching bones, we found ourselves being physically kicked by fellow prisoners, brutes known as stubbendienst or barrack orderlies.

After our ordeals of the previous five days and, in spite of the fact that our earth beds were a potential health hazard, we could have slept for a week. But there would be no rest and peace for the Jewish haftlingen of Vaivara, even on our New Year's Day. It never had been and we knew that nothing could possibly bring about any change of heart by the Germans towards us.

Tired, chilled, dazed, disillusioned and for many, bruised, we therefore woke up to celebrate the festival with a liter of black lukewarm coffee thrust at us with no more civility than swill poured into a pig trough. As soon as we gulped it down, we were once again ordered to assemble on the appelplatz.

It was still like night outside, pitch black and freezing cold. Floodlights, mounted like beady eyes on the watchtowers surrounding the camp, blazed down and illuminated the appelplatz as soon as we began to walk out of our barracks.

Once again, we were counted and after the "Mitzen ap, mitzen auf" order we were split up into different groups to form arbeitskommondos (working parties). Our group, made up of about 150 men, marched out of the camp at around 5.30 a.m.

Even then it was still pitch black. My body was starved to the marrow and my face was so numb, my lips refused to move and I could hardly talk. As we marched, I realized that we had at least 10 SS guards with us and every now and again one of them would shout: "Faster, faster! You lazy Jewish pigs."

As they spoke, they goaded the nearest prisoners with the butts of their rifles.

As long last, after all the shouting and butting, we arrived half dead at the place near some railway lines about seven kilometers from the camp. We had spent five days in the cattle truck, slept on damp earth, been awakened by the boot in the middle of the night, breakfasted on insipid coffee, marched in the bitter cold and now we were expected to work hard.

Our column was split up into five groups with two SS men and a German in uniform in charge of each group. The uniformed German was a member of the Organization Todt, a pseudo-military organization formed by the Nazis to run all construction work in occupied territories.

The group in which I found myself, together with two other groups, were told to start unloading three wagons of cement, and store them in one of the huge sheds alongside the railway lines.

The German from the Todt Organization told us to address him as Herr Meister.

He told two prisoners to stay inside the wagon and to lift the 50 kilogram sacks onto the shoulders of other prisoners below. As soon as the sack was slumped over our shoulder we had to run - not walk - and deposit it in one of the sheds. In our undernourished, debilitated condition the sacks of cement seemed to weigh tons and, with each journey to and from the sheds, they appeared to become heavier and heavier.

Our misery provided excellent sport for our German overseers. Every time a prisoner's knees buckled beneath him under the weight of the sacks, they laughed until their sides were sore.

The top man among them, on the other hand, kept running backwards and forwards making sure that we were working hard and that the bags were being stacked correctly. Now and again, the would attempt to encourage us by saying: "Soon you will get a good meal to restore your strength. Los, los arbeiten".

By that time, however, the only food we thought about was that in our stomachs and his words did nothing to boost our morale or whet our appetites.

After two hours of slave labor under the most trying conditions I collapsed on the ground and could not get back to my feet. The Herr Meister screamed at me to get up and the SS guards laughed even louder than ever. My father who was working on the next wagon, saw my predicament and, in spite of the personal dangers he knew he would face, he came running over towards me.

Simultaneously, one of the guards jumped off the stack of railway sleepers on which he had been standing and repeatedly punched by father in the face with his clenched fist. My father fell to the ground covered in blood and for good measure the SS guard kicked him in the side as he lay there, shouting at the same time something which I did not hear.

In those moments, I found a strength which I thought had deserted me. I staggered to my feet and began to plead with the Herr Meister to let me help my father. He replied: "Your father? You should be ashamed you little pig dog to cause your father so much suffering." With those words he kicked me on the backside, muttering: "Back to work, back to work you scheissdreck."

I knew then that life at Vaivara was going to be a living Hell.

Chapter 20

My "Baptism Of Fire"

At Vaivara, according to an old Yiddish saying, I paid my "rebbe gelt" – my tuition fees.

I was just 13 years old when I entered the camp and, had it not been for the war, I would almost certainly have been studying at the Lenin High School. Instead, in the fortnight that my father and I were at Vaivara, I graduated from an apprentice to a craftsman in the art of evading trouble, although it was not until my father and I left the camp that I was able to put my new-found talent to good use.

After my relatively easy life in the ghetto, I found it almost impossible to adjust to the inflexible regime of a German concentration camp. Nothing that I did seemed to go right and I cannot remember one single day during that nightmare fortnight when I was not beaten at work or on my return to the camp.

Even when I deliberately kept out of the Germans' way I attracted trouble like a honey-pot attracts bees. There seemed to be some sort of jinx on me. I was the scapegoat for the whole of my working party and suffered for everybody's "sins". It was obvious to me, from the very first day, that the meister and one of the guards took an instant dislike to me, and that they were determined to make my life at Vaivara as miserable and as painful as possible.

My father, who could do nothing apart from watch helplessly every time I was punched or kicked for my misdeeds, even tried, but without success, to transfer us to another arbeitskommandos.

I was quick to realize, however, that the solution lay in my own hands and night after night, as I lay in my barrack bunk nursing my wounds and staring into the darkness, I searched every corner of my mind for the answer which I knew must exist. There was, in fact, nothing else that one could do after a day of enforced slave labor – apart from think, and maybe dream a little too. Everyone was too exhausted even to talk to his neighbor and as soon as the lights were put out the same old thoughts came flooding into our minds.

 The answer to my own personal problem, when it eventually came to me, was simple in the extreme and I could not understand why it had not occurred to me previously. One night it suddenly became quite clear to me that many of the beatings which I received could have been avoided if I had been a little more circumspect in keeping out of the way of the Germans.

The notion came to me too late to help my immediate predicament and suffering as Vaivara, but, in the months that were to follow, the lessons I learned were to prove invaluable.

Vaivara was a baptism of fire – an initiation which, without doubt, taught me how to survive.

The work in that Hell hole was tedious, pointless and heartbreaking. For several days, we continued to unload the bags of cement, but for most of the second week we sweated and labored under the strain of thousands of bricks which arrived in one train consignment after another. Some of the less robust prisoners among us who could not keep pace with the tempo of the work were beaten to within an inch of their lives – but, incredibly, no one actually died.

Our working day at Vaivara, like in almost all other German concentration camps, started at 6 a.m., literally from dawn until dusk. After we had been dismissed, we returned almost crippled to our quarters where we endeavored to pass the time restfully and peacefully until the naked electric light bulbs, which illuminated our barracks, were switched off around 9 p.m.

Those prisoners, whose energy had not been entirely sapped by the exertions of the day, frequently discussed politics and the prospects of freedom, while still others prayed silently to themselves or joined in one of the regular secret communal services. There were no copies of the Talmud but among the prisoners there was always one or two orthodox Jews who could recite the texts from memory and who could lead the others in prayer.

As a young boy, I was preoccupied with the immediate problem of survival and with the prospect of liberation, or even escape. My youthfulness and relative good health made it possible for me to be a little more optimistic about our future than those who had had a greater experience of life. But my father, who was a rapidly ageing 37, was thoroughly dejected and downtrodden. He never ceased to worry about the fate of my mother and brother and, whenever we were together, he talked about them until his voice was choked with emotion and tears filled his eyes.

We had been at Vaivara for just a few days when a number of SS officers came unexpectedly into the camp and haphazardly began to take hundreds of men to another camp. By that time our health and strength was rapidly approaching breaking point and both my father and I prayed that we would be among those selected – in spite of the fact that we did not know where we would be taken. We assumed that anywhere was better than Vaivara.

But, unfortunately, we were not selected. On the following Sunday, however, when we were standing on the appelplatz, an announcement was made to the effect that 200 men would be needed for "important work" at a nearby camp, and that we could either volunteer or the requested number would be taken forcibly.

The phrasing of the request did not endear the prospect to us, but the conditions at Vaivara at that time were so inhuman, the required number of volunteers was surpassed in just a matter of minutes. My father and I looked at each other and decided quickly that we, too, should offer our services. Our theory seemed sound enough: if the Germans were telling the truth, we assumed that the next camp could not be any worse than Vaivara. If, on the other hand, they were lying, and we were earmarked instead for extermination, we wouldn't even then have been much worse off, in view of the fact that none of us could have survived a great deal longer under the Vaivara regime. Having resigned ourselves to this fact, we volunteered.

Everyone in the group was anxious not to be left behind and those at the back tried to push their way to the front to ensure that they were included in the transport designated to leave Vaivara. I kept as close to my father as I could. Like everyone else, we jostled for a favorable position but somehow, when the time came to be counted, we were in the last row of five.

The guards who were detailed to accompany the party restored order by pointing their loaded rifles at the swaying mass of bodies and one of the officers counted exactly 200. Those he selected were instantly surrounded by the guards and marched some 50 yards away.

The rest of us, including my father and I, were treated to a spontaneous display of concentration camp discipline at its most violent. About one dozen SS men, like uncaged wild animals, started to kick us with their jackboots and beat us with their rifle butts. They behaved like antagonized psychopathic killers let loose with pole axes among helpless children.

I learned quickly, and from bitter experience, that as soon as I was kicked or beaten, the best policy was to throw myself to the ground and stay there until the action subsided. I put my theory into practice, but those who had not learned this simple lesson and who tried to run off and hide in the barracks were pursued by the guards and beaten until the blood flowed freely on the ground.

For more than 15 minutes the guards indulged their sadistic cravings and then, like bloodhounds back from the hunt, they joined the 200 newly selected prisoners and marched them out of the camp gate.

The appelplatz looked like a battlefield. Prisoners began to help each other back to their feet and, bruised and bleeding, they struggled back to their barracks, where for the rest of the day the conversation revolved around the desirability of remaining with the devil we knew – Vaivara – rather than casting ourselves into the clutches of some new demon we did not know.

On the following day, everyone had to report for work as usual. Those prisoners who had been savagely beaten reported sick but my father and I were told by the camp officials that it would have been far "healthier" for them to have gone to work. Some of those who put on a brave face were so ill they had to be carried to their places of work.

When our meister saw the state of some of the victims he surprisingly showed some real compassion and gave them lighter work to do – making it clear to the rest of us that we would have to work twice as hard to compensate for the absence of those "softer" Jews who were unfit for work because of a "few punches that they deservedly received." He then added: "We will teach you discipline and how to earn your keep - you ferfluchte schweinhunde" adding: "Now get on with your work or I will show you what I am capable of, you cursed pig-dogs."

Our little lecture from the Herr Meister to start our day was typical of the Germans attitude to the Jews. On the one hand, he was human enough to find lighter work for those who were sick or maimed but, on the other, he threatened to cripple the rest of us if we failed to pull our weight.

The train loads of bricks seemed unending. I remember thinking to myself how thousands of years earlier our fore-fathers had slaved for the Pharaohs in Egypt and that now we were being compelled at gunpoint to do the same for Hitler.

Our meister, a short, fat, balding Nazi with a moustache not unlike that of the Fuhrer himself, was capable of the most inhuman acts. Nothing seemed to satisfy his Barbarian instincts. On one occasion when our midday meal arrived – a barrel of soup made from a few grains of corn flour and gallons of lukewarm water – he flew into a rage with a prisoner who complained that the soup was tasteless and insipid. He punched the prisoner repeatedly to the face and body and, still ranting and raving, he strode over to the barrel and emptied its entire contents into the earth, leaving the majority of us without even this poor substitute for food. Those who did not have their midday soup of that day returned to the camp that evening half dead.

A few days after this incident we heard that 500 more prisoners were needed for urgent work in another camp. Twice previously my father and I had missed an opportunity of leaving Vaivara and we hoped and prayed that it would be a case of third time lucky.

Our luck held. Some SS guards arrived at the camp and selected 500 men to work at a concentration camp at Narva and when the train left for this new destination my father and I were on it.

Never in my life had I been as glad to leave anywhere.

CHAPTER 21

Arrival at Narva

Narva, our new home, was far removed from what we had expected and our first impression led us to believe, although falsely as it transpired, that life was to become more tolerable.

Instead of the wooden barracks which had been our home at Vaivara, at Narva we were accommodated in a disused textile mill. The individual buildings were old and ramshackle, and had obviously been thrown together without the remotest notion of design and no two of them were alike. In contrast to Vaivara, too, our new home was pleasantly warm, in particular in my own quarters which were on the first floor above the rising heat of the boiler room below. Psychologically, the feeling of warmth, after the bitter cold of Vaivara, made my father and I feel as though we had survived the worst of the Nazi wrath and that there was a chance we would be left to live out the rest of the war in relative peace.

After the weary train ride to Narva and the inevitable trek from the station to the camp, we were as limp and lifeless as creaking puppets. I am sure that I could have slept for a week or more had I been left undisturbed. But it was not to be. Mein hosts, our new jailers, first wanted to see their new arrivals on the appelplatz.

A trio of German officers emerged: Kurt Pannicke, our new Lager Fuhrer, who would then have been between 28 and 30; Hans Schnabel, the assistant Lager Fuhrer, who was a few years older, and another SS man called Ernst Runde, the Sanitater, who, as his title suggests, was responsible for the sanitary arrangements in the camp. He was about 35.

Pannicke made the usual speech of welcome and both he and his two assistants smiled benignly throughout the whole of their initial encounter with the new arrivals. Those among us, and I have no doubt there were a number who felt that we were going to lead a life of relative luxury at Narva compared with Viavara, were soon proved wrong.

The initial appel over, we went to collect our daily ration of food for the day - a few ounces of stale bread, a little cube of margarine and some tepid ersatz coffee.

Ernst Runde
Photo: Courtesy of Yad Vashem

Apart from the change of scenery and accommodation, the camp procedure at Narva was identical to Vaivara. Our day started at the unearthly hour of 4:30 a.m. with the sounding of a gong on the appelplatz, and an hour later everyone had to assemble to be counted. As soon as this ritual was completed we formed the arbeitskommandos and marched out to work.

Every prisoner at Narva, as far as I could see, seemed to spend his working day digging anti-tank traps. As far as the eye could see there were rows and rows of prisoners hacking away at the frozen earth with pick-axes, often making little or no impression.

At Narva, we were more heavily guarded than at Vaivara. Members of the Organization Todt were once again in charge of the work but, compared with their counterparts at Vaivara, they behaved like saints. But while the beatings were less frequent and severe, the work itself was probably more grueling and exhausting. With nothing more than a drop of tepid soup to sustain us, we slaved for 15 hours every day and, to add to our miseries, the winter began to bare its teeth.

As prisoners at Narva we faced two basic problems: the shortage of food ant the freezing conditions – and there was no immediate answer to either of them. My father and I, like almost all the other new arrivals at Narva, simply had to learn to adjust to our new environment and the new regime.

In the evening, after we had returned from the fields, eaten our food ration, life once again seemed a little more bearable. Prisoners used to form themselves into small groups and pass the time away in conversation. One man, I remember had a pack of cards – I have no idea where he got them from - and his bunk quickly became the hub of all the social activities.

A number of ghetto administrators also shared our room at Narva, but hardly anyone ever spoke to them and, for most of the time, they sat stony-faced and thoroughly miserable either on their own or with one another. Their unpopular reign at Vilna had come abruptly to an end and in the concentration camps they were ostracized by their fellow Jews.

During the first few weeks at Narva, our guards and officers were surprisingly humane. Occasionally prisoners, my father and I included, would be at the receiving end of a Nazi fist or boot but for the most part no-one was grossly mistreated.

Unsurprisingly, it was merely a veneer of kindness and all too quickly the wooden hearts of the Germans emerged and the same old beatings started all over again. By that time my father and I had grown accustomed to concentration camp life and even the suffering reached a point where one accepted it as part of the daily routine in much the same way as a beast of burden accepts its life of toil or a caged animal, that has never known freedom, accepts its life behind bars.

November 1943 was exceptionally cold even for those who had the health and strength to endure it. But for us, with our ebbing will to live and undernourished bodies, the cold cut like blades of steel. This alone would have been painful enough to endure but, in addition, we had to brace ourselves against the ravages of Pannicke, Schnabel and company who, through lack of entertainment, devised bizarre ways of amusement at our expense.

We became human "skittles". For sheer amusement Pannicke and Schnabel used to order starved, worn-out prisoners to stand for hour upon hour on the appelplatz while from some warm vantage point they waited and gambled on those who would collapse first.

Those who did in fact keel over, and the majority did in time, were beaten with bullwhips, the Germans' favorite playthings during appels. At least two prisoners died after being thrashed by Pannicke and an SS guard I did not know.

SS Sanitater Runde was also adept with the bullwhip, especially when he was drunk—and he was drunk frequently. Runde, like the rest of his kind, needed little or no encouragement to make the fullest use of his lash. Failing to remove one's cap, slouching slightly on parade or even falling from exhaustion on the appelplatz were all sufficient reasons to prompt a beating.

First, Pannicke, Schnabel, Runde and their assistants would administer 25 strokes with the bullwhip. The prisoners, who invariably fainted and whose bodies were striped with angry weals, were then removed to the camp's bath house where an attempt was made to revive them with cold water. If this failed, as it often did, the Nazis had a ready-made place for the disposal of the body - the textile mill incinerator which was converted into a cremation oven.

Narva began to live up to, even emulate, the stories we had heard of concentration camp life. Prisoners began to die like flies, others resigned themselves to the fact that they would not survive but, for some reason I now find difficult to explain, I reacted contrary to my own expectations. As the conditions in the camp deteriorated my will to live seemed to grow proportionately stronger. I was just 15-years-old and in two years I had experienced all the tragedy, hunger and inhumanity man can suffer and I suppose that subconsciously I convinced myself that, having reached the bottom of the pit, I could only begin to crawl back to the top.

I decided that I had to try and stay alive at all costs. This much I knew; just how was a different matter entirely.

One thing, however, was obvious at Narva; a prisoner could minimize the chances of being beaten by simply keeping out of the Nazis' way. It was a lesson I had learned the hard way at Vaivara. Of course, there were exceptions - times when it was totally impossible to avoid a beating no matter how hard one tried. But for the most part I found that it was not difficult to stay out of trouble.

It certainly paid off for me and my father, too. After he was once kicked and beaten by Schnabel for being slightly out of line during an appel he decided to adopt my formula and found that, in spite of its simplicity, it was effective. For some time after this both of us avoided the boot and the bullwhip for several weeks, maybe longer.

Avoiding trouble, in itself, was not sufficient. If one wanted to stay healthy one also had to eat reasonably well. The food at Narva, like that in other concentration camps, was totally inadequate. It was too much to let you die, too little on which to live, and what was worse there seemed no means of supplementing the rations allocated to us.

Towards the end of November, I had the opportunity of transferring to another arbeitskommando and, in the hope that I might be able to improve my personal lot and perhaps secure more food, I made the move without hesitation. The work I soon discovered - digging anti-tank traps - was just as boring, just as back breaking, as I had been experiencing from the start at Narva, but it was obvious that the meisters were considerably more kindly disposed towards us. They rarely beat us or drove us too hard, and after several days in my new work place, I even managed to have a face-to-face talk with one of them. By that time my judgement had matured beyond my years and I soon realized that he could be manipulated. I came quickly to the conclusion that he was one of those Germans who detested the job he had been ordered to do and in fact felt sorry for the Jews.

It was an opportunity not to be missed. He told me that he had two boys of his own about my age and, although he did not say so, I knew that he was emotionally disturbed by the thought of my suffering. When the moment arose, I went up to him and pleaded with him to let me go over to a hut not far away that was used by the meisters of the Organization Todt during their lunch breaks.

"I just want to warm myself for a few moments," I begged.

"If you want to have a warm, you must first make a fire," he replied. I was only too pleased to oblige.

In the hut, apart from the protection it provided from the cold, I found some scraps of food and a few drops of soup left by the meisters. I devoured them voraciously, feeling afterwards as if I had dined at the Ritz.

A few days later, the fire lighting idea was taken up by other young men like myself and before long at least 15 boys about my age were employed as cleaners and stokers in the meisters' huts.

The work was far from pleasant, but there is little doubt that the spartan comforts it afforded enabled us to survive our stay at Narva and, more importantly, it renewed our chance of survival.

CHAPTER 22

Life Under Pannicke and Schnabel

The shelter and the sustenance that I found in the meisters' huts enabled me to keep my body and soul together in those dark days at Narva. But my father was not so fortunate.

Whilst I, through a combination of good fortune and opportunities, managed to shield myself from the full blast of the winter cold, my father spent most of his working day knee-deep in icy water. Nor, throughout his entire internment at Narva, did he once have any opportunity of laying his hands on extra food to supplement the meagre ration allocated to us.

Not surprisingly, this constant subjection to the twin torments of cold and hunger whittled away what little reserves of strength he had left and his health rapidly began to crack.

Whenever I went to work in the meisters' hut, I invariably obtained enough bread and scraps for a palatable "meal" and was able to give my official bread ration to my father, whose need, at the time, was far greater than mine.

The leftovers in the meisters' huts provided a useful, if monotonous, dietary supplement but I was always eager to find something even more substantial, more nourishing. This opportunity came one night when I was walking around the room and saw one of the boys, who worked in the huts during the day, eating a piece of salt herring.

"Where did you get the salt herring?" I asked. My undisguised surprise, at the sight of a concentration camp inmate eating such a luxury, was matched only by his reply. If he had been eating caviar and drinking vodka I don't think I would have been any more amazed. Ruvke, the boy in question, told me that since he had started work in the meisters' huts he had regularly been running away into Narva itself and begging from the civilian population. The older Estonian people, he said, could still speak Russian and were, on the whole, very generous to the prisoners, providing them with a selection of foods, mostly bread, herrings and potatoes.

"I'm not the only one, Abram. Quite a few of the boys regularly go to Narva. Why don't you join us and give it a try?" he asked.

The idea appealed to me and I agreed. There was always the danger that I could be caught and punished, even shot, but logically I could see no reason why I should fail if others had already been successful on numerous occasions. It was my father's poor health more than anything, however, that made me make up my mind so quickly. I felt sure that if only every few days he could have a nourishing meal his chances of survival would be greatly enhanced.

"I will join you Ruvke. When shall we go?"

"Tomorrow, if the conditions are favorable."

"I'll be there."

The following day we went to work as usual. After we had lighted the fires in our respective huts we dived into a very deep ditch and started to crawl on our bellies for more than a quarter of a mile.

When we were out of sight of the guards we emerged from the ditch and began to make our way a distance of some seven kilometers, to the outskirts of Narva where my companion led me towards an impressive-looking house.

I was trembling with fear and excitement all the time. All I wanted to do was run back to the arbeitsplatz but my friend assured me that we would be all right and that the people who occupied the house were friendly and charming and that we would be well received. He had been there the day before and I thought he was pushing his luck to return so soon afterwards, but I was wrong. We were made most welcome and after a few minutes we left with two herrings apiece and a blessing for our safe return to the camp. I could almost have cried.

My friend wanted to carry on with our begging adventure but, at this stage, I was still exceedingly nervous about the whole exercise and, having been given two salt herrings on my first call, I decided to run back to my workplace leaving him to carry on alone.

On my return, I saw no-one but almost as soon as I dropped back into the ditch I heard the sharp report of shots being fired in my direction, followed by a voice ordering me to come out into the open. I had been seen.

I had no choice. Had I stayed in the ditch and laid low it would have become my grave in a very few minutes. So, shaking with fear, I groveled my way to the surface and found myself confronted by several Luftwaffe soldiers. A barrage of questions lambasted me: "Where have you been?" bellowed one. "Why did you run away?" yelled another. "You know the penalty for trying to escape?" screamed a third. I trembled visibly and attempted to mutter something to the effect that I had not been trying to escape.

"Please don't hurt me, my father is very ill and he doesn't get enough to eat. I have only been to Narva to try and get him some food. You can see I was coming back," I said breathlessly.

They smiled, looked quizzically at each other and then began to talk among themselves. I thought to myself "kill me, kill me, get it over with quickly." But there was no violence. I fully expected a bullet through the head, or a beating at least, but instead one of the soldiers dipped his hand into his pocket and gave me two bars of chocolate. "Make sure you give some to your father!" said one of them as though he was genuinely concerned about his health. They walked away laughing.

The relief I felt on returning to the hut was indescribable. My father, who knew nothing of my begging exploits, refused to take any of the chocolate. "Chocolate is for children - your father is all right. You eat it yourself," he said. "You need the nourishment more than I do." It was not true and he knew it. After a little further persuasion, I forced him to try a little so that his palate would not lose the taste of chocolate altogether.

In December, the frost became thicker and more cruel, almost impossible to bear for very long. The camp itself was heated but far from warm. Under such deprivation it was almost impossible to survive, even had we been allowed to remain in our quarters permanently, but the prolonged and regular exposure to the piercing cold out of doors, both on the appelplatz and the arbeitsplatz, reduced our chances of survival dramatically.

On one occasion when Pannicke went away for a few days we thought that we would not have to shiver for such long periods on the appelplatz and that we would be able to return more quickly to the relative comfort of our room. It was not so. Pannicke's assistant, Schnabel, seemed to derive even greater pleasure than his superior in keeping the prisoners on the appelplatz for hour upon hour until their bodies became as numb and rigid as those on a mortician's slab. Pannicke, at least, had a sense of humor and would twist his face into a forced smile whenever he gave orders to any one of the 200 women prisoners who were at Narva. Schnabel, on the other hand, always reminded me of an undertaker at a funeral and, indeed, the simile was not far from a true representation of his function. I never once saw a flicker of joy break the sinister expression fixed permanently across his face.

After my first, and reasonably successful, begging trip to Narva - we used to call it organieziren - I became increasingly brave and began to make a habit of it, ignoring the possibility that I would be caught and punished. I was clearly aware, at the same time, that the whole exercise was fraught with a multiplicity of dangers.

By far the most serious handicap was the fact that Pannicke himself had somehow heard about the begging expeditions and, more and more often, he could be seen driving back to the camp, like a hunter returning from a safari, with one or more prisoners he had caught. The penalty they paid was 25 lashes on the backside, but even this, as painful as it was, was not a very potent deterrent compared with the counterforces of hunger pain.

Another major snag was the presence of an anti-aircraft battery on the perimeter of the arbeitplatz. Most of the Germans who manned the guns tended to turn a blind eye to our expeditions but there were always a small number of them who derived great delight in beating us with their own hands or, even worse, in handing us over to the SS guards.

I was lucky. Although I was fired upon on numerous occasions, I was never hit or handed over to the guards who, unquestionably, would have made life exceedingly uncomfortable for me.

As I became more experienced and my bravado increased, I became more selective in the houses I chose on my trips to Narva and there were hardly any occasions when I did not receive substantial handouts of food from the Russian-speaking people. As a means of providing additional nourishment the sorties were certainly fruitful but, after a while I began to look forward to them for their own sake. The daily routine in the camp seldom varied: the living conditions remained unchanged and the long appels and the torments continued relentlessly. Life was either painful or boring, and for this reason alone the begging expeditions to Narva were as much an escape from boredom as from the torments of the camp itself. Trying to keep out of sight of the police and the SS, and then returning to work unnoticed, gave us the excitement lacking in the tedious regimentation of camp life. Even though we courted death each time we ran away, we all thought it was well worth the risk.

Not all the prisoners were as lucky as I was. Several were caught red handed and severely punished.

Others, who could find no release from the misery and boredom, and could endure the conditions no longer, took the only course left open to them - suicide. One prisoner, in the bunk across the room from where I was living, committed suicide by hanging himself with his trouser belt.

He was one of many who reached breaking point at Narva and snapped.

During our stay at Narva several more people took their own lives in desperation, and the demoralizing effect it had on the rest of the camp's inmates made it even more likely that others would end their lives in the same way.

Pannicke, who behaved as if he had been made the Devil's jester, appeared to have but one mission: to laugh as we suffered. To fulfill his bloodlust and to make the appels more amusing from his point of view, he used to pick on a prisoner who had contravened some new order, force him to strip in front of the camp and then tell him to count the number of strokes that he received with the bullwhip. If he stopped counting or lost count, Pannicke would start all over again.

On other occasions, he would force all prisoners to strip to the waist for long and rigorous physical training sessions. "It will keep you fit for work," he would shout repeatedly.

Often at the end of a P.T. session he would keep us for hour upon hour in different kneeling positions and with our arms outstretched. Nothing gave him greater satisfaction than when one or more prisoners faltered and toppled over - except perhaps the administration of the 25 lashes afterwards by way of punishment. Pannicke's insistence that the exercises would keep us fit fooled no one, least of all those prisoners who returned to the camp on the point of collapse or death. Some were even too ill to collect their rations despite the hunger that ate away their shriveled stomachs.

Even on Sundays Pannicke and Schnabel would not let us rest. Often, we were on the appelplatz from 6 a.m. until 12 noon, or even later, with only brief rest periods in between. When Pannicke began to feel the cold himself he would leave Schnabel to take over. After an hour or so he would return to relieve Schnabel and return to his duties with renewed zest.

Several prisoners died during these exercise appels, and their bodies were left unattended until the order "wektretten" was given by the officer in charge. Only then were we allowed to pick up the body and carry it away for burial. The Germans refused to "soil" their hands by handling the corpses of dead Jews.

Narva began to crush us slowly. There seemed only two means of exit. One was marked Death, the other Miracle. The first seemed a highly probable means of release, but the second was too remote even to warrant serious consideration.

Chapter 23

Harsh Treatment In A Harsh Winter

The constant gnawing by cold and hunger at our flesh produced an uncanny, sepulchral sameness about the faces of the prisoners at Narva. Our hair was shaved, our skin sallow and drawn, our eyes hollow and our bodies brittle and emaciated. As we stood on the appelplatz we looked like dummies draped in rags.

Motke R. looked just like the rest of us, but, for reasons that will become clear, his face will always remain vividly imprinted in my mind. Motke, who would have been about 15, was one of the boys from the stoker brigade, as we called it, and the most regular absentee from the arbeitskommando. Almost every day he disappeared to go begging into Narva.

Time after time he succeeded in slipping back without being missed, but, on one occasion during the early days at Narva, Pannicke caught Motke while he was roaming around the streets in Narva like some Dickensian Artful Dodger thrust into another century.

Pannicke, who found the "hunt" both exhilarating and entertaining, invited Motke into his car and drove him back to the camp where, after ordering a proper meal for him, gave him 10 lashes with his bullwhip and threatened him an infinitely more severe punishment if he went absent from camp again.

Motke was not deterred. Within a few days he had resumed his exploits. More often than not he returned safely, with extra provisions for his troubles, but there were also several other occasions when he was caught by Pannicke, and on each he was punished more and more harshly.

Soon the whole exercise developed into a sort of sinister cat-and-mouse game.

Pannicke, for some reasons I never discovered, thought of Motke as his pet victim, and when he failed to find him during their game of hide-and-seek in Narva, he would even wait for Motke to return to the camp. If Motke had any food with him that he had managed to beg in the town, Pannicke would let him keep it to show off to the rest of the camp his sadly distorted sense of fair play. There were times when he made a mockery of the notion, but there is also little doubt that he was more sporting towards Motke than he was towards other prisoners who crossed his path, in spite of all the beatings that he gave him.

As a complete contrast to his treatment of Motke, one young man at Narva was shot dead by Pannicke in one of the streets in the town while trying to escape after he had caught him begging from Estonians.

His lifeless body was brought back to the camp and left on the appelplatz during the appel as a deterrent to those of us who also made a habit of running away to Narva.

But neither Motke, nor any of the stoker brigade, were in the least put off. Hunger was a far greater master then Pannicke, and, in any event, we calculated that the chances of dying from malnutrition were we to stay were as great, if not greater, then the risks we incurred by the begging trips. My father, who was very ill at the time, had also grown accustomed to the extra food and I'm sure that he would not have survived more than a few days on his daily rations had I suddenly cut off this extra source of nourishment for him.

Even the strongest among us began to break down physically after a while. An outbreak of carbuncles spread throughout the camp, and it was neither possible to contain it nor offer any real help to those who suffered from them, since there was virtually no medical treatment of any kind available in the camp. And, of course, the Germans saw no reason to provide drugs, medicines, bandages or dressings of any kind.

SS man Runde, as the official camp Sanitater, was officially responsible for the medical welfare of the prisoners, but he was more devoted to alcohol than to the job assigned to him. In any event he preferred inflicting injury and illness to healing and curing it.

The behavior of the guards and meisters towards us at Narva depended to a large degree on the successes and failures of the German armed forces at the various battlefronts. If the Wehrmach suffered a major setback, we would immediately become the whipping boys of the Nazi wrath. The guards would become noticeably wilder and vent all their anger, disappointment and hate on the defenseless Jewish prisoners.

Our fate fluctuated in this way for a number of weeks but, as New Year 1944 approached, we all hoped, illogically one has to say, that with it our fortunes would change for the better.

On Christmas Eve, we returned from work earlier than usual. On arrival at the camp we were not allowed in our quarters and instead we had to remain on the appelplatz. No one knew why but by that time we had long since realized that any deviation from routine procedure inevitably meant trouble, and, as the hours ticked by, our worst fears were realized. It was the season of goodwill but this did not apply to Jews in Nazi captivity.

After several hours and, when all but a handful of the prisoners had reached or passed the limits of endurance, Pannicke, Schnabel and Runde, accompanied by three more junior SS officers, entered the camp and lurched towards the appelplatz. We could see, even from a distance, that they had all had too much to drink.

The Lager Altester made his usual report and probably prayed to himself, like the rest of us, that the appel would end quickly and that Pannicke and party would return to replenish their empty glasses that they had obviously just left.

Our fears were not ill founded. Pannicke and his motley crew decided to inspect us. They walked staggering and swaying between the rows of prisoners, hitting one here and another there, simply because one of us was not standing to attention or for no other reason than that they disliked a certain face.

The inspection seemed to drag on for hours, and the fear it engendered, coupled with the cold, hunger and exhaustion of the day's work, caused a number of prisoners to collapse. Those who still managed to remain standing struggled to assist their fallen fellow prisoners to their feet, but it was impossible to disguise the fact from the guards all the time.

Schnabel was quick to notice one of the prisoners lying on the ground. He ordered two other prisoners to pull him in front of all the lines. He then walked further along the lines and, shouting for Pannicke and the other SS man, he came across several more Jews who had collapsed to the ground.

In all, they dragged six men in front of the appelplatz and, as we watched powerless to help, they began to kick and whip them until the last puff of wind had been beaten out of their failing lungs, and six corpses lay bruised and bleeding at their feet. They then ordered other prisoners to drag the bodies to the canal at the back of the appelplatz. There, Pannicke and his band pushed the victims into the icy water, which at one time had carried effluent from the former textile factory.

Starving and working prisoners to death was one thing, but this was wanton, cold-blooded murder.

We were told on arrival in Estonia that we would be treated well as long as we worked. It was a worthless promise and, I suppose, after our experiences in the ghetto and at Vaivara, we should not for one moment have expected more. Certainly, the murder of six innocent people, whose only crime was that they could not stand on their feet, erased from the minds of even the most optimistic among us the belief that we would ever leave Narva alive.

New Year eventually arrived almost unnoticed, certainly with no celebration or festivity. It was memorable nonetheless - for the special appel. Once again, as on Christmas Eve, we were not allowed into our quarters and were told that our Lager Fuhrer had a few words to say to us on the occasion of the New Year.

It was painfully cold and snowing heavily and, by the time that Runde and the three junior officers who had taken part in the Christmas Eve massacre arrived, we looked like whitewashed scarecrows and felt just as fragile.

Sanitater Runde, who was even more drunk than he was on Christmas Eve, started to address us: "Meine Herren und Meine Damen . . ." and continued with slurred apologies to the effect that the Lager Fuhrer could not be present and with the usual absurdities about the salvation of hard work.

I don't think there was anyone who heard or, more precisely, listened to more than a few words of his ranting drivel, but the Unterscharfuhrer made his presence felt in another way. He kept us on the appelplatz until the dawn of New Year's Day, 1944.

It was a miracle no less that anyone survived that nightmare appel, and indeed there were many who did not. For several weeks afterwards prisoners who had suffered that prolonged, enforced and totally unnecessary exposure died from pneumonia and other respiratory failures.

The whole of January 1944 was savagely cold. On the way to work our eyebrows were covered with a white matting of hoarfrost and small icicles dangled from our nostrils. Everyone, without exception, suffered frostbite, and several prisoners lost fingers and toes that had become shriveled and wasted as the blood refused to flow in the vessels that should have kept them alive. The only consolation was that our guards also had to endure the agonies of the cold but, on the other hand, they had the inner protection of regular square meals and the outer protection of warm clothing.

Pannicke, despite his abnormal intake of alcohol, seemed to feel the cold more than most other Germans and, consequently, delegated much of his responsibility to Schnabel, who took the fullest possible advantages of his position of authority. He seemed to enjoy each appel more than the one before and, like a schoolboy bully, he would select the most defenseless looking prisoner and beat him to satisfy his lust for violence, his love of inflicting suffering.

The snow that lay thickly over the countryside provided Pannicke with an interesting variation on his hunting activities in Narva. He took to hunting Motke by sledge. On one occasion, when we were returning from work,

Pannicke passed our column in his sledge with young Motke sitting beside him. At first, we envied Motke his ride back to the camp, but later we changed our minds. During the evening meal, he was given ten lashes in front of the whole camp, and then taken to the baths to be revived. For Motke, as for the rest of us, New Year 1944 offered nothing apart from a repetition of the agony and despair we had suffered during the previous year.

Chapter 24

My "Grandma" Evginia

There were many generous, sympathetic and selfless people I met on my numerous begging trips into Narva, but there is one whose memory I will cherish above all others – my "Grandma" Evginia. She was a widow, aged about 70, neither slight nor large in build, and she had lived in Narva for many years. Her white hair and pale face contrasted with the austerity of the black dress that she always seemed to wear. She lived quite alone, and was to me the epitome of the elderly Russian widow I had imagined as a boy.

Before the war she had many friends, but during the German occupation many of them were too frightened to visit her, probably because her son, her only son, was a serving officer in the Red Army. She had not seen him since 1941, and missed him dearly.

Occasionally, some of her closest friends, people about her own age, would call to see her, but their visits were infrequent and she made it transparently clear every time we met that she was overjoyed to see me and take me into her home, if only for a short time. Needless to say, the pleasure was mutual. Although she never once allowed me to return to the camp empty handed, my visits to her home were not purely materialistic from my point of view. I suppose in Evgenia I regained for a short time the love and affection which was denied to me so traumatically when my own grandmothers were murdered in Vilna prior to the formation of the ghetto, and when my mother was torn away from me by a German soldier at the time of the liquidation. Evgenia, I am sure, realized the permanent emotional scars that this could have left on me, and she always insisted that I call her babushka – grandma. I was more than happy to do so.

Her concern for me was really quite touching, and I am convinced that only Russian people are capable of such deep compassion for the persecuted. I can only assume that their attitude to the distress and wretchedness of others has been molded over the centuries by their own long and painful history of suffering.

From a purely practical point of view, and I must not for one moment deny that this was a powerful motivating force at the time, my meeting with Evgenia could not have been better timed. The clothing that my father and I had brought from Vilna, and which had remained on our backs through the winter months of 1943 and 1944, was beginning to wear thin, affording little protection against the worst of the weather.

Some of the prisoners whose clothes were in the same ragged condition as our own were fortunate in having a relative or friends among the 100 or so women prisoners in the camp who they could persuade to carry out mending jobs, and there is little doubt that they performed near miracles with needle and cotton, turning old rags into wearable items of clothing. But, unfortunately, neither my father nor I knew any of them and, since their services were already at a premium, there was no hope of our finding anyone at the camp who could repair our clothes.

My grandma Evgenia proved to be our only salvation. She knitted woolen socks from old jumpers, both for me and my father, and on one occasion, when I told her that my father's trousers were totally beyond redemption, she found an almost new pair of riding breeches that belonged to her son, and gave them to me to take back to him. I could not find the words to thank her, and overcome with emotion I burst into tears. "Don't upset yourself, my child. There is no need to thank me," she said, patting me on the cheek. "Soon the Red Army will liberate us, and we will once again be able to walk with our heads held high." I will forever cherish the memory of this fine woman for her simple kindness, her comforting smile and her soothing words quite apart from the food and clothing that she gave so willingly to me.

In camp and at work there were neither peaks nor troughs of excitement, except perhaps that the intense cold induced our guards to warm their bellies more often with liquor and, that having so fortified themselves, they tended to lose what little self control and restraint they had left in their treatment of the Jews. The first signal of a major change, however, occurred when about half our arbeitskommando was transferred to another arbeitsplatz and, together with prisoners from another arbeitskommando, we formed a new working group. By sheer coincidence my father and I found ourselves in the same group.

My father was still weak and sickly as a result of the ill treatment he received at his previous workplace, but the fact that we were together again during the day made life more bearable for us both. My former meister, one of the few Germans I met who was capable of genuine sympathy, was put in charge of our group, and once again I was appointed stoker of the meister's hut.

It was certainly comforting to work alongside my father but, at the same time, it saddened me to see him laboring in such obvious distress and, after much deliberation, I plucked up courage and asked my meister if he could find him some lighter work. In spite of his previous kindness he was no saint, and I fully expected that he would clip me around the ear, or put his boot into my backside, but in fact he did neither. His former soft heartedness had not deserted him and, with no further persuasion, he arranged for my father to be transferred to a section whose job it was to push small wagons to another part of the field. It was considerably less arduous work.

With the extra food that I managed to bring back home from Narva, the warmer clothing that my "grandma" Evgenia gave to us, and the lighter work, my father slowly regained his health. After a few weeks, he looked more like the robust man I had known before the war, the ghetto and the concentration camps began to take their toll. I could once more talk to him rationally when we returned to the camp in the evening. Our chitchat touched on a thousand and one topics about our past, present and our future but it was my father's unending store of stories about our family that never failed to arouse my interest.

He would tell me about the lives they used to lead before the war, about their social life, their likes and dislikes, their idiosyncrasies. For every piece of information that he volunteered, there was always something else I wanted to know. It was as though my future was barren, empty and, to compensate, I wanted to fill the void with a surfeit of our past. Strangely, I was fascinated most of all by his stories of those relatives whom I had never met, and who, as fate had it, I never did meet.

No matter how we began our reminiscences, we inevitably ended up on a sad note, discussing the whereabouts of mother and my young brother. The thoughts that rushed to mind always brought tears to his eyes, but even when he was most despondent he never gave up hope that we would all ultimately be reunited, or if he did, he never transmitted his worst fears to me. Somehow, too, his optimism spread to me, and I began to feel that the yoke of Nazism which pinioned us to a life of slavery would soon be lifted from our shoulders, and that life would once again become normal, or as normal as was possible bearing in mind the grave losses of life which had irretrievably decimated the Jewish population.

One morning during the appel, Pannicke asked for volunteers to go to another camp not far from Narva, preferably skilled tradesmen such as joiners, plumbers and electricians. A few men shuffled forward, but only a fraction of the numbers Pannicke required. The poor response incensed him and, in temper he started to whip all those prisoners near at hand. When he calmed down, he again asked for volunteers.

This time, fearful of the consequences, about a half of the prisoners stepped to the front. Pannicke beamed all over his face and shouted: "That's better." Then, accompanied by his aides, he began to walk along the volunteers like an Eastern potentate inspecting slaves before the start of a street auction, and said: "That is good, very good. But now we have too many. Some of you will be moved to another camp; the others will remain here. We Germans are humane people. We do not want to cause any unnecessary suffering by separating families. So, if you have a relative among the volunteers stand together. Fathers, brothers, sons and other relatives move together. Now!"

Several prisoners moved from the spot on which they were standing. The Germans watched without making a move. It was the lull before the storm. After a few minutes, they made their first move, and we realized that their kindness was nothing more than calculated, sickening trickery. Instead of allowing kith and kin to stay together, they deliberately separated all those prisoners who were related. Pannicke then counted 200 men and, under the hail of rifle butt blows from the guards, we were marched out of the camp with the anguished cries of our remaining relatives still ringing in our ears.

My meister's face looked grim. Now and again he would say a few words to me. Once, in a moment of bravado, I asked him why he was so morose, and when no one was in earshot, he replied: "What is there to be happy about? My wife is dead. I haven't seen my children for ages, and the way things are going at the front I will soon be a prisoner myself in the hands of the Russkies." Then he added: "You won't be around here much longer. The front is getting nearer all the time. Only be careful and keep your mouth shut about this."

When I saw my father after the appel that night I could not keep the news to myself and excitedly told him what my meister had said about the approach of the Red Army. We agreed that it was good news but, although we wanted to shout it from the rooftops, we were too frightened to pass it on. Neither of us mentioned it to anyone. However, as it turned out, my father and I were not the only ones to hear that our move from Narva was imminent. There were whispers of it everywhere, and each day they grew more audible until I am sure it was universal knowledge in the camp.

Outwardly nothing changed, but when the appels were over we would return to our quarters to work out in our minds all the possible permutations of our future. Some of the guesses were wild and without logical foundation;

others were more reasoned and plausible. There were those who thought that when my meister said we would "not be around much longer," he meant that we were to be shot – destroyed like scuttled ships in the sight of an advancing army. Others seemed convinced that we would be returned to the Vilna ghetto, and still more – the more pessimistic of the prisoners – suggested that we would be taken to an even more hideous place than Narva, a concentration camp in Germany. As it transpired, none was correct.

After several days of agitated, tense speculation, it was announced that all the inmates of Narva were to be transferred to two other camps not too far away, and that Narva itself was to be closed. The mere thought that we would shortly see the backs of Pannicke, Schnabel and Runde for the last time brought an immediate flutter of relief to our hearts, but it was not possible to feel any more profound sense of joy. It was unlikely, we knew, that our new masters, whoever they were, would be any more brutal than the trio at Narva, but from experience we had learned the folly of pinning our hopes too high and, in any event, we could not be certain that the Germans were telling the truth.

During what was to be the last of more than 200 appels at Narva, our notorious Lager Fuhrer, Pannicke gave a repeat performance of the appel to which 200 prisoners, many of the prised apart from their closest relatives, were removed forcibly to another camp. He assured us again that he did not wish to separate families but that it was incredibly naïve of him to expect us to believe him a second time and, indeed, no-one did. My father and I stood as far from each other as we could and all those who still had relatives in the camp adopted the same policy.

Pannicke tried several times to reassure us that fathers, sons and brothers should stand side by side if they wanted to go to the new camp together but his words fell on deaf ears. Nobody listened to what we knew were idle promises.

Eventually, the hour of our departure came. Our SS guards, under the overall control of Pannicke himself, started to form us into two groups, taking prisoners from opposite ends of the rows of five in which we were standing. Our fate at that state was in the lap of the Almighty.

My heart thumped like a battering-ram inside my chest and I clenched my fists so tightly, my nails almost dug into the flesh of my palm. If it is possible to will something to happen then I did just that. For after several minutes of agonizing tension, I saw my father being pushed toward the group in which I was standing.

Altogether, in our group, there were about 200 men and 50 women who left Narva on that day. The intense relief we felt as we walked through the gate for the last time was blighted by just one more fact. None of us knew our destination and, in ignorance, it is a human weakness to fear the worst.

CHAPTER 25

Arrival At Kivioli 2

Our new home, Kivioli 2, was a miserable little chicken coop compared with the vastness of Narva. There were a few barracks thrown together to form a compound, four guard towers manned by Estonian SS men armed with machine guns, and the whole little pathetic parcel of a place was tied up in the inevitable strands of barbed wire.

Kivioli was characterless, claustrophobic but the concentrated confines we suffered within its barbed wire walls were a small price to pay for the absence of Pannicke, Schnabel and Runde.

Not that Kivioli was a Colonia Toz, it wasn't. We had hardly time to take stock of the hovel in which we had to live - or die as the case might be - when we were taken, under guard, to a nearby forest and immediately ordered to start work. Almost without exception all the male prisoners, including my father and I, spent our working days at Kivioli cutting down trees, sawing them up into more manageable lengths and then man-handling them out of the forest. No-one really knew what they were for, nor cared, but it was unquestionably more pleasant work than in the frozen wastes around Narva and for that alone we were thankful.

In charge of the tree felling was a meister from the Todt Organization, a Belgian, whose demeanor and attitude towards us changed from day to day but, on the whole, it was not totally impossible to work for him without being beaten.

If, in fact, we had received sufficient to eat our existence at Kivioli 2 would almost have been tolerable, certainly by comparison with our treatment at Vaivara and Narva. Unlike Narva, where we slept in long communal bunks, in Kivioli we were accommodated in twin bunks which afforded a good deal more basic comfort. The women, who were employed mostly as cleaners, cooks, and laundresses, were housed in a separate sector of our barracks nearest to the gate. During the day, my father and I worked together and at night we occupied adjoining bunks.

The Camp Commander was a spineless, colorless individual with the rank of Unterscharfuehrer (Corporal). He gave us the impression that he was doing the job more out of necessity than because he had any stomach or affection for the work. We saw him only during appels and I often wondered, and still do, how he spent the rest of his time.

Our accommodation was cramped but tolerable. The work was exhausting but not intolerable and our new meisters, whilst mean and unpredictable, were for the most part not the fiends we had known elsewhere. The most insoluble problem at Kivioli was the food. There was never anything like enough and at first there seemed no way of starting up the begging missions.

Both my father and I, and all those who had depended previously on the spoils of the begging expeditions to Narva, greatly missed the nourishing little extras. The rations at Kivioli consisted of a small army loaf, often stale, which had to be divided among four, a small cube of margarine, a liter of soup made from frozen swedes *(the English name for Swedish turnip or rutabaga)* given to us at work or coffee which was received on alternate days after the evening appel.

It was grossly insufficient and I spent much of my time relieving the boredom by churning over in my mind ways of supplementing our starvation diet.

After my experiences in Narva, I had become an expert in absconding from work unseen and no matter what avenues I explored I always came to the conclusion that there was only one way of laying my hands on the food we desperately needed. I decided there was no alternative but to try my luck again in the new environment. But first I knew that if I was to stand a chance of succeeding I had to equip myself with certain vital information. The movement of the guards had to be observed carefully and the surrounding terrain reconnoitered. Observing the guards presented no major difficulty but the second problem seemed, at first, to be insoluble until, by a stroke of incredible good luck, my dilemma was solved more than satisfactorily.

An Estonian farmer called one day at the camp and said he wanted some work carried out on his land. Our guards, after haggling with him for some time, eventually agreed to let five prisoners visit his farm in return, I have no doubt, for some small consideration or favors.

I was fortunate enough to be included in the group and it gave me an invaluable chance to acquaint myself with the surrounding area.

I quickly discovered that in the immediate vicinity of the camp there were two small villages as well as several farms. We worked on the farm for several days but we did not grow fat. Our farmer was not over-generous to say the least. All we received from him for our labors was slightly better soup than we were given at the camp or at work in the forest and, at the end of the day's work, he gave us two pieces of dry bread each. But even this little helped.

When our contract came to an end on the farm I resolved to make a break from work and test out my new-found knowledge of the area as well as the generosity of some of the other Kivioli farmers.

My first attempt was as successful as it was uneventful. At the first farmhouse, I was given a kilogram of bread and a piece of salted pig-fat. I was so pleased with myself I decided to make my way back to work fearing all the time that I had been missed. I did not want to overburden my initial good fortune.

Once back at the camp my father and I had a feast of a meal. A banquet could not have tasted better.

For several weeks after that first trip I regularly absconded from work and arrived back in time for the count of prisoners which was made at noon just before the soup was dished out.

On one occasion, I took two friends with me. Our short journey to the village was uneventful but when we reached it we were horrified to see some of our guards in the main square talking to local farmers.

We panicked thinking that they had seen us and darted into a nearby barn to hide, fully expecting that it was only a matter of time before we would hear the thumping of jackboots and the sound of German voices. We were scared for our lives and sat almost motionless in the barn for more than two hours. When we eventually emerged, the guards had gone and my friends and I decided that since the immediate danger had passed we might as well attempt to beg for food from the local population as we had originally intended.

We lost all sense of time and, during our absence, the guards at the Arbeitaplar began to look for one of the boys who was with me. When they could not find him, they ordered a roll call of all the prisoners – and discovered that two more prisoners, including myself, were also absent.

A massive search was mounted at once. Every corner of the forest was scoured and, when it proved fruitless, several guards were posted on the approach to the workplace in the forest where they waited patiently for us to return. Having realized that we were not at work, they felt sure that we had absconded and that we would return by the spot where they lay in ambush. They were right.

As we approached the forest, each of us carrying a small bread sack full of food that we had managed to beg, three Estonian SS guards stepped, seemingly from nowhere, into our path and pointed rifles at our hearts. They were obviously prepared to shoot.

We begged for mercy. What else could we have done.

One of the guards, speaking in German, said that we knew the penalty for running away and we were going to pay for it. The three of them raised their rifles and cupped their fingers around the triggers.

I shut my eyes so I would not see my assassin at the moment of death. But nothing happened. I continued to breath. Instead of the shots a voice, a voice in German shouting: "Don't shoot." Nothing else, just that. It had an official, severe ring to it.

That voice – the voice of the man who saved my life and the lives of my friends – belonged to none other than the head of all the concentration camps in Estonia, Obersturmfuhrer Otto Brenneis *(in Alan Weiler's original notes he recalls the name as Breneisen but current research has shown that this was incorrect. Brenneis was reportedly killed in action in Heide, Schleswig-Holstein, Germany in 1945, aged 45)*

I opened my eyes to see him standing there just a few feet away. The relief was indescribable. "Why did you run away?" he asked, obviously expecting an instant and truthful answer. And he got it. Shaking and stammering as we spoke, we told him the truth: that we had gone begging and had absconded from the camp simply because we had not sufficient to eat.

Brenneis said nothing. Then, after a moment or so, he strode over to the barrel which contained our food. He peered into it like some witch pouring over her cauldron, mixed it for a few seconds, tasted it – and finally spat it out on the ground. "Swill," he shouted and in temper he tried to push the barrel over but it was too heavy and he could not manage to tip it. Even more furious, he then summoned two guards who helped him to upset the barrel and spill its foul contents on to the earth.

As the puddle of soup sank into the soil, Brenneis ordered us to assemble and marched us back to camp where he promised a meal which would conform to regulations. That day we had our first taste of descent soup since our arrival at Kivioli.

The food continued to be more palatable for a few days when but when Brenneis was out of reach our unscrupulous Lager Fuhrer resorted once again to the abhorrent practice of selling food on the black market which was intended for us, while we had to survive on soup which was indistinguishable from water.

Despite the food problem – the common denominator of all concentration camps – the morale among the prisoners at Kivioli was a great deal higher than at Valvara or Narva. As a diversion from the macabre and the monotonous, some of the prisoners even used to organize cultural activities, and almost every night Yiddish ghetto songs were sung in the barrack block. Temporarily, the camaraderie with ones fellow Jews made us forget the tragic situation we were in.

Brenneis had saved my life, and for that I will always think of him with as much charity as one can have for a Nazi but, after his visit, it became impossible to run away on begging trips. The camp security was tightened up and at work we were counted several times each day.

We had been at Kivioli 2 some time when my father learned that some of his closest friends were in Kivioli 1, our sister camp, which was only a few miles away.

One day, while he was at work, he met a group of prisoners from Kivioli 1 who had a message for him. They told him that he should try and visit the following Sunday and they would be able to help out with some food. This was not totally impossible because, as a special concession for good behavior and hard work, 50 prisoners from our camp were allowed to visit Kivioli 1 on Sunday afternoons. The camp was about 15 minutes' walk away.

After no more than three or four weeks, however, the privileges were withdrawn. On the first occasion, almost everyone wanted to take advantage of this rare opportunity to go "Sunday visiting", if only to another concentration camp. As a result, there was a great deal of jostling and pushing among the prisoners, all of them hoping to be included among the chosen few.

My father, after making several unsuccessful attempts to visit Kivioli 1, decided in desperation to abandon the idea.

I, on the other hand, joined the group early and was right up at the front by the time that the Lager Fuhrer, a man named Diller, a German Jew I first met at Narva, counted us. I had been pushed to the back with several other prisoners and was not among the privileged 50.

In anger and disappointment, I complained to Diller and pointed out as plainly and placidly as I could that I had been unfairly treated. His response was unsympathetic to say the least. Without hesitation, he hit me several times on the nose and chin and, within a few seconds, my face was swimming with blood like a slaughterhouse sluice.

My father, who had watched this ugly scene, could not contain himself. He ran over to where Diller was standing and floored him with a single blow. But the pleasure that my father must have experienced in that moment of triumph and paternal glory was, like every other pleasure, short-lived. He paid dearly for his rashness in the shape of a brutal beating from the Lager Fuhrer. As he administered the blows he warned my father that Diller was his representative inside the camp and that his orders had to be obeyed to the letter, adding that if anyone so much as laid a finger on Diller he would be shot immediately.

Diller, who as a German Jew was allowed the privilege of having his wife and children with him in the camp, was never popular among the prisoners but after his attack on me he was hated even more.

The following Sunday, with the cuts and bruises of the previous week's episode still on my face, I turned up again in the hope of a visit to Kivioli 1. It was, I suppose, a gesture of bravado, or defiance, and never for one instant did I think I would be among those selected for the Sunday visit. I was wrong. Diller had atoned and, as if nothing had ever happened, he included me in the group of 50.

When we arrived at Kivioli 1 the camp was feverish with the news of a tragedy which had just occurred. A prisoner had been found hanged in the camp toilet. "Who was it?" I asked. "Meilach Widecki," came the reply.

I was struck dumb. Meilach Widecki, my father's friend who, with his wife Sarah and their two children, Sonia and Moiszele, had been with us day and night in the same room in the ghetto for over two years, was dead.

People who knew him at Kivioli told me that he had been talking of committing suicide for a long time. He had said how he missed his family and did not want to go on living without them.

I could not really believe that I had come to Kivioli 1 and had heard such sad news. It was altogether too tragic. Even the food which my father's friends gave to me did not help to ease the grief I felt in the knowledge that Mr. Widecki had been driven to kill himself.

My father, on hearing of his death, could not control his emotions and started to cry silently until he could cry no more.

After a time, our Lager Fuhrer became exceptionally ill-tempered and on one particular Sunday during an appel he decided, for some inexplicable reason, to check if we were clean. I remember it was a warm day but he made us put on our overcoats to check if they, too, were clean.

The method he employed for the inspection was both painful and bizarre. He used to hit us with his bullwhip. If no dust billowed out he would leave you alone but, if just a few particles were whipped into the air, he would continue beating until all the dust had dispersed. In fact, the Sunday dustings took the place of the "outings" to Kivioli 1 after the Lager Fuhrer withdrew the concession.

Early in June the Lager Fuhrer suddenly disappeared. At the time, I don't think I gave the matter a great deal of thought but I have learned since that he was removed from his position of authority because of an association he had with a Jewish woman prisoner in the camp.

Soon after his disappearance we were told to pack what miserable possessions we had left and once again we were on the move to another camp.

CHAPTER 26

Arrival At Aseri

It was mid-June, when we arrived at Aseri, another small camp consisting of a few wooden barracks a short distance from some sheer cliffs which overlooked the wild Baltic coast.

I had never seen the sea before. In the happy days of my childhood in Vilna and at this time of the year, under different circumstances, I would have made my way to the river and run barefoot along the edge of the water.

But all thoughts of this kind evaporated instantly from my mind when, as our transport arrived, we were confronted once again by Pannicke and Schnabel. I almost vomited physically, realizing that we were once again at the mercy of these two arch-Nazis.

Pannicke began by bellowing out the same lies that I had heard so many times before. Work hard, obey regulations and you will be treated well. Blatant, scandalous dishonesty and most of us knew it.

We listened because we had no choice but to listen, but as soon as he had finished we were put to work. A handful of prisoners remained in the camp to handle the administration and the cooking, but the rest of us were taken under guard to the cliffs perched high above the noise and swell of the Baltic breakers.

The work at Aseri consisted mainly of breaking large stones into small ones. It was back-breaking, unrewarding work at the best of times but at Aseri it was nothing short of sheer torture. That, in fact, was the only purpose the work fulfilled. We never found out what the stones were used for and apart from the pleasure our suffering afforded our tormentors, we were convinced that both Pannicke and Schnabel organized the work so that they would be spared from being drafted to the Russian front where, for them, the dangers would have been considerably greater.

On the few ounces of bread and the watery soup we received twice a day we were expected to hack away at the stones for 12 hours a day with just one break.

The lack of food and the torture of the work was a lethal combination and, after only a few days at Aseri, people began to become ill. Before long almost everyone had painful carbuncles and many had high feverish temperatures and were obviously unfit for work.

Pannicke showed no compassion. In the morning, he used to drag everyone out of their bunks irrespective of their illnesses, regardless in fact of whether they were fit or unfit. Our guards, too, were easily the worst we had met. Almost all of them were Estonian volunteers to the SS and, in most cases, they were far more cruel than the Germans themselves.

One of the guards, in particular, excelled himself in his ability to create the maximum suffering for the Jews at Aseri. He was a wiry, whippet-like man with white eyes and pink eyebrows who we all knew as The Albino. A quirk of nature, a genetic mutation, had made him physically different from his fellow human beings and, to relieve the grudge he felt, he kicked us as often and as hard as he could. Whenever he was in charge of the work group he not only yelled insanely and incessantly at us to work, but at the same time, and for no reason, he would strike any prisoner who came within striking distance. There was certainly not the remotest chance of slipping away to beg for food while The Albino was in charge.

Fortunately, he was not always about and there were several occasions when, in his absence, I managed to break away from the work group to get some bread and a few potatoes from the villagers. On one occasion, my friend Rafael came along with me. We had a miserable morning. At every farm, we visited we were refused food and, thoroughly dejected by our failure, we decided to head back to the camp empty-handed. There was just one place we had not tried – a farm on the way back to the camp that we had visited on previous trips and had been received favorably.

Rafael and I decided to give it another try. For a few seconds, we paused at the gate. Then as we approached the farmhouse, a woman dashed out ahead of us and began waving in an agitated manner. Rafael and I took no notice and continued to walk up the path towards the house. Only then did we realize that the frantic gestures had not been to deter our begging but to save our lives. For there, sitting with his back towards us and his arm around the farmer's daughter, was The Albino.

The farmer himself, who appeared theatrically a moment later from one of the outhouses, realized that if The Albino had seen us we would have been shot on sight. He thought and acted quickly. With courage and composure, he called The Albino over to where he was standing and without turning around he got up and walked over to the farmer. Those few seconds were all that we needed. Rafael and I raced back as fast as could to our work group. We had no food but at least still had our lives, and survival at Aseri was always the first priority.

The sing-song evenings at Kivioli seemed to be an eternity away.

On some days, in spite of the incessant goading by Pannicke and Schnabel in trying to force the sick from the bunks, there were more prisoners left in the camp than there were at work. Even the women, who at other camps were permitted to undertake the less arduous domestic chores, had to join the stone-breaking gang like hardened convicts.

The morale at Aseri was lower than at any of the previous camps and even those with the most resilient constitutions began to crack under the constant pressure and strain.

Sometimes, there would be a brief respite; a moment of victory which would temporarily restore our will to live and our confidence that others were fighting for our liberation.

On one occasion, as we slaved on the cliffs with bleeding fingers, several Soviet planes swept low over Aseri as though they were searching for a target. Our guards, whose bravery went no further than the end of their bullwhips, panicked like timid hares. They ran for cover and did not emerge until the air raid had passed.

Angels to us could not have been more welcome. There were three German ships in the Aseri harbor and for more than half an hour the Russian aircraft darted and danced over the water like fireflies entertaining us to an exhibition of bombing. Soon all the ships were blazing fiercely and one of them began to sink. One of the planes was hit by anti-aircraft fire and it plummeted into the sea but the rest flew off having hit the Germans a hard and costly blow.

That night, when we returned to the camp, everyone seemed a little more cheerful. Although optimism was a luxury we had learned to deny ourselves, we could not help feeling that, if the Soviet planes could attack German ships without encountering any opposition from the Luftwaffe, our liberation by the Red Army was imminent.

Of course, we had to pay dearly for the treat we observed from the cliffs at Aseri. For several days after the raid our guards were even more brutal. They accused us of making signals to the planes and, although we had seemingly watched passively and motionless, the Germans made us pay for our "crime" in sweat and blood.

If nothing else, the air attack provided some relief from the acute boredom, although from my own point of view I was still, at that time, preoccupied with the need to beg for food. During one of my escapes I called at a farm where the farmer, although an Estonian, knew Russian quite well. He was a kindly man and invited me into his house. The farmer's wife made me something to eat and I noticed that she had tears in her eyes every time that she looked in my direction.

As I devoured the food I told the farmer about some of the wicked impositions that we had to endure. He listened with a sympathetic ear and then told me to wait for a few minutes while he spoke to his wife in private. When he came back into the room he had a benign smile on his face which was almost paternal.

"My wife and I have been thinking, we have room enough here and we would be pleased if you would stay with us until the war is over," he said quite plainly.

My first reaction was to accept his offer but I felt I had to warn him of the perils that he would face if he were to be caught harboring an escaped Jew. It would have been certain death for us all. He smiled again and said: "You need have no worries for us. We have a safe hiding place for you where you would not be found. You can be sure of that."

With these reassuring words, I made up my mind to stay. I was taken down to the cellar and the farmer said he would camouflage the room in such a way that it would be practically impossible for the Germans to find me.

I stayed in the cellar for several hours thinking all the time that my father would not know what had happened to me and would assume that I had been caught and killed. It was a great temptation to stay and bury myself away until the cancer of the war had healed, but the more I thought about it, the more I realized that I would not be able to live with myself. Having reached this conclusion, I surfaced from my hideout and reluctantly told the farmer and his wife that I had decided I must return to my father.

They could not believe that I was rejecting their generosity but they realized that I was determined to leave and that it would have been quite useless to try and change my mind. He gave me some bread and a few potatoes and let me go with his good wishes.

I knew that I would have been missed and I was right. When I returned to the arbeitsplatz I was beaten black and blue by one of the SS men who told me that I was lucky not to have been shot. For a week afterwards I was too ill to go to work.

One morning, after I had recovered, I got up as usual only to find that we were not allowed to go to work. No-one knew the reason for this change in routine but, without exception, we were all curious to know the answer. We all assembled on the appelplatz and waited, and the longer we stood around, the more our curiosity was aroused. No-one had the remotest idea what was happening.

Eventually, Pannicke and Schnabel made their entrance and told the Lager Altester to give his customary report. It was only then that we learned that some Nazi VIPs were coming to inspect the camp.

Shortly afterwards, a Dr. Franz von Bodmann, the head doctor for all the concentration camps in Estonia, arrived at the camp followed by his entourage. He had been head physician at Auschwitz and Majdanek concentration camps where he had personally killed inmates by injecting them with Phenol and had carried out similar experiment at other camps. One look at his clinical eyes filled me with dread. I knew that as far as the Jews were concerned, he was more interested in homicide than healing, and that he was the sort of Nazi doctor capable of the vilest forms of human vivisection and experimentation, allegedly in the interests of science.

He walked up and down the lines of prisoners. The Lager Fuhrer then announced that the Third Reich needed strong workers, and proceeded to select some 50 prisoners – the older men, the sick, who he dragged from their bunk along with a few youngsters. My good friend Nionia Antokoletz, who was standing next to me, was among them.

Dr. Bodmann halted in front of me several times and looked me up and down. "Flex your muscles," he ordered. I flexed my muscles and he gripped my biceps. Then, without uttering a word, he walked towards the center of the appelplatz and announced that he was taking the people he had selected to a medical rest camp so that they would regain their strength and once again be fit to slave for the Fuhrer.

Under a heavy guard they marched out of the camp where they were shot in cold blood a short distance from the gate. We were all stunned. Nionia, who perished that day, was a neighbor of ours before the war. His father, in fact, owned the building in which we lived at Kwaszelna 11 in Vilna. He and I had always been great pals.

Another 50 Jews had been exterminated senselessly but, as usual, we were not allowed to brood over such "insignificant" tragedies. A few days later, Pannicke announced that we were to be moved to yet another camp and, as if the information would reassure us, that he and Schnabel would be coming with us.

Chapter 27

Arrival At Goldfiltz

With our clothes encrusted with lice and our bodies erupting with carbuncles, we arrived in a stinking open truck at our new camp – Goldfiltz.

It was the beginning of September, 1944 and almost a year of our lives had been spent in concentration camps. There were about 200 of us who arrived that day at Goldfiltz and none could see any obvious reason why we had left Aseri for a place which was almost identical in appearance and which, we had little doubt, would perform the same function. We could only assume that it was in some way relevant to the self-preservation of our guards.

At Goldfiltz, with the exception of several small work parties which left the camp each day, most of us had no work to do at all, and for most of the time we occupied our days crushing the lice and discussing the position at the front.

Pannicke and Schnabel, as well as our SS guards, seemed nervous and tense, and we deduced from their strange, uncharacteristic behavior that the Germans were suffering heavy defeats at the hands of the Russian armies. But it was totally impossible to come by any more precise information. The Goldfiltz camp was situated at the edge of a large and dense forest and there was no chance of any news filtering through to us. The prisoners in our group were the only inhabitants of the camp at the time, but there were signs that other Jews had lived there before us. Names and messages had been scratched or written on the barrack walls in the remote hope of some chance communication with other prisoners, perhaps even a relative or a close friend. As my father and I cast our eyes over the walls in the hope of recognizing a name, we could not help thinking that the authors of those poignant messages were now dead and that the words they wrote were, in effect, their own epitaphs.

Although we were at Goldfiltz for only 10 to 14 days, we felt more isolated, more helpless, and more frustrated than at any of the other camps. Towards the end of our stay, a small group of Jews were put to work outside the camp. They returned with ashen faces and news which hit us in the pits of our stomachs.

It seemed that one of the Estonian SS men, with a little more compassion than his colleagues, had advised one of the prisoners that he should try and save his life by running away. He said that at another camp called Klooga, the

SS had started to shoot and burn all the Jews rather than be forced to stand back and witness the humiliating experience of their liberation by the fast advancing Red Army.

The news paralyzed us. We felt there was nothing we could do. This numbness stayed with us until one of the prisoners, whose first name was Shmuel, threw us a "lifeline" which, for a short time at least, helped us to drag ourselves out of the depression into which we were sinking rapidly.

While using the camp toilet he had noticed that it would not have been too difficult to dig a hole under the toilet and wriggle through it into a deep ditch which ran parallel to the barbed wire on the outside of the camp.

From the end of the ditch to the forest – and comparative safety – it was only a few meters.

Shmuel made a tour of the barracks, asking his fellow Jews if they were interested in his discovery as a possible means of severing the Nazi shackles. Several of them were and joined him in a sort of escape committee but, while everyone naturally wanted to save their own skin, only a handful were prepared actually to take the risk of making an escape bid. The committee included two of my father's friends, Szymon Keiden and another man, Kushiel P. who I believed, also survived. I tried to persuade my father to join them. But he declined, maintaining that it was our duty to try and survive for the sake of my mother and brother and that we should not risk our lives in any foolhardy adventures. He said that the escapers would probably be gunned down by the guards before they even reached the end of the ditch.

Despite what he said, I still wanted to take a chance but, after giving the matter some very careful consideration, I decided to take his advice and abandoned it.

Those prisoners who decided to take the chance made their way to the toilet early one afternoon. Several others, who were not planning to escape, joined them in the toilets and then made their way back to the barracks so as not to arouse the suspicions of the guards. As long as large numbers of prisoners went in and large numbers came out, the guards were always satisfied that nothing was amiss.

This procedure was repeated for approximately two hours until a total of 42 prisoners had slipped under the barbed wire and were safely in the forest. The plan had been executed without a hitch.

Diller, our Lager Altester, who knew nothing of the escape or the preparations for it, found out just before 5 p.m. when we began to assemble for the evening meal and it was noted that 42 prisoners were missing.

The discovery placed him in an almost impossible position. He did not know whether he should attempt to conceal the escape from the Nazis or report it at the appel and risk being murdered by those Jews who remained in the camp. His loyalties could not have been stretched more painfully had they been placed on the rack, but eventually he agreed to do all he could to conceal the escape by forming us at the appels into rows of four instead of the normal five, giving Pannicke the impression that all the prisoners were present. It was naïve in the extreme to expect that Pannicke would not notice that 20 per cent of the prisoners were missing, but there was no alternative but to give it a try. When the Lager Fuhrer, accompanied by Schnabel, entered the camp, Diller made his usual report saying that all prisoners were present and correct. There were times when Pannicke did not bother to count but, on that occasion, there were gaping spaces in our ranks and we all noticed the snarling expression on Pannicke's face as he became aware that something was radically out of order and began to count our heads.

The discovery, a few moments later, that 42 prisoners were missing, turned him white with rage and he began to scream obscenely at Diller. Diller's pleas of innocence went unheeded. Pannicke and Schnabel took turns at kicking him and, when they were satisfied that he had had enough, Schnabel said; "We will catch every single one of them. You cannot get away from us so easily."

Immediately after the appel, a pack of SS guards set off for their frightened quarries, and later that evening Pannicke called another appel to announce, with pleasure, that all the escaped prisoners had been caught and shot. After the war, I discovered that that, in fact, that Pannicke had not told us the whole truth and that eight of the 42, including my father's two friends, Kushiel P. and Szymon Kejdan, had managed to find lasting freedom.

Despite the wretchedness we felt on hearing Pannicke's announcement, there was no time to mourn. The dead were dead and we had long learned that we needed all our energies to devote to the living and staying alive ourselves. The deaths did, however, reaffirm a universal uneasiness, a feeling of tension, throughout the camp that something was about to happen. It did.

About 10 p.m., six lorries drew up in front of the camp. Pannicke, Schnabel, and several Gestapo men in leather coats and jackboots and all carrying whips or truncheons, stormed into the barracks.

"Juden Raus! Make your way to the gate at once," shouted one. Normally we would have obeyed like frightened children. But this time, as if by some prearranged sign, every single prisoner refused to move from his bunk.

Rage spread like a forest fire over the Nazi faces. They were not used to their orders being ignored and they reacted in the only way they knew – with violence. When most of us had taken a beating, the united resistance we had offered disintegrated and slowly we all began to file out of the barracks. Two Gestapo men stood on each side of the door and repeatedly struck us as we came out, just to ensure that no-one escaped punishment. As we reached the gate and began to drag ourselves to the waiting lorries, we were beaten for a third time.

The sight of blood and brutality was by then nothing new to us, but the severity of this insane episode branded my mind permanently, and I have had nightmares about it ever since. The images that rushed to my mind were so vivid that for 16 years after the war, I used to wake up night after night screaming with beads of sweat erupting over my face. Happily, as I have grown older and the memories of Goldfiltz have become dulled, the nightmares have been less and less frequent, but I doubt whether they will ever disappear entirely.

All the guards and Gestapo men were armed. All reeked of alcohol. It was a bad omen and it led us to only one conclusion: that we had but a few hours to live. One rumor, which went around the camp, suggested that we were being taken to Kloza to be shot.

Slave labor or slaughter – those seemed to be the alternatives which faced us as the lorries moved off. The journey was unpleasant but without incident at first. Then, as we reached a crossroads, someone shouted hysterically that we were without doubt on the Klooga road.

In a matter of seconds there was uncontrollable panic and, like suicidal lemmings, we began to throw ourselves over the side of the moving lorries onto the side of the road. A blaze of machine gun fire followed us as we fled into the darkness and the undergrowth. My father and I, together with many more prisoners, crouched in a potato field hoping that a stray bullet would not seek us out.

As quickly as it began, the firing stopped and the sound of the shots was replaced by the equally unwelcome sound of Pannicke's voice booming through a loud-hailer. We had nothing to fear, he screamed, the lorries had taken a wrong turning. We were being taken not to our deaths at Klooga, but to work for the Third Reich at Tallinn.

"If you do not return voluntarily, you will all be shot when the dawn breaks and we can see you," he said.

No-one moved. The Gestapo guards remained alongside the lorries with their fingers poised over the triggers of their guns. Occasionally, we saw the flare of a match as they lighted a cigarette to pass away the time. The cats waited for the mice, but the mice did not stir.

At first light, Pannicke once again assured us that it would be in our own best interests to return to the lorries immediately. We realized that, in fact, there was no alternative for us, short of committing virtual suicide.

Cautiously, and still half afraid that Pannicke was lying, we rose like ghosts from the potato field in which we had spent the night, and slowly, one by one, we trailed back to the lorries. By the side of the road we saw the bloodstained bodies of six prisoners who had never reached the relative safety of the field. As we clambered back into the vehicles, we were once again beaten by truncheons and punished for delaying the evacuation to Tallinn.

CHAPTER 28

On The Road To Tallinn

Dusk was slipping rapidly into night when, after travelling for a whole day in the lorries, we halted outside our new home. It looked almost indistinguishable from Goldfiltz but I have been unable to discover its precise name or location.

Pannicke said that we would be given some food and continue our journey to Tallinn the next day. By that time, we had not eaten for 24 hours and the slice of bread and bowl of soup we received was devoured ravenously.

It began to look, for once, as though Pannicke was telling the truth. Had the Germans intended to kill us they could have done so any time that day on the pretext that we had attempted to escape – not that any pretext was needed.

With the griping hunger pains in our stomachs appeased a little, we found a place to rest our heads for the night and, for some hours, nothing was heard except sporadic snoring.

Early the next morning we were given a slice of bread and a mug of Ersatz coffee and told to assemble on the appelplatz. Pannicke announced that we would have to complete the rest of the journey on foot as the lorries had been requisitioned by the Wehrmacht for more important work.

When we started to walk towards Tallinn we realized from what we saw that the Russian armies must have been quite near. There were thousands of German troops all marching dejectedly in the same direction as us and it became obvious that they were all leaving Estonia in a hurry.

The German troops did not look in much better condition than us. Almost without exception they were dirty, unshaven, tired and drawn and, collectively, gave us the impression that they had been given a thorough hiding from the Russians. Some of them even looked as though they were sorry for us and one German soldier who passed our column gave me a bar of chocolate and whispered: "Have courage." Other prisoners were given small packets of cheese and crusts of bread.

The Wehrmacht, as we saw them that day branded with the scars of war, looked shadows of the invincible conquerors that they had been three years earlier.

In the afternoon, when our feet would not carry us another step, Pannicke gave us permission to stop for a short respite by a Wehrmacht field kitchen.

The aroma of soup that was cooking smelled like nectar but none of us thought for an instant that we would be allowed to sample it. Yet as soon as we sat down by the roadside the German Unteroffizier, who was in charge of the kitchen, approached Pannicke and asked permission to give us some soup. To our amazement Pannicke agreed. We drank gratefully, finding it hard to believe that there were still some Germans with a shred of humanity in them.

We marched on through the afternoon and by early evening we reached the docks at Tallinn where, as if it had been timed for our benefit, we found ourselves in the midst of an air raid. It was only the second time we had seen Soviet aircraft and the sight of them lifted our morale to such an extent that we forgot to take cover.

I suppose we had a sort of blind faith that the pilots could distinguish between friend and foe and that we had a natural immunity to Russian bombs and bullets.

A few seconds later the planes turned around, swooped low and started machine gunning in our direction. The whole length of our column dived underneath a goods train and took cover. German anti-aircraft spluttered skywards and, after a few minutes, the Soviet planes flew off having left their mark on the quayside. All went quiet and no-one moved.

I decided to take a chance and emerged from beneath the railway carriage and, to my amusement, all the prisoners and our guards had their heads under the train but their hind quarters were protruding unprotected into the air. I suppose it was the case of trying to protect one's head but to Hell with one's backside. Certainly, it was one of the few comic incidents I can recall during all my years in the hands of the Nazis.

The planes returned once more but, this time, they did not fire on us and when they had, so to speak, flexed their muscles to the Germans they flew off again. We then marched on to the quayside where we were confronted with a scene of utter chaos.

There were only two large ships in the docks - one of them I believe was called the "Mar del Plata" - but there were literally thousands of German soldiers, Russian prisoners of war and Jews from concentration camps like ourselves. The whole docks area was surrounded by heavily armed Gestapo SS troops and military police.

The German soldiers were the first to go on board and, in long bedraggled crocodiles, they climbed up the gangplank into the belly of the vessel until it was almost busting at the bows. When the capacity point was reached there were still several thousand soldiers left on the quayside and, when they realized that their long wait had been to no avail, they became impatient and several of them tried to rush the other ship. The SS guards and the Gestapo barred their way and, for quite some time, there were angry, hostile scenes as the Wehrmacht fought with the SS. Shots were fired to prevent the fisticuffs developing into a fully-fledged insurrection.

A high-ranking Wehrmacht officer pleaded for law and order and in a few minutes, all was reasonably peaceful again, although one could sense an explosive atmosphere amongst the rank-and-file troops.

I overheard one German soldier speaking to one of the guards. With tears streaking down his cheeks he said: "Why don't you leave these prisoners here and let those who fought for the Fatherland return to their families in Germany?" The guard merely shrugged his shoulders and said nothing.

First the Russian POWs were taken on board. There were thousands of them and they all looked as if they had been through the seven stages of Hell. They looked desperately ill, their clothing was in tatters and it was clear for all to see that they had been drained of their last drop of fight. If it had been possible for anyone to suffer more than the Jews it was the Russian POWs. Their faces told us more vociferously than words about all the beatings the Nazis had meted out to them and for a short time I forgot my own problems.

As soon as the Russians had been herded aboard, it was our turn. Each of us was given half a loaf of bread for the journey, but the wretched looking Russians, who needed it as much as if not more than we did, were given nothing.

I was in the last group of Jews to go on board and, as I walked up the gangplank, I could still hear the Wehrmacht pleading with the SS to take them on the ship.

It is an accepted fact that, in times of tragedy and distress, people tend to help their own kith and kin more readily than in times of peace, yet at Tallinn the German command chose to leave their own people to be taken prisoner and decreed that the only ship available for the evacuation be used for the transportation of Russians and Jews into slavery. Sometimes, the Germans were capable of the most inexplicable paradoxes. Their whole basic ideology was based on the extermination of the Jews and anyone else who stood in their path of victory but, on occasions such as this, they could completely reverse their entire thinking and sentence their own troops to almost certain incarceration instead.

The ship was so tightly packed it was impossible to move, without treading on someone. The Russians, who always received the roughest end of the stick, were pushed into the lower deck and throughout the voyage the Wehrmacht ensured that they were kept separate from the rest of us.

For some hours we sailed uneventfully towards Germany. Then we heard the droning of aircraft flying low, followed by the sound of exploding shells in the immediate vicinity of our ship. It was a nightmarish experience. We were a proverbial "sitting duck" and what made matters even worse was the fact that we knew that no one would have bothered to rescue us had we been hit and thrown into the sea.

We were lucky. The shells peppered the water around us but not a single one made a direct hit. But we discovered later that at the time of the raid we were near the port of Riga and that another ship, not very far from ours, was hit and sank with the loss of everyone on board.

It was my first voyage on an ocean-going ship and the seasickness I felt was not alleviated by the nausea that came over me every time I realized that at any moment I could have been flung into the water and drowned.

Several hours later, and still in one piece, our ship docked at Dantzig just before noon. We disembarked quickly with the SS and the Wehrmacht guards speeding up the process by goading us with their rifle butts. On the quayside, we regained our land legs and were marched to a huge field not far from the docks where thousands of lifeless looking prisoners were already assembled, surrounded by more SS men than I had ever seen during my whole period of captivity.

For the month of September, it was unusually hot and by about 1 p.m. the heat was almost unbearable. All the prisoners were either lying or squatting on the ground and their tongues were parched for the want of water. Repeatedly we asked our guards for a drink. Not only did they refuse but for daring to ask we were beaten in the bargain. Thirst is a wicked tormentor and after some time we were on the point of collapse for the want of water.

Our salvation came in an unexpected and novel way. One of the prisoners discovered that if he dug a small hole in the ground, it filled up from underneath with muddy water. The word quickly spread and, in no time at all, the thousands of prisoners had turned the field into a lifesaving well.

By late afternoon parties of prisoners were assembled and marched off into the unknown. We also hoped that our group would be taken to some camp so that we might not have to spend the night under an open sky and where we might be given a little food or, at least. clean water.

By nightfall our turn came. We were ordered into a tram and taken on the short journey from Dantzig to Stutthof, one of the biggest concentration camps in Germany. That much we knew, but nothing more.

CHAPTER 29

Arrival At Stutthof

When I first saw Stutthof palls of choking smoke were belching into a breathless, hot September sky from a chimney that stood in the middle of the camp compound.

I was struck instantly with crippling terror. Was this finally one of the Nazi gas chambers and crematoria about which I had heard such horrific stories? Was this where it was all going to end? Would the unmistakable smell of burning human flesh soon be rising and dissipating into the stinking air? As I was goaded through the gates by the guards the thoughts embedded themselves in my mind like poisoned arrows and it was obvious from the horror on their faces that my fellow prisoners had been overcome by the same fears.

A few minutes later the relief we felt was as profound as the fears that had preceded it. As we went through the door it became clear that the barracks was not, in fact, a gas oven but merely a delousing chamber.

Almost as soon as the last Jew had entered the barracks we were told to strip off our clothes and shoes and enter a large room bristling with dozens of showers. There must have been several thousand prisoners waiting to be deloused on the day we arrived and, consequently, we were not allowed to spend more than a few seconds under the cleansing jets of water. A group of prisoners who at been at Stutthof for some time, and who were given the job as camp barbers, shaved off the hair on our bodies, both on our heads and around our private parts.

For the first time in our captivity we were issued with a concentration camp uniform, a blue and white striped jacket, trousers and a cap to match. Outside the delousing chamber there was a mountain of shoes from which we had to help ourselves. When my turn came around I was surprised to see a number of prisoners fighting and squabbling over the shoes which they had selected. A small group from the Vilna underworld paraded up and down scrutinizing the shoes which each prisoner picked from the pile – and under threats of violence took several pairs away from them. Only later did I realize the significance of their strange behavior. The underworld mob had hidden gold coins in the hollowed-out heels of their shoes and they were making sure no-one else got their hands on them.

Two views of the Stutthof Concentration Camp
Photos: Courtesy of Yad Vashem

Although we were not given any food or drink on our first night, we had compensation of another kind. One of the walls of the barracks allocated to us for the night had dozens of signatures and messages from women who had been taken away to concentration camps at the time of the liquidation of the ghetto a year earlier.

Some prisoners even came across messages from their wives and daughters and most of the names were familiar to someone. The thought that the women had been through the camp so recently boosted our morale, and made it possible for us to forget our hunger and thirst for at least a few hours. There were no messages from my mother but my father and I were a little more hopeful that she was still alive.

Our first full day at Stutthof was spent on the appelplatz. We were issued with a steel mug and spoon. We all had to undergo a medical examination. There was also a registration procedure at which each of us was given a camp number. Mine was 35,535.

After the formalities were completed, we were marched off to block number 2, which was to be our home during our short stay at Stutthof. The barracks were permanent brick buildings which, at one time, had been an army camp. In each barracks, there was a large room with toilets, washbasins, as well as showers. Compared with the accommodation we had previously, Stutthof was luxurious.

At least two government ministers were incarcerated in another block where, I have no doubt, they were given privileges of one kind or another. The two I know were there were Leon Blum, the French Prime Minister before the war, and the President of the Lithuanian Republic, a man named Antanas Smetona. They were both allowed to wear civilian clothes.

(Both men survived the war. Leon Blum, who was born into an Alsatian Jewish family in 1870, was Prime Minister of France on three separate occasions, the last being for a brief period after the war in the transitional post-war coalition government. He was released from Nazi captivity in May 1945. He died, aged 77, in 1950 at Jouy-en-Josas in France.

Antanas Smetona, who was born in 1874, was the most important political figure in Lithuania between World War 1 and World War 2. He served as the country's first President from April 1919 to June 1920 and again as the country's last President from December 1926 to June 1940 before its occupation by the Society Union. He and his wife eventually settled as private citizens in Cleveland, Ohio, USA where they lived with their son Julius' family. He died tragically in a fire at the house in 1944).

Leon Blum
Photo: courtesy of Yad Vashem

Our stay at Stutthof, we were told, was for quarantine reasons. We were given strict orders not to leave the camp, but there were quite a number of prisoners who did not comply with the regulations and we heard that there had been a surprising number of escapes. Soon after our arrival another prisoner made a bid for freedom, and when the Lager Fuhrer discovered that he was missing, he announced that we would all have to remain on the appelplatz until he was found. He kept his word. For 29 hours, more than one whole day, we were kept standing there until the missing prisoner, a Russian, was caught and brought back to the camp. On his return, he was forced to march around the camp with a sign around his neck which read: "I shall not escape again."

He didn't. At 11:00 a.m. he was hanged from hastily erected gallows in the middle of the appelplatz watched by thousands of helpless and demoralized prisoners, including my father and myself.

Somehow, despite the more pleasant surroundings, it was far worse to stay in camp than to go out to work. One had nothing else to think about apart from thirst and hunger. The rations at Stutthof were similar to those we received in the other camps, but the system of distribution was quite different.

At midday, the soup was brought from the central camp kitchen and poured into a huge wooden trough which stood outside the barracks. Two by two we then used to go up to the trough to receive the soup, but rarely had a chance to gulp more than a mouthful or two of it. Each prisoner had a bowl, but as there were only 50 of them for 500 prisoners, they were snatched from our hands by the guards before we had an opportunity to drink our share. Consequently, we became like animals, fighting with one another for the pitiful dregs which invariably were left at the bottom of the trough, much to the amusement of the guards. Every so often, when they were bored of this degrading spectacle, they would set their alsatian dogs on us to restore order.

I did, however, have one memorable "feast" at Stutthof. One day, another young prisoner, whose name I cannot remember, and I were lurking in the vicinity of the camp kitchen in the hope of being thrown a few scraps of food. We had been there for some time when an SS guard, carrying bread and a large salami sausage, walked passed and noticed the hungry look in our eyes. "You are hungry, yes? Would you like to try some bread and sausage?" he said. At first, we thought he was joking. But his offer was genuine. There was, however, one important condition. We could each have a feast of bread and sausage, but we had to devour every last morsel. If we left just one crumb he said he would kill us, and we knew that it was no idle threat.

Each salami sausage weighed about two and a half pounds, and the loaves of bread were large, but we were so hungry and so sure of our appetites that we agreed to the German's proposition. "Come, follow me," he said, and proceeded to lead us to his barracks just outside the camp where, with a broad grin on his face, he explained to some of his comrades that he had some sport to entertain them.

The salami and bread were placed in front of us. The Germans gathered around to watch like spectators at a cockfight, and then the command was given for us to start eating. At first, we ate slowly and cautiously, but before long both my partner and I began to choke on every mouthful. The dry bread tasted like sawdust, the salami like spicy rubber. Our "benefactor" and his friends were in hysterics.

I asked for some water, but my request was turned down by the SS man, who first pointed his gun at the bread that was left on the table, and then at my mouth. Somehow, I managed to struggle through, but my friend was not so fortunate. His gut seemed to regurgitate every mouthful and, in the end he was forced to capitulate in spite of the fact that he knew that death was the penalty for failure. He waited for the bullet to put him out of his misery, but it never came. Our performance seemed to please our audience, and my partner was let off with a severe beating. The price one had to pay for a full stomach was always high, whether one begged, stole or behaved like performing animals.

Soon after this unpleasant episode, Stutthof began to fill up with new arrivals. One of the largest groups to arrive were women prisoners from the Lodz ghetto, a Polish textile town at least three times bigger than Vilna. Thousands of them were kept for several days in an open field surrounded by barbed wire and a heavy SS guard. To my knowledge they were not given any food or drink, and some of the men wanted to pass them scraps of bread and some water. The guards opened fire and refused to let anyone go near the women. Two or three days later, hundreds of the women from Lodz were lying dead on the ground.

It soon became clear that we would have to move from Stutthof. The camp administration began transferring prisoners from one block to another and, on the days before our departure, an SS medical commission arrived during an appel to carry out a selection in the men's camp. Hundreds of prisoners were segregated from the younger ones and led out of the camp to waiting trains that we found out later took them to Auschwitz and their deaths.

Wizyta Himmlera w Stutthofie 23. XI. 1941. Himmler w towarzystwie komendanta obozu Pauly'ego z oficerami S.S., pełniącymi służbę w Stutthofie

SS Chief Heinrich Himmler inspects the guard at Stutthof
Photo: Courtesy of Yad Vashem

When the medical commission had pruned away all the older prisoners, they began to look for youngsters not old enough or fit enough to work. They selected 500 boys between the ages of 12 and 17. I was one of them.

All that night we were kept locked up in a separate barracks and, in the morning, we were led, accompanied by the leech-like SS guard, towards the camp gate. There we were told to sit on the ground. Among the Jewish prisoners at Stutthof there were a number of highly accomplished musicians who were formed into a small orchestra by the Germans, and ordered to play at the camp gates while the evacuation was taking place. It no doubt appealed to the Nazi's sense of humor to prepare for a mass murder to the strains of the classics, especially when the instruments were being played by Jews.

I realized with great acuity of mind that I only had a very few seconds in which to save my life. I knew more certainly than I had known previously that if I did not make a break for it there and then, my hours on earth were numbered.

I watched and waited. Suddenly, the guard nearest to me turned his head for a split second. Like a frightened gazelle, I darted away from the group and began to weave in and out of the rows of barracks. I was missed almost immediately, and pursued by a pack of alsatian dogs with an acquired liking for the taste of human flesh, and no knowledge of fair play. The guards themselves quickly followed.

Instinctively, I ran towards my father's barracks. There I saw men squatting in two groups and, almost at the same instant I arrived, I heard my name and number being called out. "Present," I shouted automatically, and went over to the group that had already been checked. My father was called next and a moment or so later we were together. He embraced me, and with tears rolling down his face, said: "Thank God you managed to get here in time. It must be fated that we live through this nightmare together." I learned then that when he had registered he had given my number – 35,535 – as well as his own – 35,536 - believing that by some quirk of fate, it would improve our chances of staying together. Rarely, can such incredible forethought and good luck have combined so fortuitously.

Had I arrived at my father's group a few seconds earlier or later, I would without doubt have perished in the gas chamber at Auschwitz. A few seconds later and I would not have been there at the time my number was called. And if, by the same rule, I had been forced to wait any length of time, my pursuers would have caught up with me. As it was, I was secure in the group that had been checked ready to move off to another camp by the time that the guards and their dogs arrived. Since we all tended to smell the same at Stutthof, the alsatians had very little chance of sniffing me out.

They failed to find me, and eventually they went away. We were then packed into a cattle train, and we set off on a long and exhausting journey to Schomberg in the Baden Wurttenberg province of Germany.

Survivors visit the Stutthof crematorium
Photo: Courtesy of Yad Vashem

The crematorium at Stutthof in 1945
Photo: Courtesy of Yad Vashem

The gas chamber at Stutthof
Photo: Courtesy of Yad Vashem

Chapter 30

Arrival At Schomberg –

And The "Scourge of Dautmergen"

There were times during the two days it took us to travel from Stutthof to Schomberg when we forgot who were our friends and who were our foes.

The confusion was caused by the incessant air raids which bedeviled our journey from start to finish, and which made it necessary for our train to come to a halt on countless occasions while we took cover alongside the line. To the Allies it was a German enemy target: either a train almost certainly carrying German troops or supplies of food, or ammunition for the German Army. It rarely, if ever, occurred to the pilots that the wagons were packed with thousands of innocent Jews. As the shells exploded around us, it was sometimes hard to accept the fact that the planes were fighting for our cause.

On one occasion when the train was stopped at a place called Halle, we did not even have time to take cover and we remained in the wagons during the raid. A number of nearby trains were set on fire by the falling incendiaries, but just as we had avoided being hit on the crossing from Tallinn, we escaped a direct hit on this occasion, too.

After the raid, we were allowed off the train in small groups to get water for the first time during the entire nerve wracking journey. At some point near our destination, several trucks were uncoupled and, together with their cargo of prisoners, they remained at a tiny railway junction. The other wagons, which included my father and me, continued to Schomberg. There we were met by new guards who marshaled us roughly into a long column, and told us to march quickly.

The countryside in this part of Germany has a charm and beauty all its own. The fields are rich and fertile, the pastures like green velvet. During our short walk to the camp we walked along a road lined on both sides with apple and pear trees. Sadly, however, our impression of this magnificent piece of nature's handiwork was marred, as always, by the nagging hunger in our stomachs, the aching in our limbs and the fears in our hearts.

As we headed towards the camp, a number of prisoners tried, when they thought that the guards were not looking, to pick up some of the apples or pears which had fallen to the ground. They soon learned that such pickings were not for the haftlingen of the Third Reich. On that short stretch of road, we soon became aware of the fact that our new guards were more vicious than in Estonia. Those who attempted to help themselves to the rotting fruit were beaten so brutally it left us in no doubt about the sort of existence we could expect at Schomberg.

To illustrate the point, our future Lager Fuhrer, a tall, bent man named Stefan Kruth, shot a prisoner simply because he was too exhausted and could not keep up with the rest of the column. The closer we came to the camp, the less hospitable the scenery became. The fruit trees became more and more sparse and, on the approach to the camp itself, they had all but disappeared. At the end of the short track we came face to face with Dautmergen - Schomberg, one of the most feared concentration camps in the infamous Natzweiler K.Z. group.

Survivors file passed exhumed body remains at Schomberg after the war
Photo: courtesy of Yad Vashem

Human remains found in a mass grave at Schomberg
Photo: courtesy of Yad Vashem

The inevitable guard towers rose menacingly above the barbed wire that encompassed the camp. Inside the atmosphere was one of instant gloom, of past sorrows and future tragedies. The smell of death lurked in every corner and crevice. As we expected, Kruth, our new master, counted us, and after we were dismissed we were moved into one of the barracks.

I thought that it was advisable to reconnoiter the camp at the first possible opportunity and, on my first fact finding sortie, I unearthed several fascinating, albeit horrifying, facts. Polish prisoners I met told me that there had been an unsuccessful uprising at Warsaw, and that those Poles who had not perished in the bunkers or under the rubble of shelled buildings had been rounded up by the Nazis and some were brought to Dautmergen. The Poles from Warsaw had in fact established the Dautmergen camp. The Polish prisoners looked so ill, it was heartbreaking even to look at them, not to say ominous for our own futures. I could not help thinking that if the Germans at Dautmergen managed to reduce young, strong Polish underground fighters into bloodless skeletons in just a matter of weeks, then the Jews of Estonia, already half dead, would have precious little chance of survival.

The inmates of Dautmergen were of mixed race and blood. Apart from the Poles and Jews, there were Russians, Yugoslavs, Hungarians, Germans, gypsies and even one Italian.

We were accommodated in a large wooden barracks containing three-tiered bunks and one blanket per person but, without doubt, the most notable single feature of Dautmergen was the appelplatz, a veritable quagmire of mud which in places was knee-deep. A kind of catwalk was built in front of some of the barracks to enable us, and of course the guards themselves, to walk in and out.

Unlike other camps, a system of segregation was also practiced at Dautmergen for most of the time. The German prisoners were accommodated in block No 1, the Poles in No 2, the Jews in No 3 and so on. In fact, the only barracks which contained all nationalities was the schonungs block – the hospital recuperation bay. All in all, I suppose there have been some 2,000 prisoners in the camp and about 60 guards.

The morning after our arrival we were awakened at 4:30 a.m. by the sound of a gong. About 20 of us were selected to go to the kitchens to bring our breakfast: coffee, a slice of bread, a small knob of margarine and one added luxury, a spoonful of cream cheese mixed with jam. At 5 a.m. prompt we were ordered to assemble in front of the barracks to be counted. Then, after about half an hour, the Kapos – the leaders of the work group – came over to our group and each one picked some additional men for inclusion in their arbeitskommandos.

I was selected by a Kapo called Helmut, a lanky but muscular man with ginger hair.

Helmut, who already had 150 prisoners in his command, selected a further 150 from among the newcomers. My father was chosen to work in another group.

All the arbeitskommandos at Dautmergen consisted of between 200 and 300 men and all of them were led by the Kapos – in almost all cases German nationals who in one way or another had "sinned" against the Nazi regime. But despite their distaste for Hitler's genocidal madness, they were not the most saintly of men. Whenever they had an opportunity to beat or maltreat a prisoner they did so with obvious relish and invariably, if the opportunity did not arise, they were more than accomplished at creating them.

Our workplace was about seven kilometers from the camp and the work itself consisted of digging up earth in one place and loading it on trucks to be removed and tipped in another part of the same field. It was futile and a complete waste of time and energy, quite apart from the fact that it contributed to the deaths of hundreds of men. Our daily ration at Dautmergen comprised one-fifth of a German Army loaf per person with a bowl of coffee, before the morning appel, and a bowl of soup made from frozen swedes (*Swedish turnip or rutabaga*). The cream cheese and jam we had on arrival was missing for most of the time or, to be more accurate. it never reached us. More often than not, the camp administrators used it to trade for cigarettes and tobacco for themselves, and there was really nothing we could do to put an end to the practice. On return from work all we were given was coffee.

Dautmergen soon claimed its first victim from among the Vilna Jews. He was 29-year-old Leib Aronovitz who died at the camp on October 16, 1944. Cause of death: starvation

I worked in Helmut's group for about six weeks and I cannot recollect any one day when prisoners did not collapse from maltreatment, beatings or sheer hard labor. Anyone who stopped digging for more than a few seconds was pounced upon by the guards and kicked until they fell in a helpless heap on the ground.

The digging for me had one compensation. I discovered a type of groundnut embedded in the soil. These nuts, which I never have been able to identify botanically, were bitter and unpleasant to the taste and few and far between, but they helped to keep me alive – and indirectly saved me from being beaten for resting on my pick or spade. Every so often I would come across a patch of earth where the rewards were plentiful but at other times I could shift a ton of soil and not find even one nut. This insatiable eagerness to find them eventually cost me my health. I consumed more energy in searching for them than I conserved by eating them and after my six weeks spent in Helmut's arbeitskommando I was not fit for work. No-one else seemed to be feeling much better.

The atmosphere in barracks No 3 was like that in a morgue and to give the likeness even greater credence we soon faced an epidemic of deaths.

After Aronovitz's death, people seemed to drop like flies. By the end of October, 10 people had died and by the end of November the number had risen to more than 80. By that time, we had shared the ordeals of Estonia and when each death occurred it was like losing a member of one's own family.

Stefan Kruth became the "Scourge of Dautmergen". Whip in hand and with his head perpetually bent forward, he used to scurry erratically around the camp, often running from one end of the compound to the other just to make use of his whip. He was soon nicknamed "Zayontz"' – "The Rabbit" - but if one had considered his behavior rather than the peculiarities of his movements, "The Vulture" would have been more appropriate. During appels he would whip anyone who did not remove their hats quickly enough or, as was so often the case, for no reason at all.

When I became too sick to work I was transferred from block No 3 to the schonungs block for a few days. Every morning Kruth used to come in and select sick, dying men who could hardly stand on their feet for some of the most grueling laboring tasks. One morning he dragged me from my bunk, shouting all the time that I was shamming illness because I was too lazy to work. Altogether, he dragged out about 20 men and told us to stand in front of the barracks.

I discovered that during the night someone had stolen one of my wooden clogs. I explained to Kruth that I could not go to work until I found it. His response was a vicious punch which knocked me to the ground. With his hefty jackboot, he then proceeded to kick me into the mud until my head was buried and I began to suffocate. I thought I would die but, just as I was about to relinquish my grip on life, his attention was distracted by some activity elsewhere and he walked away – not knowing or caring whether I was alive or dead.

A Polish Stubbendiest – a "room service" attendant – lifted my limp body out of the mud. When he realized that my heart was still beating he carried me back to the barracks and revived me as best he could.

I suppose I never came closer to death than I did on that occasion.

CHAPTER 31

The Death Of My Father

One of the few comforts that my father and I shared at Dautmergen was the chance to talk and confide in each other when we returned from work in the evenings. But after my beating from Kruth even that was denied us. My father was confined to block No 3 and I was too ill to leave the schonungs block.

On one occasion, however, he managed to come and see me. Although I was overjoyed to see his face once again, his visit left me feeling even more depressed and dejected than I had been before he came. He said nothing to worry or upset me but there was something in his general demeanor which suggested me that he had finally abandoned his fight for survival. Throughout our concentration camp life in Estonia his health and morale had risen and fallen with barometric predictability but at Dautmergen he went steadily and rapidly downhill.

מחנה דארטמרגן . נמסר ע"י חיים גולני
2852/208-ג

Figures wander around the camp area at Dautmergen
Photo: courtesy of Yad Vashem

About the time of my encounter with Kruth my father discovered that a number of prisoners, desperately in need of food like himself, used to exchange their bread ration for apple pulp that had been used in the fermentation of cider. By the time that they received it, it was a dark brown, vile-looking, vile-smelling mass which had been rotting for weeks and which contained absolutely no food value whatsoever. But, temporarily, its sheer bulk filled the empty void of their stomachs and the starving prisoners were convinced that they were getting a good bargain for their bread.

I tried on several occasions to convince my father that he would have derived more nutriment from his bread ration, as meagre as it was, but he failed to see the sense of my argument and carried on trading it in for the apple remains.

Ironically, in view of the advice which I had given him, it was an apple which indirectly brought about his final downfall. On November 23, 1944, he went to work as usual. On his way, he saw an apple lying in a ditch and, in a momentary lapse, he allowed his hunger to be master of his mind. Without pausing to think of the consequences he bent down and picked it up.

An SS guard saw him and repeatedly hit him with his rifle butt until my father collapsed on the ground. The guard then ordered two other prisoners to carry my father to work.

When they arrived at the arbeitsplatz he was still unconscious so the guards ordered him to be left on the frozen earth until the column was ready to return to the camp at least seven hours later. There were some 150 prisoners in my father's group and the guards, who refused to carry Jews themselves, found that there were no volunteers at the end of the day to carry him back to the camp. In the end a Yugoslav prisoner, who was himself very ill, volunteered to undertake this act of mercy when he overheard one of the guards say: "If none of this stinking lot will carry him back I will shoot him."

Back at the camp he was thrown into the schonungs block and placed in a bunk not very far from mine. His face was swollen and distorted and it was not until he regained consciousness and spoke to me that I was certain he was my father.

I heard him cry out in his bunk for water. One of the stubbendiest brought him some but it was not enough. His mouth and throat were burning savagely and his breathing was labored and irregular.

I pleaded with a Polish friend of mine to use what little influence he had with the doctor at the camp hospital to try and persuade him to admit my father for treatment. The doctor agreed and a few hours later my father was transferred from the schonungs block to the hospital. Had the necessary drugs and medicines been available there would have been every likelihood that he would have made a full recovery but the facilities were little better than in the schonungs block itself and on the morning of November 24, 1944, he died.

I learned later that only seconds before taking his last anguished breath he had pleaded for a drink of water but his request fell upon the deaf ears of the hospital orderlies. For the rest of my days I will always carry this picture of my father painfully mouthing a cry for water and dying with the words hovering unheeded on his lips.

When the hospital doctor, a Polish Christian, told me of my father's death I was struck dumb. He gave me a drink of coffee to help soothe my nerves and told me that I would have to accept his death like a man. He added: "You must try and be strong if you want to see your mother again." He said that if ever I should need help I should not hesitate to contact him and for that I was grateful.

I tried to take his advice but my mental and physical state was already low and the effort proved disastrous. My condition deteriorated. I developed a very high temperature and felt desperately weak. Once again, I sent for the doctor who took one look at me and had me carried off immediately to the camp hospital. I had typhoid fever.

The only medicine available was quinine and it was made clear to me that my survival depended almost entirely upon how much I wanted to live.

For three weeks, I walked a tightrope between life and death – I believe nearer to death – but amazingly I pulled through. The quinine undoubtedly helped but, to this day, I am convinced that the most important single factor in combating my illness were some oranges that I received from a man from Luxembourg named Karl. He was a voluntary farm worker who contracted typhoid and was sent to the hospital as there was no isolation hospital in the vicinity. His status was different from ours and, as such, he was allowed to receive parcels from home sent through the Red Cross. The life-saving oranges came in these parcels. Karl himself sadly did not survive the typhoid epidemic which raged through Dautmergen and I will always regret the fact that I was not able to thank him for his kindness. When I was feeling a little stronger and the fever crisis had passed I was taken back to the schonungs to recuperate.

My health gradually improved and soon I was discharged as being fit for work. Through the initiative of my father's friends, who had promised him that they would look after me, I was appointed by the Block Altester as a stubbendiest. My duties consisted of helping to hand out the food ration and keeping the barracks clean and shipshape.

The typhoid epidemic was still rampaging through the camp and claiming many victims every day. Most of them died in the schonungs block and every day we had to drag at least 20 or more corpses out of the bunks and pile them in front of the barracks gates. After the appeal, the Lager Fuhrer would call, accompanied by a "dentist" who carried pliers and a small black bag. The dentist would then prise open the mouths of the corpses and, if he found any gold teeth or fillings, he would remove them and hand them to the Lager Fuhrer. The plundered corpses were then removed by a specially-appointed death squad known as the Leichenkommando. By the cartload, like victims of the Great Plague, the limp, emaciated bodies were taken out of the camp and dumped in a communal grave, a deep pit which had been dug specially to receive them. In return for this sordid chore, the Leichenkommandos received extra rations of bread and soup.

Dysentery also took its toll of life at Dautmergen. Unlike typhoid, which could strike a sudden and lethal blow, it was a slow, miserable death, the tragic finale of weeks of debilitating illness. Prisoners would spend night after night running feebly between their bunks and the latrines which consisted for the most part of wooden planks or beams straddled over a stinking hole in the ground. It was not uncommon for those too tired or weak to support themselves to overbalance and drown in the quagmire of human excreta. It hardly bears thinking about that any man, no matter what his crime, and least of all those who had committed no crime at all, should take his last breath in this way.

The food ration in the schonungsblock was worse than for the rest of the camp. Instead of providing us with added nourishment to help us regain our strength, the Lager Fuhrer took the view that it was a waste of good food on an unproductive element. Everyone in the schonungsblock suffered as a result of this stringency, but the Hungarian gypsies suffered more than most and, in sheer desperation, were driven to acts of cannibalism. Whenever any of the gypsies died, and scores of them died, their bodies were torn apart by their starving neighbors who devoured raw, what little flesh covered the brittle bones. Several times they were ordered to leave their dead intact, but their hunger cancelled out all their reason and the warning went unheeded. Certainly, there was no more damning indictment of the Nazi regime than the depths of degradation to which these poor, wild creatures were forced to sink.

During the time, I was on the schonungsblock, the bread ration on some days was one large loaf for six people, and at other times it was shared between ten. The order from the Lager Fuhrer was that before collecting the bread from the kitchen all the dead had to be removed from the camp to ensure that only living prisoners shared in the allocation.

The gypsies however found an ingenious way of hoodwinking the authorities. They used to prop up a dead man between two living ones and so claim the dead man's bread. Since the dead were virtually indistinguishable from the living, their deception frequently went undetected. Only after the Block Altester inspected them and discovered their deception did they throw the corpses out of the bunks.

During the typhoid epidemic, we were isolated from the world outside. The whole camp was closed and no one was allowed in or out. By the time the epidemic was over and the camp reopened, the fever had caused hundreds of deaths. From the Vilna group alone more than 150 people died during the epidemic.

At the tail end of it, the Lager Fuhrer concluded that it had been caused by our personal lack of hygiene – our "dirty habits" – as he put it, and to prevent a repercussion he said we would all be disinfected and bathed. The delousing chamber and bath was about a kilometer from the camp. In groups of 50, we had to run from the camp to the bath, deposit our clothes in a disinfection chamber, wash and have all our hair shaved off. Then, stark naked the SS guards made us run back to the camp through the snow and the freezing December air. The bath episode took place during the last days of the month – I think December 28 – and the following day there were 63 corpses in the schonungsblock, 18 of them from the Vilna group.

The month of December was the most tragic of our whole stay at Dautmergen, with more prisoners dying of typhoid, dysentery, cold, hunger and ill treatment than in the remaining months of its existence. Quite apart from the indignities we had to suffer at the hands of Kruth and his comrades, we also had to endure the torments of vermin in the textbook, zoological sense of the word. The luxury of hot water and a clean change of clothes were unknown and, as a result, our vulnerable bodies quickly became desirable breeding grounds for lice. Vast seething colonies of them encrusted under one's armpits and in one's hair, and could be torn away by the handful. Some of the prisoners, for identification purposes, had a bald stripe shaved from their foreheads to the napes of their necks which became known as "Louse Street." Every so often the lice would emerge from the adjacent hair and race like performing fleas up and down the street. Out of revenge, other prisoners would sit up all night removing the lice from their skin and crush them between their fingers like peanuts. But the exercise was pointless, for the scratches which they made on their skin simply opened up new areas of colonization by these tiny, but vicious verminous hordes.

After the typhoid epidemic, the schonungsblock was so overcrowded that there was no room to accommodate the scores of prisoners who were unfit for work. The capacity of the schonungsblock was about 750, but at one stage the number must have exceeded 1,000. It was, therefore, inevitable that Kruth would discover this unhealthy overcrowding and select the weakest for extermination. So, it was. The Block Altester was forewarned of his visit and, when the news reached me, I decided to hide under a bunk just in case Kruth remembered my face from the time he thrashed me within a hair's-breadth of my life. He missed me. But 350 other prisoners were not as fortunate. They were removed for a one-way trip to the gas chambers. When he had gone, life in the schonungsblock returned to normal – cannibalism, dysentery and lice hunting.

I began to think I was doomed to endure this suffering forever, and that would have been a fate worse than death. I began to look for a way out. I had been hardened to the most horrible sights, but the sight of humans devouring humans or, for that matter, of men sitting by a hole in the barracks floor all night waiting for rats for food, were even too much for me, by then a thick-skinned halfling of the Third Reich.

Chapter 32

Dautmergen Under Kruth And Schnabel

Emotionally, the Nazis were succeeding in making me sterile, but the cannibalism of the schonungsblock sickened me beyond belief, and I knew my first priority was to find a way out. My father's friends continued to be very helpful, in spite of the fact that they had problems of their own. When I discussed my troubles with one of them he promised he would do all he could to find me another job outside the schonungsblock.

I never thought for an instant that his influence would carry any weight but, a few days later, I was called into the camp office and told quite bluntly that I could start work immediately as the Lager Pförtner – the gatekeeper.. I asked no questions, but accepted gratefully. The job consisted mainly of opening and closing the camp gate whenever any groups of prisoners, or the Germans themselves, were either coming in or going out. Kruth, who walked in and out of the camp several times a day, fortunately did not recognize me. Perhaps he thought that I was dead. Had he done so I had no doubt at all that he would not have let me keep my job.

Opening and shutting the gate, I discovered, formed only part of my duties. Quite apart from that, when the columns had gone to work in the mornings I had to run errands for the camp administration staff. It wasn't exactly the most stimulating of jobs, but it was infinitely better than being forced to hump around soil, break rocks or carry sacks filled with cement as I had done before. It was also more palatable than playing nursemaid in the schonungsblock.

There was a more important compensation, however. For the first time since my captivity I had no difficulty in obtaining additional food to supplement my rations. Anyone who worked on the camp's administrative staff was entitled, as a special privilege, to extra food. Needless to say, we all took advantage of the chance.

There were drawbacks, too. One was that I had to get up half an hour earlier than the rest of the prisoners in the camp to sound the morning reveille, a gong which was situated between the schonungsblock and the block in which the Russian prisoners were housed. The gong was simply a piece of metal suspended from a wooden post. I had to strike it with a hammer, and it made a deafening noise.

After making sure that everybody had heard it and was awake, I was allowed to go back to sleep, but before doing so I first had to notify the camp secretary that I would not be attending the appel. This was quite permissible. My name used to be included on the "commandiert" list – the list of people on office duties excused from attending the appels. Rising early, however, was a small price to pay for the relief I felt in being out of the schonungsblock for most of the day. Unfortunately, I had to return at night and witness once again the cannibalism of the gypsies, the lice destruction and all the accompanying scenes of utter wretchedness. The dawn never came quickly enough, and there were times when the days did not differ greatly from the nights, when the "landscape" outside the schonungblock was no more inviting than it was inside.

One morning, as I was standing near the camp offices, I noticed Kruth running in his characteristic, ungainly fashion across the muddy appelplatz towards the camp toilet. A Russian prisoner suffering from dysentery had annoyed him because he had seen him go to and from the latrines too often. Kruth went berserk, kicking and punching the poor Russian until he collapsed on the ground. When he was lying there, powerless to offer one spasm of resistance, Kruth kicked him on the head and proceeded to hold him down with his boot until the last breath of life left his lungs. Kruth then turned on his heels and walked briskly back towards the office.

As he headed back, I ran back inside the office in case he saw me and realized that I had witnessed this cold-blooded murder. A few moments later he walked through the door muttering the phrase "Russian pigs" over and over again. I pretended to be busy sorting through some file, but I could think of nothing but the murder which I had just seen committed. In mitigation, the Nazis have said a thousand times since the end of the war that they acted under orders from their superiors. In some cases, I have no doubt that this was true. In others, such as this savage killing of a helpless Russian by Kruth, there could have been no excuse whatsoever.

The Germans have always thought of themselves as a cultured people with a noble heritage and a palate for the delicacies of art, music and literature. This being so, they perpetrated what must surely have been the most inexplicable paradox in modern history: the extermination and humiliation of millions of Jews under the motto "Gott mit Uns" – God is with us. Therefore, I can only assume that the period during which they perpetrated these unparalleled atrocities were indeed God's sabbatical years.

Some short time after the young Russian was suffocated under the Dautmergen mud, Kruth was replaced by a new Lager Fuhrer, a Nazi of long standing named, Franz Hofmann. His arrival did not have the slightest effect on the daily routine of the camp but, for a brief period at the start of his administration, we came to the conclusion that he did not possess the same murderous instincts as his predecessor.

Hofmann, like all his other collaborators, soon proved us wrong. One freezing cold day a lorry pulled up in the camp and dumped a load of frostbitten potatoes at the side of the kitchen barracks, directly opposite the office. Hofmann was standing near the glass window in the office door and, from that position, he saw a prisoner stuffing the potatoes into his jacket. He darted out of the office, and I moved quickly towards the door to see what had made him run so fast. When I reached the door, I saw a terrified youth, no more than 16 or 17 years of age, dropping the potatoes on the ground while Hofmann stood over him seething and puffing at the gills. As the first potato fell to the ground, Hofmann told the youth to run towards the gate. The young man obviously thought that the Lager Fuhrer was in a lenient mood and he turned and ran. But before he had gone more than a few paces, Hofmann pulled out his revolver and shot him dead.

The Lagerschreiber pulled me quickly away from the door. "If you value your life get back to work you numbskull. You have seen and heard nothing – remember," he said. I took his advice, but I found it extremely difficult to carry on as if nothing had happened. I was growing accustomed to witnessing such senseless killings but, on this occasion, I knew the victim. I knew him as well as I knew my own brother. The body lying on the freezing earth belonged to Chaim Laskov, one of my playmates from my school days in Vilna.

At dinner that night, Hofmann brought me some soup. I accepted it, but I spluttered and choked on every mouthful. It was illogical, I suppose, that one could witness or hear of the slaughter of thousands of Jews and still be able to eat what little we received with relish, but that the death of one friend should make it impossible to keep the food in one's stomach – but that's the way it was at Dautmergen. Hofmann noticed that I was behaving oddly and asked why my normally healthy appetite had deserted me. I could not very well have told him the truth. I said simply that I was feeling unwell and that I was off my food.

I don't know whether Hofmann was gullible or whether I was especially plausible but he seemed to accept my answer and even seemed genuinely concerned for my well-being. He sent me to my barracks to lie down with orders not to return to the office until I was fit and well again. I still cannot find a logical explanation for Hofmann's contradictory behavior. One moment he could murder a starving Jewish boy for taking a few miserable potatoes; the next he could show real concern for me.

Since that day in the ghetto when, in the market place in Vilna, I first saw at close quarters the contorted faces of dead men, I had seen the executions of more Jews than I care to remember, but the slaying of Chiam Laskov upset me more than any other and made me physically ill. I felt like crawling into some obscure corner of the camp and blotting out all this inhumanity behind a haze of tears, but I knew that it was a short sighted and impractical solution to my problems. Even had I reported sick I would almost certainly have lost my job. There was only one course of action left open to me – to carry on working.

I must have been more ill than I imagined because one evening I could not summon up even enough energy to inform the camp secretary that I would not be attending the morning appel so that I would not be included on the komandiert list. I assumed that my name would have been included automatically.

The day started normally. I sounded the gong at the appropriate hour and, having done so, returned to my bunk to go back to sleep. During the roll-call it was discovered that one of the prisoners was missing. Hofmann and the camp Wurtschaftefuehrer – the quartermaster – a squat, toad-like SS man with a few strands of spiky hair on his head, counted and recounted the prisoners until they were satisfied that they had not made a mistake. They had not. Hofmann and the quartermaster paced the appelplatz like two lions waiting for their pounds of flesh, and the assembled prisoners were told that they would have to remain transfixed to the spot on which they stood until the missing man was found.

All the time I slept on obliviously and unaware that anything was amiss. I knew nothing in fact until the Block Altester, who had the presence of mind to see if my name was included on the komandiert list, came up to my bunk and shook me awake. He did not need a reply. He would tell by the expression on my face that I had not and before I leapt from my bunk he ran off to inform Hofmann that the missing man had been found and that the rest of the prisoners need no longer be kept on the appelplatz.

The Wurtschaftsfuehrer, who had taken an instant dislike to me from the first moment that we met, could not wait to make me pay for the unnecessary confusion that I had caused. He came over to the schonungs block and kicked me all the way to the appelplatz and then pushed me into a column that was about to leave the camp.

As I walked through the gate, convinced that I had made a blunder which would cost me my life, Hofmann pulled me out of the column and ordered me back to the office.

The relief I felt at that moment was matched only by the disappointment and annoyance which the Wurtschaftsfuehrer found impossible to disguise.

CHAPTER 33

Increase In Allied Air-Raids

Thoughts of escape persistently exercised our minds at Dautmergen. Elsewhere in the remote regions of Estonia the camps had been in the middle of cruel wildernesses where the perils that existed outside the barbed wire were almost as great as those inside it.

But at Dautmergen the position was very different. It was close to the Swiss border and, as such, the protective arms of a neutral country.

Like every other prisoner at Dautmergen I was frequently impassioned with near physical lust to tread the sweet Swiss soil but I knew that, even at Dautmergen, the chances of crossing the border were more than remote.

Two prisoners I knew well and who lived in the schonungs block, decided that, despite all the attendant risks and hazards, they would try and reach the haven of Switzerland. They took me into their confidence and asked me to join them. I was honored that they should consider me a worthy partner but their plans were vague, complicated and fraught with disaster and, after some careful reflection, I declined their offer, wishing them all the luck in the world if they decided to undertake the escape did without me.

Although it was always pleasant to deliberate on such plans there were several immovable stumbling blocks which made it foolhardy, if not suicidal, to think seriously of trying to reach and cross the Swiss border. Although we knew that the border was near, we did not know precisely how near. A matter of a few miles and the chance of a run to freedom might have been practical, but if it was 50 or a 100, or even more, the chances, to say the least, would have been slim. Quite apart from that we knew nothing of the terrain, apart from the fact that the whole area was heavily guarded simply because of the camp's proximity to Switzerland.

In spite of all this, irritating vestiges of doubt lingered in my mind about my decision not to join my two friends. But they were soon dispelled.

One morning there was a phone call from a village not far from the camp. The caller said that he had seen three prisoners hiding in a barn. Our Wurtschaftsfuerer immediately called three SS guards and asked me to accompany them as their interpreter.

When we arrived at the village the tree prisoners, all of them Russians, were being held by a mob of farmers who eagerly handed them over to the guards. Almost at once I was ordered to ask the three Russians why they had escaped and if anyone in the village had helped them. They told me, as I anticipated, that they had escaped from their workplace that morning and had made their way to the village in the hope of finding some food and some information about the safest route to Switzerland. They were quick to add that none of the German population on whom they had called had given them any help at all.

Disillusioned, they had decided to hide in the barn until nightfall and then, under the cover of darkness, make a dash for the Swiss border.

I translated what the Russians had said and the guards, satisfied with their answers, marched us all back to the camp. There the Wurtschaftsfuehrer, eager as ever to spill a drop of blood, did not waste a moment. As soon as the guards and I had left the camp he organized a team of joiners and ordered them to erect a gallows.

When we returned from the workgroup it had been completed and the appel took place, as though nothing had happened, with all eyes focused fearfully upon the black timbers. I guessed what it was for but most of my fellow prisoners did not. Like me, all the office staff knew the course of events that was to follow – but they were too scared to breathe a word to anyone.

The next day was Sunday and as usual the appel, no doubt so that the Germans could enjoy an extra hour in bed on the Sabbath, was an hour later. After the roll-call had been taken we were ordered to remain in our places and wait for an announcement by the Lager Fuhrer. A few minutes elapsed and the three Russians were brought on to the appelplatz and walked under guard up to the gallows. They knew they were about to die and every movement they made, every muscle which twitched, transmitted the fear which savaged their guts at the moment. It was all so utterly futile apart from anything else. Such a waste, a shameful waste of life.

The Wurtschaftsfuehrer, exhibited the characteristics of a Roman general at a gladiatorial orgy. He was about to throw three men to the "lions" and he could hardly wait to witness the agony of the death throes. He was all but slavering at the mouth as Hofmann announced that the three prisoners were to be hanged as a punishment for trying to escape and that anyone else attempting to emulate them would suffer the same fate.

As soon as Hofmann finished his little speech, the Wurtschaftsfuehrer told the three men to climb on to the platform in front of the gallows. SS guards then placed the nooses around the prisoners' throats and, after a brief pause, no doubt so that he could savor the full sadistic pleasure of the moment, the Wurtschaftsfuehrer pulled the ropes.

One could only hope that the fall broke their necks cleanly and quickly and that their deaths were not agonizing and lingering. All we could be certain of was that as we walked away from the appelplatz three limp bodies spun on the end of the ropes like straw-filled dummies on a bayonet practice range.

So ended the only attempt to except the Hell of Dautmergen and, in the bargain, any ideas that any other prisoners might have had of making their own bid for freedom.

Death seemed the only sure way out. By the end of February, 1945 the Vilna group alone had lost 376 men out of the total of around 500 who arrived at the camp. The disappearance of Kruth for a short time eased conditions temporarily but it was too late to make any lasting or significant improvement on the rate at which we were dying.

Most of the prisoners had been reduced to skin and bone and were incapable of supporting their own frail bodies, let alone fit for strenuous physical work – but in spite of this the SS insisted that the work had to continue to assist their war effort. No doubt they derived great satisfaction from rubbing salt into our wounds, by forcing us to expend our last breaths, spill our last drops of blood in the name of the Third Reich. During this period of austerity scores of prisoners died but our Nazi masters, who at that stage still had delusions that they would win the war, had no difficulty in replacing the victims. Several replacement transports arrived at Dautmergen, the largest of them being Jews from Radom in Poland. They were mostly housed in the bunks formerly occupied by the dead Vilna Jews and, after the comparative comfort of life in Radom, they did not find it easy to adjust to the deprivations of life in a concentration camp – Dautmergen no less.

They soon began to die like flies and, in after just a matter of weeks, only the hardiest among them had survived.

In March, the weather, which in the winter months made our suffering so much harder to bear, began to improve. The sun began to generate a little warmth and, with the imminent spring, the seeds of eventual liberation once again began to germinate in our hearts. In the camp office, we heard whispers that the Allies were making steady progress and other prisoners also heard while they were at work, favorable reports of the war in other parts of Europe. All these pieces of information seemed to fit neatly together into a patchwork of hope which spontaneously raised the morale among the prisoners and each day the will to survive grew stronger and stronger.

I have often doubted the validity of the will to live as a concept but there was little doubt that the newly-found strength and its accompanying lighter frame of mind, led to a marked drop in the number of deaths at Dautmergen. From the Vilna transport, only four people died during the whole of March and the Leichenkommandos were once again envied their easy job and the extra rations which went with it. The Allied air-raids became more and more frequent and the sound of their engines was like sweet music to our ears.

It was obvious to the Nazis that we had all become increasingly confident that we were soon to be liberated and, as intolerant as ever of anything which brought a little pleasure to our hearts, they decided to dampen our spirits with a public demonstration of murder.

A group of 22 Russian prisoners, who were waiting to be executed in a civilian prison, were brought to Dautmergen for the purpose. During the evening appel they were put on the appelplatz alongside Block No 2 and a German staff car, carrying Hofmann and Kruth, pulled in and halted between the cookhouse and the office. The car headlights were switched on to provide illumination and unceremoniously the order was given to fire.

Eleven of the prisoners hit the ground stone dead. The second group of 11 were then moved into position and another blast of shots rang out. This time only 10 of the Russians died instantaneously. The eleventh began to stagger about like a paralytic drunk clutching his gut and about to vomit. A repeat order was given to shoot and the last of the 22 was thankfully put out of his misery.

No one really knew for certain why these prisoners had been brought to Dautmergen for their execution. We could only assume that the execution had been arranged especially by the Nazis to aggravate our distress at a time when we were beginning to see a little chink of light in our "dungeon" wall.

This was Kruth's first appearance at Dautmergen since his brief period of leave and he was quick to demonstrate that his feelings had not changed towards us and that he has not in any way mellowed.

For reasons known only to himself he hanged a prisoner by his feet from a protruding beam outside the camp toilet with strict orders that no-one was to go to his aid. Like a piece of squirming, writhing bait at the end of a fishing hook he hung there all one night, the blood rushing to his brain until his head felt it would burst and his ankles blanched and numb as the course ropes dug into his flesh. The following morning Kruth simply cut him down and walked away. I remember the incident as though it was yesterday but I never knew the prisoner involved or found out what became of him.

Quite naturally, the slaughter of the 22 Russians and hangings of this kind shook our morale but it was generally felt that the atrocities reflected the Nazi's defeats at the front and that they were trying to assert their remaining authority.

The air-raids by the Allies became more regular than ever and it did my heart good to watch our SS "heroes" – the leaders of the Master Race – run to their well-constructed shelters as soon as the air-raid sirens started to scream out their warnings. Hofmann literally used to sprint the few yards to his shelter opposite the camp gates. In fact, he was so scared he lost his appetite completely. Practically every day he told me to collect his meals for him from the SS kitchen and eat them myself.

By the beginning of April 1945, it became clear to all those working in the camp office that something of great importance was bound to happen – and happen soon. Hofmann and his companions looked haggard and grim faced and nothing like the hand-rubbing, gloating, unshakable tormenters we had known during our early months at Dautmergen.

Something was going to happen – that much we were sure of – but I believe we were all taken by surprise by the suddenness and the speed of the events which followed. Without any warning, 20 SS guards surrounded the schonungs block and several hundred extremely sick prisoners were driven out of the barracks, assembled on the appelplatz and told by the Lager Fuhrer that they were being taken to an erholungs lager – a rest cure camp. We all knew what was meant by that. The only interpretation was a trip to the gas chambers – though it was doubtful whether some of the sick, emaciated, dying men who were dragged from their bunks that day, cared whether they lived or died. In truth, many of them might have preferred the quick death of the ovens to the slow painful one of the schonungs block.

Gradually, the camp population was whittled down. Kruth made several more selections within a few days and even sent reasonably fit men to the erholungs lager. I kept out of his way as far as was possible under the circumstances and, on one occasion, a friend pushed me under a bunk and nailed some boards over the front of it so that I would not be seen. I felt as though I was being buried alive and, as it turned out, I suffered the discomforts unnecessarily. Kruth collected his required number of victims before reaching my corner of the schonungs block.

CHAPTER 34

The Evacuation Of Dautmergen

With the Allies beginning to breathe down their necks in April of 1945, the Germans largely turned their attention away from us to the more pressing issue of self-preservation.

I clearly remember that during the second week of that month, shortly after several prisoners had been killed at work during one of the Allied air raids, the Germans evacuated 250 other prisoners from the camp. The 750 prisoners who remained were all but forgotten by their frightened masters and, on one occasion, even Kruth was absent from the camp – preoccupied, like the rest of his comrades, with taking steps to save his own skin.

By that time, we were certain that the war and our suffering were coming to an end, but this did not inherently imply that we would survive long enough to see our liberation. For many thousands of prisoners before us, their suffering had ended with a bullet through the head or in the gas ovens of an extermination camp and we were well aware of the fact that the same fate could have been planned for us. Yet the feeling of optimism among us, as sick and wasted as we were, was undeniable and, in itself, self-perpetuating. The favorite topic of conversation was just how soon after liberation the Red Cross would be able to take over the camp and begin healing our wounds, filling our bellies and generally restoring our lost sanity.

Quite suddenly, as the speculation continued, Dautmergen was closed and no prisoners left the camp to report to the arbeitskommandos. There was nothing to do apart from exercising our minds with dreams and plans for the future in the eventuality of our liberation – although it was a luxury we denied ourselves for most of the time. Our lives previously had been lived on the basis of surviving each day, maybe a week or perhaps even a month, but no one dared to look further ahead than that into the future.

This state of inactivity lasted until April 17 when the silence was shattered by exploding shells dropped by Allied aircraft in the vicinity of the camp. The raid lasted for some minutes. We stayed inside the barracks, listening and waiting. Suddenly, there was deafening explosion close by followed by a mushrooming quiet. Cautiously, everyone in the camp's administrative offices went out on to the appelplatz to see what had happened. But before we had a chance to reconnoiter, Hofmann and some SS guards came around to ask for our help. It soon became clear what had happened. One of the shells had scored a direct hit on the camp's generator. It had been reduced to a pile of smoldering rubble and two SS guards' barracks had also been partially demolished.

Six Germans were killed outright and there were at least 20 others wounded, some them trapped beneath the bricks, masonry and twisted metal.

The Herrenfolk regarded the Jews as subhuman and beneath their dignity to have any form of social contact with them but, in their hour of need, they cast aside their prejudices and were only too ready to seek our help. For almost two hours we burrowed into the rubble with picks, spades and even our bare hands and as each SS man was dragged half-dead from the building, he was taken to the camp hospital on a shuttle service of stretchers.

As soon as Hofmann was satisfied that the last of the guards had be extricated and removed for treatment to the hospital, he called all the camp staff back and announced that Dautmergen was to be evacuated immediately. He had had enough and could not bear the thought that, on any subsequent raid, he himself might have been killed or seriously injured.

The Lager Altester asked Hofmann where we would be taken. He simply replied: "Get the prisoners assembled and ready for departure. We have no time to lose."

So, after six months of untold suffering and deprivation we were to leave Dautmergen behind us. We were also leaving behind our dead – 1,755 fellow prisoners, 385 from the Vilna transport alone.

The panic-stricken Germans, in their haste to flee from the advancing Allies, forgot to provide us with food. The camp administration remembered, however, that there were nearly 400 loaves of bread in the cookhouse and, as the prisoners were being assembled on the appelplatz, they hurriedly cut each of the loaves in half to ensure that each of us had something to eat for the journey.

In no time at all, all 750 prisoners who were being evacuated that day each received their bread ration. Hofmann and Kruth then ordered us all out of the camp and, as we marched through the gates, we were comforted by the thought that our next home, wherever it was to be, could not be as bad as the one we were leaving. For me the relief was tarnished only by the fact that my father did not survive long enough to be with me on the day we left the Hell of Dautmergen.

After marching for a few hours, I realized that the SS officers, who had been with us from the start, were no longer with us – that they had disappeared at some point along the way. As it began to get dark everyone was completely exhausted and many complained that they could not walk another step but the macabre sight of several hundred dead prisoners lying in ditches along the roadside enabled them to find reserves of energy which they did not know they had. The bodies we saw were covered loosely with the only possessions they had – dark grey blankets – and here and there we could clearly see the striped concentration camp uniforms protruding from underneath.

We marched on in silence, much as mourners at a funeral. To cause the deaths of innocent people is always the most unpardonable of crimes, but to be slaughtered like this in the eleventh hour was tragic in the extreme. What was more, the freshly-slain bodies revived in us the fear that we were merely being led by the Germans to some convenient and desolate spot where we, too, would be disposed of as so much useless ballast slowing down the Nazis' escape.

When it became quite dark we were taken to a large farmhouse and given accommodation for the night in the barn. Our guards warned us not to touch anything but one Russian prisoner could not resist the temptation. He caught and killed a chicken, and was just preparing to have a feast when one of guards noticed him plucking the feathers from its breast.

Without waiting for an explanation, the guard beat the Russian to death with the butt of his rifle.

Several other prisoners, including myself, found some new laid eggs and, despite the risks, we ate them in the dark. In the morning, our march to nowhere started once again. The countryside in that part of Germany, while gentle on the eye, had a marked uniformity and, as there were no obvious landmarks, we came to the conclusion that we were marching for the sake of marching and that we were simply going around in circles.

The monotony of this futile merry-go-round was broken after about an hour when the area once again came under attack from the air. The guards told us to take cover in the nearby woods. Within a few minutes the immediate danger passed, but there were sporadic raids throughout the rest of the day and, with empty stomachs, we had to sleep as best we could among the trees until nightfall.

At night the raids stopped and, as we wearily dragged ourselves back on to the road, the guards told us that we would thereafter continue to lead this topsy-turvy existence, sleeping during the day, marching at night.

That first day we marched continually with just one short break.

At first our rest periods were merely for a few hours but on April 19, the air raids began at dawn and continued throughout the whole day. From sunrise to dusk, until the droning of the engines stopped, we laid low among the trees but at night, when it was safe to emerge and begin our nocturnal trek, everyone was too weak to move. None of us had eaten a morsel since the half a loaf we received on leaving Dautmergen.

With some persuasion from the guards' bayonets we eventually began to stir ourselves but for some the woods by the of the road were literally the end of the line. Even the prodding of the bayonets could not get them to their feet. They were finished and died as peacefully as was possible among the trees in the sweet-smelling air of a German wood.

During the break that night I was approached by a prisoner, who I knew vaguely, with a plan to obtain some bread. It was fraught with potential disaster but, by that time, I was so ravenous I agreed to take the risk. The plan was that I should keep one of guards talking while my friends rummaged for bread in a bag which the SS man kept on his back. To enhance our chances of success we selected a guard with one eye. The other was covered with a black patch. It worked like a charm. My friend removed the bread without the guard feeling a thing and before he realized that it was missing we had eaten every last crumb of it.

When he did eventually find out that he had been robbed he went berserk. Every prisoner was searched and others, suspected of the robbery, were given a beating. But the bread was safe in our bellies and ironically when he had calmed down a little he asked me if I knew who was responsible. I told him that I had no idea. He then went on to tell me that he had been saving the bread for me and that he had been waiting for an opportunity to give it to me when no one else was around.

The stolen bread was a great tonic and that night I finished the march in remarkably good spirits.

The following morning, we reached a road that had been hacked out of the dense forest and once again we rested and slept under the cover of the trees for most of the day. Several prisoners, shattered beyond redemption, simply lay down to die and when the order was given to resume the march their worn-out bodies remained motionless on the damp earth.

Death was all around us. We could not seem to escape from it. As we set off again, leaving the dead of our column behind, we passed the bodies of scores of other dead prisoners lying along the roadside. Again, we wondered just how long it would be before we, too, were murdered by our guards.

On April 12, shortly after dawn, a German army dispatch rider passed our column. One of the guards waved him down and asked how far we were from the front. "Eight kilometers," he replied, and drove off.

We pressed on, but minutes later there was an air-raid yet again and we ran for cover into the forest. The raid lasted for a long time. Some bombs hit the road not many yards from where we were and huge slabs of asphalt and earth were blasted all around us. In the confusion, some Polish prisoners I knew well at Dautmergen came up to me and, with persuasive intensity in their voices, asked me if I would like to try and escape with them. They said they needed someone who could speak German in the event of any awkward confrontations en route. I had previously refused an offer to escape from Dautmergen – though I have no regrets about that – but this time I did not hesitate in accepting. We gripped each other by the shoulders like brothers to seal the contract and then waited with thumping hearts until the raid was over.

When the planes disappeared in the distance the guards gave the order for our column to reassemble on the road, but my six Polish friends and I moved instead out of sight of the guards and, when we heard the sound of marching feet, we sank deeper into the protective oblivion of the forest in our bid for freedom.

Chapter 35

Our First Taste Of Freedom

Our first sweet taste of freedom obliterated the hunger pains in our stomachs and the aching in our bones and, until sheer exhaustion forced us to stop, we ran and stumbled through the trees like exuberant children.

We were free, we were free, we were free – the thought kept cancelling out everything else in our minds and as we sat down to rest we breathlessly congratulated one another on our initial success. Had we escaped earlier from one of the workgroups there would not have been the remotest chance that we would not have been missed when the roll call was taken. But this time it was quite different. So many prisoners in our group had died along the march from Dautmergen, there was very little chance that the guards would have missed another seven – and, in any event, they were more concerned with saving their own miserable skins.

Having rested and found our second wind, we began to head deeper into the forest – and to our horror immediately came face to face with a group of German soldiers. Could fate deal us such a cruel blow? Surely no-one could have such damnable luck. We were terrified and totally incapable of moving as they approached us.

"Do any of you speak German?" said one of the group, a sergeant.

"I do," I stammered.

"Good – tell your comrades that they have nothing to fear. We will not harm you. We are deserters. As far as we are concerned the war is over. We will give you some food but after that you must keep away from us."

Nothing it seemed was predictable. One moment we expected that our short-lived freedom was at an end. The next we were being given tins of pork and handfuls of cigars. It was an unreal and in many ways, I suppose, a very pathetic situation. We thanked the Germans for their gifts of food and the cigars, wished one another a safe and speedy end to the war and parted company.

A few yards further along we came across a clearing and sat down to a hastily consumed meal hardly believing our incredible good fortune. Having eaten we continued to put more miles between ourselves and our former guards.

The forest seemed as dark and as unending as our former years of slavery and, when the rapidly failing light made traveling hazardous, we stopped and started to make some sort of shelter for the night. With twigs, branches and leaves we started to construct a makeshift, kennel-like hut, but our attempts were thwarted by torrential rain which cascaded like a waterfall through the trees. Our clothes, which at the best of times provided little protection against inclement weather, were soaked through and in the cold night air we all began to shiver uncontrollably. In my low state of health, it was too much for me to stand and I asked my companions to keep moving and walk on slowly in the dark to try and find a way out of the forest. I thought that at least this would prevent our joints from stiffening up and keep our blood circulating. But they declined. They said they preferred to stay where they were and suffer the cold discomfort rather than take the chance of being caught and shot at the last moment.

Thoroughly miserable and with my nerves in ribbons, I therefore set off alone. But when I had gone no more than a few paces one of my friends, who was older than I, decided to accompany me so that I would not get lost. We kept running simply to prevent the damp cold from eating into our bones and we soon reached the edge of the forest.

In the distance, we could see the lights of a farmhouse. I looked at my friend and he looked at me and without uttering a word we realized that we were in agreement about our next move – to make our way towards it and hope for the best.

As soon as we came within earshot we could clearly hear the chatter and laughter of drunken German voices. This was enough for us. Without pausing to find out the reason for the revelry we turned on our heels and started to run away. But we were too late – we had been seen. The door of the farmhouse blasted open and the farmer came running out slamming it shut behind him. His demonic appearance, however, belied his general demeanor and, when he spoke to us, his tone was one of kindness and sympathy.

"What is it you want here at this time of night?" he asked.

"We were just looking for food and shelter for the night, nothing more," I replied.

He came closer, looked us up and down and I could see in his eyes that our sorrowful state and our honest answer to his question, that he would respond sympathetically. "You're very lucky, very lucky indeed. My house is full of SS deserters. If you had come in there's no knowing what might have happened. Now follow me quickly," he said.

It was obvious that he knew we were escaped prisoners and there was no need to tell him more. He led us to a barn and told us that we should keep out of sight and at daybreak we should leave as soon as we woke up. At first my friend and I were frightened to enter the barn but, after a little discussion, we decided that if the farmer had intended to do us any harm he only had to call the drunken SS men out of his house.

I slept like a contented child, oblivious to everything until the cock crowing in the farmyard woke us up at sunrise. We picked ourselves off the straw and made our way to the barn door where the farmer himself met us with a large jug of milk and a large loaf of bread.

"Please leave as soon as possible – before my guests start to wake," he said, concerned both for our safety and his own.

We thanked him profusely and made our way across his land back to our other five companions in the forest. They were soaked, frozen and as we approached we could hear them coughing. Their flimsy shelter had collapsed on top of them and they had spent almost the whole of the night under what was nothing more than a pile of sodden rotting leaves and twigs. My friend and I had spent a reasonably comfortable night in the barn and we used the additional strength our good night's sleep had given us to massage our companions back to life. When the blood in their veins slowly began to circulate again, we all set off slowly, eating the bread which the farmer had given us as we went.

After about a half-an-hour we saw some farmworkers running towards us. They embraced us all in turn and excitedly they kept repeating: "You are free, you are free, we are all free..."

When we had all calmed down, the farmworkers explained that they had all been brought to the area after the Warsaw uprising and forced to work for the Nazis, adding that French troops had, for the past 48 hours, been in occupation of the little town of Salgau, a mere three kilometers away. The farmworkers, who were intoxicated with their freedom, thought that the occasion called for a liberation party and generously invited us to join them. But reluctantly we declined. We did not doubt the validity of their story for an instant but, after so long in captivity, we felt that we could not celebrate adequately until we had seen the Allies with our own eyes. Only then would we believe that we were really free.

We arrived at Salgau to find the streets practically deserted. Every now and again we would see a French Military Policeman and, after standing, so to speak, in the wings for some time, one of our group, a doctor from Warsaw who could speak French, approached one of the policemen, explained that we were Polish ex-concentration camp prisoners and asked him if he could find us anywhere to stay.

He was completely overcome with emotion began to kiss us and weep like a baby. At first, we thought that he was in some way mentally unbalanced but in a few minutes, he regained his composure and, in perfect Polish, he replied: "My dear brothers – I am so happy to meet you. You are the first Polish survivors of a concentration camp I have met. Of course, I will help in any way that I can."

My friends, who were interested only in returning to their families and Poland as quickly as possible, wasted no time in seizing the helping hand he offered. They asked him if he could find them some bicycles. He promptly took us all to the local police station, where there was a compound of assorted bicycles and, without approaching anyone for permission, he invited us to help ourselves to whichever machines appealed to us. When we had made our selection he gave us dozens of tins of pork and, with more embraces and fond farewells, we said goodbye to him and set off on the northward journey to Poland and home.

Our plan was to follow in the wake of the Allies and within a few days we reached the outskirts of Wurtzburg.

The excitement of being free and the grueling pace we tried to keep up made me feel quite ill. I had a high temperature and could not stop shivering. I bedded down for the night in the classroom of a small school and, without success, I tried to find a little warmth and comfort. In the morning, my travelling companions wanted to leave early but I could not raise myself from the floor let alone pedal a cycle.

They knew how horribly sick I felt and I begged them to wait a day or so until I was fit enough to travel but they would not listen and insisted that I went with them there and then – or not at all.

One of them Wladyslaw K., who helped me at Dautmergen on more than one occasion, looked me in the eyes and said: "You ungrateful Jew. I helped you to survive so that I could take you to Poland to exhibit you as our country's last surviving Jews and this is how you repay me – by not wanting to return."

"Just a day or so more. That's all I ask. We are safe here. Then I will come with you gladly," I said.

But my pleading was pointless. He was so angered by the thought that he would lose in me a steady income after the war – by showing me off as a sort of freak – he kicked me viciously in the ribs, took my bicycle and walked out together with his friends.

As he went out I pulled myself up off the ground and begged him once again not to leave me. Wladyslaw turned and spat a sentence at me: "Stop mithering you dirty little Jew", and as a final gesture he punched me in the face.

I felt at that moment only contempt for a man who could behave in such a despicable way after he himself had suffered so wickedly at the hands of the Nazis.

A German woman, who saw the whole disgusting spectacle, helped me back into the classroom and, out of sheer compassion, asked me to stay in her own home. I accepted gratefully and for the next few days she nursed and fed me until I was strong enough to leave.

When I did eventually leave her home, I managed to hitch a lift on an American army lorry back to Wurtzburg where I made my way to the town Mayor's office. A young Greek girl, who worked there as an interpreter, looked up at me and asked me what I wanted.

I told her who I was and that I was looking for some Jewish people who would give me a temporary home.

"It must be your lucky day," she said, adding that the man she worked for, an American army colonel, was Jewish and that she was certain he would be pleased to help me in any way that he could.

She took me through into his room. He was a well built, well preserved man with greying hair and, as I walked hesitantly into his office, he was puffing cigar smoke in my direction. I stood silently a few yards from his desk as the interpreter explained that I was a former Jewish concentration camp prisoner and that I needed food and lodgings.

"Shalom Aleichem," said the colonel apologizing straight afterwards for the fact that he could not speak Yiddish. He then turned to the Greek girl and told her to give me half a loaf of bread, a tin of pilchards and, afterwards, to take me to a Displaced Persons camp in the center of Wurtzburg.

"Shalom Aleichem," he said again. The tone of his voice and the expression on his face made it clear that my little interview was at an end. I thanked him politely and left.

How vastly different the first few days of freedom turned out from the way in which I had dreamed they would be during all those dark, deathly nights in Hitler's death camps. Not only were there no comforting, healing hands from the Swiss Red Cross, but there was very little compassion either.

The Wurtzburg D.P. camp was as overcrowded as the schonungs block at Dautmergen and the American military administration of the camp could not supply sufficient food for the number of displaced persons who daily kept swelling their numbers.

This led to outbreaks of fighting and squabbling among the inmates, each of them desperately trying to obtain their share of the little that was available. Had I been bigger and stronger I might have succeeded in getting my share, too, but I was weak and small at the time and found myself constantly being ousted from my rightful place in the queue.

Being a Jew only made matters worse. When the other DPs found out that I was Jewish they not only pushed me away physically but accompanied their bullying tactics with anti-Semitic obscenities.

After 46 months of suffering, beatings, hunger and degradation in the ghetto and, afterwards in the concentration camps, I had to contend with ex-prisoners whose own sufferings had failed to teach them that all human beings, irrespective of race or religion, are equal and have the inviolate right to live without being persecuted.

I left the Wurtzburg camp after only a few days, still wearing my striped concentration camp uniform.

I walked out of the town dazed and disillusioned and after a few hours I reached a crossroads. There were no signposts and I had no way of knowing which way to turn. I sat down and cried silently.

The next thing I remember was a French army ambulance pulling up beside me. The driver wound down his window and asked me where I wanted to go.

"Anywhere where there is no hatred or prejudice," I replied.

The end

INDEX

Important Note: The INDEX below does not include names in the appendex that follows, so please review that list separately.

Appendix

List of Vilna Jews ז"ל who perished at Dautmergen

1	Leib	Aronovitz	1915	October 16, 1944
2	Simon	Diker	1905	October 16, 1944
3	Itcik	Chwoles	1899	October 26, 1944
4	Eliash	Rubin	1910	October 27, 1944
5	Israel	Freiman	1903	October 28, 1944
6	Isser	Jacobson	1913	October 30, 1944
7	Joel	Dworcman	1897	October 30, 1944
8	Aron	Shenkman	1914	October 29, 1944
9	Chaim	Bartman	1918	October 29, 1944
10	Jacob	Bandas	1898	October 31, 1944
11	Moses	Wyszynski	1906	November 1, 1944
12	Wolf	Stoluff	1909	November 1, 1944
13	Reuben	Minsker	1902	November 1, 1944
14	Chaim	Siskind	1906	November 1, 1944
15	Chanania	Tsamerski	1900	November 2, 1944
16	Baruch	Warszawczyk	1904	November 3, 1944
17	Michal	Seidel	1895	November 4, 1944
18	Ephraim	Kesselman	1898	November 5, 1944
19	Shleime	Dregetz	1904	November 7, 1944
20	Shleime	Ditkowski	1921	November 7, 1944
21	Moses	Bitter	1907	November 8, 1944
22	Abram	Abramowitz	1900	November 8, 1944
23	David	Sakowitz	1906	November 10, 1944
24	Ber	Turgel	1920	November 10, 1944
25	Joseph	Rybek	1900	November 12, 1944
26	Abram	Szenkier	1898	November 12, 1944
27	Rachmiel	Katz	1905	November 12, 1944
28	Scholem	Adelson	1915	November 13, 1944
29	Berl	Katz	1910	November 14, 1944
30	Isaiah	Lewin	1905	November 14, 1944
31	Tuwie	Zusmanowitz	1904	November 14, 1944
32	Betzalel	Stoler	1915	November 15, 1944
33	Jacob	Pesker	1905	November 15, 1944
34	Owsiej	Sher	1921	November 15, 1944
35	Leib	Minsker	1915	November 15, 1944
36	Gedalie	Gelman	1898	November 16, 1944

37	Hersh	Milikowski	1900	November 17, 1944
38	Wolf	Schapiro	1902	November 17, 1944
39	Chaim	Szkelnicki	1905	November 17, 1944
40	Joseph	Pilowski	1914	November 17, 1944
41	Ber	Epstein	1901	November 18, 1944
42	Ber	Levinson	1907	November 19, 1944
43	Meilach	Koplman	1905	November 20, 1944
44	Baruch	Swirski	1910	November 21, 1944
45	Israel	Bobrowski	1909	November 21, 1944
46	Joseph	Garbacki	1903	November 21, 1944
47	Jehuda	Bolberg	1898	November 22, 1944
48	Tsodek	Pervdominski	1904	November 22, 1944
49	Abram	Lewin	1910	November 22, 1944
50	Leib	Cheifetz	1905	November 22, 1944
51	Baruch	Lubocki	1898	November 22, 1944
52	Ephraim	Rechetz	1911	November 22, 1944
53	Moses	Krom	1907	November 24, 1944
54	Ber	Geler	1907	November 24, 1944
55	Scholem	Weiler	1906	November 24, 1944
56	Rachmiel	Seider	1904	November 24, 1944
57	Chaim	Band	1908	November 25, 1944
58	Gedalie	Chaietowitz	1905	November 25, 1944
59	Meier	Chaiet	1912	November 26, 1944
60	Abram	Nabroszczyk	1918	November 26, 1944
61	Beny	Dalin	1907	November 26, 1944
62	Leon	Bendas	1914	November 26, 1944
63	Jakub	Trupianski	1909	November 27, 1944
64	Idel	Kinkulkin	1906	November 27, 1944
65	Berl	Salwowicz	1904	November 27, 1944
66	Szloime	Starodwerski	1914	November 27, 1944
67	Daniel	Rimszinet	1905	November 27, 1944
68	Joel	Lewin	1904	November 28, 1944
69	Betzalel	Rudnik	1908	November 28, 1944
70	Benjamin	Zupraner	1899	November 28, 1944
71	Idel	Balasz	1895	November 28, 1944
72	David	Lev	1926	November 29, 1944
73	Feyvel	Trupianski	1904	November 29, 1944
74	Joseph	Leikin	1906	November 29, 1944
75	Isak	Wapnik	1907	November 29, 1944
76	Chaim	Grodzinski	1905	November 29, 1944
77	Chaim	Gurwicz	1910	November 29, 1944

78	Max	Kodesh	1903	November 30, 1944
79	Leib	Berlin	1912	November 30, 1944
80	Samuel	Pogorzelski	1900	November 30, 1944
81	Israel	Kravetz	1906	December 1, 1944
82	Abram	Badanowski	1925	December 1, 1944
83	Szewel	Portney	1905	December 1, 1944
84	Szloime	Gitel	1900	December 1, 1944
85	Idel	Golumsztek	1910	December 1, 1944
86	Yankel	Kinkulkin	1908	December 2, 1944
87	Nachum	As	1909	December 2, 1944
88	Chaim	Kaplan	1919	December 2, 1944
89	Motel	Kowarski	1915	December 2, 1944
90	Wolf	Pinski	1911	December 2, 1944
91	Adam	Gorfein	1908	December 3, 1944
92	Szymon	Sztersz	1907	December 3, 1944
93	Szymon	Durgiel	1913	December 4, 1944
94	Szloime	Scholem	1915	December 4, 1944
95	Ascher	Lewin	1915	December 4, 1944
96	Zanwel	Kahn	1900	December 4, 1944
97	Benjamin	Elmer	1924	December 4, 1944
98	Szluime	Gordon	1925	December 4, 1944
99	Peretz	Szpicberg	1909	December 5, 1944
100	Lejzer	Misziker	1900	December 5, 1944
101	Samuel	Dlugacz	1913	December 5, 1944
102	Mordechai	Wilkomirski	1909	December 5, 1944
103	Isak	Gofman	1905	December 5, 1944
104	Moses	Aabramowicz	1909	December 5, 1944
105	Zisman	Krieger	1900	December 5, 1944
106	Joseph	Goldstern	1906	December 5, 1944
107	Abram	Aren	1924	December 6, 1944
108	Samuel	Minsker	1912	December 6, 1944
109	Reuben	Zarembek	1925	December 6, 1944
110	David	Maszanski	1907	December 6, 1944
111	Lejzer	Cepelewicz	1922	December 7, 1944
112	Israel	Borowak	1905	December 8, 1944
113	Nachum	Romm	1923	December 8, 1944
114	Chaim	Cymbal	1911	December 8, 1944
115	Joseph	Jergod	1911	December 8, 1944
116	Aba	Katz	1925	December 8, 1944
117	Leib	Abramowicz	1913	December 8, 1944
118	Chaim	Feigelson	1914	December 8, 1944

119	Henech	Lewin	1912	December 8, 1944
120	Berl	Rajwencz	1900	December 8, 1944
121	Szymon	Zacharan	1902	December 9, 1944
122	Hersz	Lewin	1924	December 9, 1944
123	Michal	Lewin	1920	December 10, 1944
124	Hersz	Gechman	1907	December 10, 1944
125	Abram	Tarakinski	1909	December 10, 1944
126	Natan	Szukstulski	1905	December 10, 1944
127	Eliyahu	Sznajoman	1910	December 10, 1944
128	Motel	Szachman	1924	December 10, 1944
129	Israel	Najfield	1908	December 11, 1944
130	Hersz	Sznajdman	1905	December 11, 1944
131	Lejzer	Gezenda	1904	December 11, 1944
132	Isak	Zas	1904	December 11, 1944
133	Joseph	Mulnar	1927	December 11, 1944
134	Pejsach	Kurt	1926	December 12, 1944
135	Szloime	Losowski	1918	December 12, 1944
136	Saul	Getzkes	1908	December 12, 1944
137	Mates	Polarski	1907	December 12, 1944
138	Chaim	Griner	1906	December 12, 1944
139	Miszka	Jar	1891	December 12, 1944
140	Feywel	Lewin	1917	December 13, 1944
141	Chaim	Tejkin	1906	December 13, 1944
142	Abram	Brezin	1908	December 13, 1944
143	Mendel	Hofsztein	1905	December 13, 1944
144	Lejzer	Gurwicz	1921	December 14, 1944
145	Scholem	Rudomin	1910	December 14, 1944
146	Leib	Zalkin	1912	December 15, 1944
147	Nachum	Dodones	1896	December 15, 1944
148	David	Jadlowker	1901	December 15, 1944
149	Szmerl	Gurwicz	1908	December 15, 1944
150	David	Elizerowicz	1909	December 15, 1944
151	Abram	Kropiwek	1907	December 15, 1944
152	Wikter	Daniszewski	1908	December 16, 1944
153	Rubin	Daniszewski	1908	December 16, 1944
154	Joseph	Lewicz	1923	December 16, 1944
155	Gerszen	Kagan	1924	December 16, 1944
156	David	Kaplan-Kaplanski	1899	December 16, 1944
157	Pejsach	Szeres	1922	December 16, 1944
158	Abram	Geler	1909	December 16, 1944
159	Emanuel	Czesli	1912	December 17, 1944

160	Samuel	Wolpow	1920	December 18, 1944
161	Pinchas	Dawiszen	1920	December 18, 1944
162	Abram	Chastman	1919	December 18, 1944
163	Jehosha	Szernocki	1910	December 18, 1944
164	Benjamin	Abramowicz	1919	December 18, 1944
165	Abram	Blinder	1904	December 18, 1944
166	Saul	Fleiszer	1910	December 19, 1944
167	Mejlach	Szulman	1919	December 19, 1944
168	Szloime	Kamen	1908	December 19, 1944
169	Noah	Weiner	1924	December 19, 1944
170	Abram	Gunszar	1912	December 19, 1944
171	Eliyahj	Damen	1900	December 19, 1944
172	Reuben	Elsztein	1905	December 19, 1944
173	Arnold	Dajches	1912	December 20, 1944
174	Jakub	Arens	1909	December 20, 1944
175	Szepsel	Rentacint	1908	December 21, 1944
176	Moses	Zalkind	1908	December 21, 1944
177	Moses	Dworkan	1921	December 21, 1944
178	Jechezkel	Rezman	1906	December 21, 1944
179	Israel	Drozie	1907	December 21, 1944
180	Tzedek	Gordon	1916	December 21, 1944
181	Szloime	Orman	1898	December 21, 1944
182	Issak	Maiael	1912	December 22, 1944
183	David	Sz mid	1905	December 22, 1944
184	Ber	Meszelnik	1909	December 22, 1944
185	Aba	Berger	1920	December 22, 1944
186	Idel	Kusznir	1909	December 23, 1944
187	Moses	Farber	1906	December 23, 1944
188	Alexander	Szlosberg	1926	December 23, 1944
189	Yudel	Mirom	1907	December 23, 1944
190	Reuben	Sorokin	1919	December 23, 1944
191	Feywel	Don	1914	December 23, 1944
192	Issak	Daniszewski	1926	December 23, 1944
193	David	Berger	1905	December 23, 1944
194	Leibusz	Gercler	1895	December 23, 1944
195	Israel	Segalowicz	1907	December 24, 1944
196	Sender	Szneider	1916	December 24, 1944
197	Gerszow	Kreicer	1915	December 24, 1944
198	Moses	Zaks	1905	December 24, 1944
199	Moses	Niemenczynski	1925	December 24, 1944
200	Joseph	Lewinson	1908	December 25, 1944

201	Leizer	Szulman	1908	December 26, 1944
202	Isak	Dworozan	1905	December 26, 1944
203	Abram	Bobrowski	1906	December 26, 1944
204	David	Wigushin	1921	December 26, 1944
205	Rubin	Berkowicz	1903	December 26, 1944
206	Isaiah	Guszanski	1910	December 26, 1944
207	Idel	Gol	1905	December 27, 1944
208	Szymon	Zamoszczyk	1910	December 28, 1944
209	Nachum	Slucki	1914	December 28, 1944
210	Natan	Szimelowicz	1917	December 28, 1944
211	Szymon	Blinder	1899	December 28, 1944
212	Alex	Percowski	1905	December 28, 1944
213	Samuel	Kupelowicz	1903	December 28, 1944
214	Wolf	Stolper	1906	December 28, 1944
215	Leibusz	Weisman	1906	December 28, 1944
216	Alexander	Grodzenski	1915	December 29, 1944
217	Wolf	Nager	1906	December 29, 1944
218	Nachum	Kapelowicz	1905	December 29, 1944
219	Hersz	Rabinowicz	1926	December 29, 1944
220	Lipe	Gurwicz	1907	December 29, 1944
221	Cemach	Feldsztein	1896	December 29, 1944
222	Aba	Abramowicz	1925	December 29, 1944
223	Jakub	Aron	1907	December 29, 1944
224	Emanuel	Notik	1901	December 29, 1944
225	Leizer	Trubaczyst	1926	December 29, 1944
226	Abram	Gamarski	1919	December 29, 1944
227	Abram	Kramer	1906	December 29, 1944
228	Mordechai	Zalmanowicz	1906	December 29, 1944
229	Chaim	Portney	1926	December 29, 1944
230	Joseph	Miler	1905	December 29, 1944
231	Moses	Blitz	1918	December 29, 1944
232	Levi	Stolicky	1910	December 29, 1944
233	Israel	Gurewicz	1912	December 29, 1944
234	Abram	Gordon	1904	December 29, 1944
235	Nachum	Ring	1907	December 29, 1944
236	Scholem	Weiner	1902	December 30, 1944
237	Jakub	Muszke	1910	December 30, 1944
238	Abram	Kagan	1913	December 30, 1944
239	Ascher	Abramowicz	1926	December 30, 1944
240	Lipe	Mindel	1908	December 30, 1944
241	Isak	Czeski	1908	December 30, 1944

242	Jakub	Gurwicz	1906	21/31/1944
243	Betzalel	Pacowski	1924	January 1, 1945
244	Joseph	Lapidus	1916	January 2, 1945
245	Meier	Gelbard	1923	January 2, 1945
246	Moses	Rubin	1911	January 2, 1945
247	Isak	Marin	1906	January 2, 1945
248	Wolf	Grinblat	1922	January 2, 1945
249	Benjamin	Kowner	1923	January 2, 1945
250	Zalmen	Nachimowski	1906	January 2, 1945
251	Rafael	Abramowicz	1911	January 2, 1945
252	Azriel	Szames	1921	January 3, 1945
253	Heszl	Balon	1904	January 4, 1945
254	David	Kinkulkin	1904	January 4, 1945
255	Leib	Reis	1918	January 4, 1945
256	Rubin	Rodaszewski	1914	January 4, 1945
257	Moses	Gelfer	1923	January 4, 1945
258	Mendel	Milchiker	1926	January 5, 1945
259	Idel	Zeger	1905	January 5, 1945
260	Boris	Pevsner	1906	January 5, 1945
261	Eliyahu	Suzan	1922	January 6, 1945
262	Szloime	Weinberg	1911	January 6, 1945
263	Idel	Gefen	1913	January 6, 1945
264	Leon	Sokoliski	1913	January 6, 1945
265	Kalmen	Kliaczke	1910	January 6, 1945
266	Benjamin	Kliaczke	1920	January 6, 1945
267	Scholem	Kaplan	1920	January 7, 1945
268	Chaim	Pupke	1920	January 7, 1945
269	Samson	Brezlin	1906	January 8, 1945
270	Chaim	Laskov	1926	January 8, 1945
271	Paul	Szuster	1906	January 8, 1945
272	Rubin	Szapiro	1906	January 8, 1945
273	Abram	Szlos	1923	January 8, 1945
274	Baruch	Kabacznik	1923	January 10, 1945
275	Zelig	Kabacznik	1913	January 10, 1945
276	Nachmen	Blumental	1911	January 10, 1945
277	Leib	Kahn	1926	January 10, 1945
278	Max	Kowalski	1908	January 10, 1945
279	Gedalie	Buszel	1907	January 10, 1945
280	Efraim	Landsman	1920	January 10, 1944
281	Hersz	Beigel	1925	January 10, 1945
282	Szloime	Szarapey	1904	January 10, 1945

283	Kalmen	Aszayev	1905	January 11, 1945
284	Gedalie	Aronowicz	1927	January 11, 1944
285	Owsiej	Twerdin	1925	January 11, 1945
286	Feywel	Cukier	1923	January 12, 1945
287	Wolf	Kurian	1922	January 12, 1945
288	Tanachum	Gordon	1907	January 12, 1945
289	Isak	Nurkd	1921	January 13, 1945
290	Yechiel	Perski	1912	January 14, 1945
291	Leib	Diker	1909	January 14, 1945
292	Joseph	Winiski	1905	January 14, 1945
293	Gerszen	Lewin	1896	January 14, 1945
294	Feywel	Pol	1914	January 15, 1945
295	Moses	Nisanelewicz	1925	January 16, 1945
296	Isak	Szardonski	1922	January 16, 1945
297	Chaim	Nik	1910	January 16, 1945
298	Meier	Federman	1905	January 16, 1945
299	Joseph	Kowarski	1901	January 17, 1945
300	Leib	Szif	1903	January 18, 1945
301	Henech	Frost	1921	January 18, 1945
302	Eliyahu	Pupke	1922	January 19, 1945
303	Benjamin	Weitzman	1925	January 19, 1945
304	Baruch	Gurwicz	1926	January 19, 1945
305	Moses	Arenowicz	1906	January 19, 1945
306	Betzalel	Friedman	1901	January 22, 1945
307	Moses	Weinberg	1906	January 22, 1945
308	Jakub	Szulkin	1906	January 22, 1945
309	Pejsach	Bernsztein	1901	January 24, 1945
310	Leib	Scholem	1908	January 24, 1945
311	Szepsel	Lukaszek	1905	January 25, 1945
312	Samson	Daniszewski	1923	January 25, 1945
313	Israel	Madeiski	1910	January 27, 1945
314	David	Gurwicz	1909	January 28, 1945
315	Abram	Berkan	1899	January 29, 1945
316	Isak	Dworski	1912	January 30, 1945
317	Mark	Perewoski	1926	January 31, 1945
318	Hersz	Zilber	1906	January 31, 1945
319	Aron	Mil	1908	February 2, 1945
320	Michal	Weisberg	1924	February 2, 1945
321	Isak	Lewin	1926	February 2, 1945
322	Jakub	Berger	1916	February 3, 1945
323	Samuel	Leibman	1913	February 3, 1945

324	Natan	Listowski	1924	February 3, 1945
325	Israel	Lewicz	1908	February 4, 1945
326	Lazar	Kanturowicz	1915	February 6, 1945
327	Leib	Chodosz	1910	February 6, 1945
328	Isak	Breinin	1919	February 6, 1945
329	Isak	Braude	1911	February 7, 1945
330	Marek	Hofman	1926	February 8, 1945
331	Sioma	Sakowicz	1918	February 9, 1945
332	Idel	Feigelson	1917	February 22, 1945
333	David	Segalowicz	1922	March 3, 1945
334	Hersz	Kiowicz	1908	March 8, 1945
335	Nisn	Dworkin	1922	April 6, 1945
336	Markus	Breitbard	1906	April 7, 1945

List of Jews from the Vilna Area who perished at Dautmergen

1	Chaim	Szainer	1900	October 4, 1944
2	Szloime	Elkind	1902	November 3, 1944
3	Joseph	Swirski	1908	November 7, 1944
4	Benjamin	Poczter	1902	November 7, 1944
5	Natan	Janiski	1912	November 12, 1944
6	Kusiel	Chodosz	1905	November 17, 1944
7	Idel	Goldman	1897	November 25, 1944
8	Henech	Mirski	1921	November 26, 1944
9	Isak	Abramowicz	1923	November 27, 1944
10	Szloime	Reznik	1904	November 28, 1944
11	Chone	Berger	1907	December 14, 1944
12	Mates	Kezlowski	1913	December 6, 1944
13	Leib	Szainer	1925	December 8, 1944
14	Moses	Nuchimzen	1904	December 8, 1944
15	David	Taboriski	1910	December 8, 1944
16	Samuel	Kuricki	1900	December 9, 1944
17	Zisle	Taboriski	1905	December 11, 1944
18	Pejsach	Rudnicki	1905	December 11, 1944
19	Szloime	Grup	1902	December 12, 1944
20	Aren	Perewoskin	1909	December 13, 1944
21	Joseph	Rauch	1906	December 16, 1944
22	Lelek	Zlotejablke	1906	December 16, 1944

23	Yossel	Berman	1905	December 18, 1944
24	Mordechai	Leskes	1926	December 19, 1944
25	Szewach	Gumitz	1905	December 20, 1944
26	Leizer	Liskowicz	1903	December 20, 1944
27	Isaiah	Laskow	1904	December 22, 1944
28	Jankiel	Lifszic	1911	December 24, 1944
29	Max	Krawczynski	1907	December 24, 1944
30	Aron	Leibman	1910	December 25, 1944
31	Zalmen	Alperowicz	1923	December 28, 1944
32	Michal	Fiszer	1904	December 28, 1944
33	Joseph	Wolf	1906	December 29, 1944
34	Rubin	Greis	1904	December 29, 1944
35	Tevie	Osziwowski	1909	December 29, 1944
36	Natan	Mirski	1906	December 29, 1944
37	Simche	Chodosak	1912	December 30, 1944
38	Hersz	Siskind	1925	December 30, 1944
39	David	Rudnik	1917	January 2, 1945
40	Meier	Bunimowicz	1913	January 8, 1945
41	Szymon	Kuricki	1926	January 12, 1945
42	Isak	Benwemanetz	1924	January 17, 1945
43	Feywel	Ancelewicz	1926	January 26, 1945
44	Lazar	Niemenczynski	1910	January 1, 3045
45	Abram	Katz	1905	February 5, 1945
46	Chaim	Rudin	1910	March 28, 1945
47	Aron	Rudnicki	1915	March 31, 1945
48	Gerszon	Abramowicz	1921	April 5, 1945

www.ingramcontent.com/pod-product-compliance
Lightning Source LLC
Chambersburg PA
CBHW050411110426
42812CB00006BA/1864